SAVE energy SAVE money!

SAVE
energy
SAVE
money!

201 Do-It-Yourself Projects, Tips, and Ideas

From the Editors of **The Family Handyman**®

Reader's Digest

The Reader's Digest Association, Inc.
Pleasantville, New York

A READER'S DIGEST BOOK

FOR THE FAMILY HANDYMAN
Project Editor: Spike Carlsen
Assistant Editor: Mary Flanagan
Graphic Designer: David Simpson
Copy Editor: Dinah Swain Schuster
Indexer: Stephanie Reymann
Archive/Finance Manager: Alice Garrett
Design Director: Sara Koehler
Editor in Chief: Ken Collier

Editorial and Production Team: Donna Bierbach,
Steven Charbonneau, Roxie Filipkowski, Jeff Gorton,
Keith Kostman, Travis Larson, Peggy McDermott,
Lisa Pahl, Becky Pfluger, Judy Rodriguez, Bob Ungar,
Gary Wentz, Marcia Wright Roepke

Photography and Illustrations: John Keely, Mike Krivit,
Phil Leisenheimer, Don Mannes, Ramon Moreno,
Frank Rohrbach, Eugene Thompson, Bill Zuehlke

FOR READER'S DIGEST
U.S. Project Editors: Barbara Booth, Kim Casey
Associate Art Director: George McKeon
Executive Editor, Trade Publishing: Dolores York
Production Manager: Liz Dinda
Vice President, U.S. Operations: Michael Braunschweiger
Associate Publisher: Rosanne McManus
President & Publisher, Trade Publishing: Harold Clarke

Library of Congress Cataloging-in-Publication Data

Save energy save money: do-it-yourself projects, tips, and ideas/
the Family handyman.
        p. cm.
    Includes index.
    ISBN 978-0-7621-0902-9
1. Dwellings--Energy conservation--Amateurs' manuals. 2. Dwellings--
Maintenance and repair--Amateurs' manuals. I. Reader's Digest
Association. II. Family handyman.
TJ163.5.D86S279 2007
644--dc22

2007034550

Address any comments about *Save Energy, Save Money!* to:
The Reader's Digest Association, Inc.
Adult Trade Publishing
Reader's Digest Road
Pleasantville, NY 10570-7000

For more Reader's Digest products and information, visit our website:
www.rd.com (in the United States)
www.thefamilyhandyman.com

This book is printed on environmentally friendly paper certified by FSC (Forest Stewardship Council).

Printed in China

1 3 5 7 9 10 8 6 4 2

A Note to Our Readers
All do-it-yourself activities involve a degree of risk. Skills, materials, tools, and site conditions vary widely. Although the editors have made every effort to ensure accuracy, the reader remains responsible for the selection and use of tools, materials, and methods. Always obey local codes and laws, follow manufacturer's operating instructions, and observe safety precautions.

Introduction

Congratulations on making one of the smartest investments of your life—this book. Smart, because between these two covers you'll find more than 250 pages of energy-saving and money-saving ideas you can put to work TODAY.

When it comes to saving money, there are lots of areas where the situation is out of your control. If you need a gallon of milk, a postage stamp, or a ticket to a baseball game, you pretty much have to pay the going rate. You could drink less milk, deliver your letter by hand, or buy a cheaper seat, but in all those cases there's a downside.

But the energy zone is an area where you can save money *and* wind up with an upside. With a small initial investment of time or money, there are hundreds of ways you can lower your energy bills and reap side benefits to boot. A compact fluorescent lightbulb doesn't only save you $36 over its lifetime, it lasts 5 to 10 times as long. A well-insulated house isn't only cheaper to heat, it's quieter and more comfortable. Fixing a drippy faucet leads to both a lower utility bill and a better night's sleep. And on a broader scale, saving energy helps save natural resources and the environment.

Let's not completely sugarcoat things. Sometimes there are tradeoffs. Using a programmable thermostat may mean a cooler trip to the kitchen for that midnight snack. Installing insulation means putting up with the scratchy stuff for a day or two. Purchasing a high-efficiency furnace may mean not recouping your initial additional investment for five years or more. But, for the most part, these are small prices to pay for a lower utility bill and a cleaner world.

This book isn't just filled with ideas for saving energy; it's filled with simple step-by-step instructions on how to implement those ideas. Whether it's tuning-up an air conditioner, weatherstripping a window, or installing a storm door, *Save Energy, Save Money!* will give you the hands-on information you need to do just what the title promises.

So read on and save!

Contents

Saving Energy:

Making your home more energy efficient without a game plan is like taking a trip without a road map: You'll eventually reach your destination, but it will take you longer, be more of a hassle and cost you more.

Having the big picture in mind is important. It will help you prioritize what to do first based on which projects have the biggest impact and quickest payback. Having a game plan will not only help you lower your utility bills faster but also help you maximize your comfort level, increase the safety of your home and leave more cash in your checkbook at the end of the day.

This first section will help you set your priorities based on the condition and location of your home, your budget and your skill level. Those with a $100 budget will have a different approach to saving energy than those with a $10,000 budget. Those living in Miami will be more interested in energy-

The Big Picture

efficient cooling strategies than those living in blustery Minneapolis. And those who are do-it-yourselfers will look at things a little differently than those who are more comfortable with "point and pay."

Whoever you are and wherever your house is, make sure to pay close attention to the section on carbon monoxide poisoning starting on p. 22. Sealing up your home changes the way it breathes. You want a house that's not only energy efficient but safe as well.

An 8-step energy-savings strategy

If you wince every time a gas or electric bill arrives in your mailbox, take heart. You can easily reduce energy use in your home. And we don't mean by wearing three sweaters, taking cold showers and shuttering the windows. Energy efficiency and a pleasant indoor environment work hand in hand. You'll not only reduce the drain on your bank account but also find your home more comfortable.

Here, we'll give you the BIG picture on how to evaluate your home's energy performance, determine where the biggest savings lie and maintain a healthy indoor envi-ronment. Other articles in this book deal with the specific simple steps you can take to save energy and money.

We'll tell you right off that big energy savings aren't as easy to get today as they were 30 years ago. During the energy crunch of the 1970s, many homeowners added insulation and caulked around windows and doors to capture the biggest savings. And since then, new homes have been built to higher energy-efficiency standards. Still, if you follow these simple steps, you'll find plenty of savings out there.

Figure A How energy is lost

The biggest culprits are air leaks (infiltration) and poor-performing windows. But every home is unique. An energy auditor will tell you where the biggest savings lie in your home.

- 35% Air Leaks
- 18% Doors and Windows
- 17% Floor and Basement
- 13% Walls
- 10% Ceiling

1
Hire an energy auditor

It's worth hiring a pro to evaluate your home and help you sort out the many possible energy-saving strategies. Call your local utility company to find energy auditors. It may supply this service for free or recommend an auditor.

An energy audit typically costs $250 to $400, but sometimes community programs subsidize the bill. The energy auditor will inspect your home and rate its current performance in terms of insulation levels, air leakage, condition of heating or cooling equipment and other criteria. (You can also conduct a somewhat crude energy audit yourself by going to www.homeenergysaver.lbl.gov.)

> **tip** Schedule a time when you can walk through your home with the auditor. Ask lots of questions. You can learn a ton about your home and how it works.

The auditor can then tell you which upgrades are cost-effective and estimate your energy savings. Cost-effectiveness is the key. You can spend thousands of dollars for upgrades that won't save you much, and a good auditor will steer you away from those. For an improvement to be worthwhile, the estimated savings should cover the cost of the improvement in about seven years. For example, adding $200 of insulation to your attic will be worth it if the estimated savings are about $30 per year ($210 after seven years). But installing a new efficient window for $200 won't be worth the cost if you save only $10 per year ($70 after seven years). The auditor's report should clearly specify the estimated savings.

> **tip** Have the auditor tell you which improvements you can do yourself. That eliminates the labor cost and makes many more upgrades cost effective.

Keep in mind that as energy costs go up, more retrofit ideas become cost-effective.

Quick tip*

SAVE BIG BY WASHING COLD. When you use your washing machine, 90 percent of the total amount of energy used goes into heating the water and only 10 percent into operating the actual appliance. Use cold water and cold-water detergents whenever you can.

2
Reduce air leakage

Think of the warm air leaking out through gaps, cracks and holes in your home's walls and ceilings as your energy dollars floating away (Figure A). Sealing these openings is one of the most cost-effective ways to save energy.

Stopping air leaks in the attic is usually enough. You don't have to work your way through every room caulking every crack, inside and out. Just get the largest and worst offenders, which are almost always in the attic.

> For do-it-yourself information on sealing attic bypasses, see p. 54.

You'll notice that your house feels more comfortable too, because you'll have fewer drafts. The less warm air that leaks out, the less cold air that leaks in to replace it.

*Sealing air leaks is one of the most effective ways to save energy **and** money.*

3
Conserve energy

There are hundreds of energy-saving steps that cost little or nothing. Some ideas involve a small investment of time and money—for example, installing a programmable thermostat or caulking around windows. Others involve a small investment of energy—yours. These simple steps include lowering the temperature setting on your water heater and closing the curtains.

> See pp. 30-33 for simple energy-saving tips

4
Buy high-efficiency windows

(when it's time to replace them)

Windows are the weakest link in your home's outer defenses against heat loss, accounting for about 18 percent of the heat loss in the typical home. But windows are also expensive, so it isn't cost effective to replace them just to save energy. If they're worn out, however, it's cost effective in all but the southernmost regions to upgrade to double-pane windows with low-E coatings. Your window specialist will help you choose the type of coating that works best, depending on whether you mostly need to slow heat loss or reduce solar gain.

See "Saving Energy: Windows & Doors," starting on p. 114, for more complete information.

Windows are the weakest link in your home's outer defenses against heat loss.

Quick tip*

WHAT'S U-VALUE? The National Fenestration Rating Council tests all new windows and assigns each a "U-Value." The lower the U-Value, the more energy efficient the window.

5
Add insulation

Add 6 in. of insulation to an uninsulated attic and you'll reap substantial energy savings. Add 6 in. more and you'll get additional energy savings, but to a lesser degree. To find the point of diminishing returns, consult the Department of Energy charts at www.owenscorning.com or www.certainteed.com. The recommended values are based on climate, fuel costs and other factors. Adding more than the suggested amounts will result in a longer payback period for your investment.

50%
Space Heating

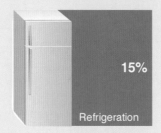

22%
Water Heating

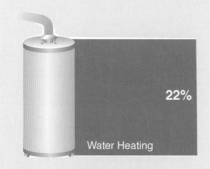

15%
Refrigeration

Figure B Where energy goes

About half of the energy consumed in the average home goes to space heating and/or air-conditioning. But all areas are targets for energy improvements as energy costs rise.

13%
Appliances and Lights

6
Shade your home

Shading is the best way you can save energy dollars in the summertime with your own sweat equity. Shading saves energy because it blocks out direct sunlight, which is responsible for about 50 percent of the heat gain in your home. Most of it strikes the roof and works its way through the attic, then down through the ceiling; the rest comes in mainly through windows. If you upgrade your attic insulation to at least 12 in. thick (about R-36) and make sure to buy light-colored roofing next time you reroof, you'll stop most of that roof heat. And steps like planting trees, attaching awnings and extending roof overhangs will shade the most vulnerable south-facing windows as well as those facing east and west. Most of these are low-cost, do-it-yourself strategies.

See "Cooling with shade," p. 86, for more on cooling strategies.

Shading saves energy because it blocks out direct sunlight, which is responsible for about 50 percent of the heat gain in your home.

7
Stop air conditioner duct leakage

Studies have shown that an average duct system loses 10 to 40 percent of the cool air through gaps in the duct joints. This cooling is wasted when the ducts run outside the interior conditioned space, in an attic or a crawlspace. While sealing ducts is a common practice now, few air-conditioned homes have had this done. Sealing ducts is difficult. You'll have to rely on professional services (see "Air-Conditioning" in your yellow pages) to test the ducts for leakage and to retest to show the effectiveness of their work.

Quick tip*

LIGHT-COLORED SHINGLES SAVE ENERGY. Installing white shingles (which reflect heat back into the sky) instead of dark shingles (which absorb heat) can reduce the cooling load in a home by up to 20 percent.

8
Protect your health and the health of your home

Energy-efficiency improvements can increase the risk of carbon monoxide (CO) poisoning. This can occur in homes with devices that burn gas, oil or wood and in homes with attached garages. At a minimum, install a CO alarm.

Watch your windows for excessive condensation. Most energy-saving measures reduce air leakage, allowing excessive moisture to build up inside. This moisture can cause mold and rot and an unhealthy indoor environment. Condensation on windows is common at the beginning of the heating season but should largely disappear except during cold snaps. Usually the best prevention strategy is to find the moisture sources (some of the worst culprits are improperly vented dryers, bath fans and the rooms they're in) and eliminate them or improve ventilation.

See "Prevent carbon monoxide poisoning" on p. 22 for information on alarms and placement.

Save $$ with an energy audit

If high energy bills are causing you shock and frustration, take heart. There's something you can do—call your local utility company and ask for an energy audit.

An energy auditor will come to your home and conduct a series of tests to provide detailed information about your home's energy usage and energy loss. A report, generated at the conclusion of the two- to three-hour audit, will detail:

- The condition and efficiency of your heating and cooling system
- The overall efficiency of your home, including the primary areas of air leakage in your exterior walls and ceilings
- Low-cost ways you can improve energy efficiency and save energy
- Larger upgrades that will pay back their cost with energy savings within a relatively short period.

Here, you'll walk through a professional energy audit with Erik Lindberg, a Minnesota state-certified energy auditor, whose company, Enervision, has performed more than 12,000 audits. An audit typically costs $250 to $400, but most utility companies offer a rebate to reduce the cost to you. The house shown here was built in 1979.

"An energy audit addresses *five* priorities:

First is home safety. If your house isn't safe, energy efficiency doesn't matter. Second is durability. Finding and fixing moisture problems and rot helps the house last longer. Third is comfort. The audit identifies drafts and cold spots. Fourth is to set up the best action plan to make your home more efficient, especially things you can do yourself. Fifth is cost benefit, which tells you what it'll cost to make improvements, and how long it'll take for the savings to pay off those costs."

Erik Lindberg,
Certified
Energy
Auditor >

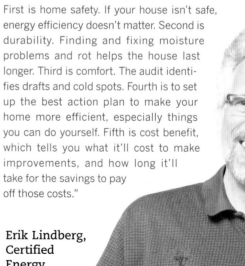

Checking heating and hot-water systems

The audit starts with a furnace combustion efficiency test. With the furnace running, Erik inserts a gas analyzer in the furnace's draft diverter (Photo 1). If there's no draft diverter, he drills a small hole in the flue for the wand, then later patches it. The analyzer provides an immediate reading. Our furnace had a 76.9 percent combustion efficiency—not bad considering furnaces at least 15 years old are usually 55 to 68 percent efficient and this unit is 27 years old (typical lifespan is 15 to 20 years).

This test also measures:

- The amount of carbon monoxide in the flue gases
- The draft pressure in the flue to determine if gases could leak into the house.

These are safety issues. If waste gases aren't being drawn up the chimney, then moisture, carbon monoxide and other pollutants could be flowing into your home. Common causes of vent problems (allowing gases to "backdraft" into the home) are birds' nests in the vent pipes and vents that have come apart. Erik often finds these problems. He notes one common clue: "If you have moisture on your windows, the first thing to check for is backdrafting in the furnace and water heater flues."

Erik tests for backdrafting in the water heater flue as well by holding a flame or a smoke stick next to the draft diverter (Photo 2).

The check of the heating and hot-water systems concludes with a visual inspection. Rust particles (called "scaling") inside the furnace heat exchanger indicate corrosion, which will eventually lead to holes and combustion gas leakage. Scaling may also be visible on top of the water heater around the draft diverter.

Erik looks to see if the furnace filter is clean and installed correctly. "Clogged filters can cause a moderate increase in heating costs, but more significantly, cause the heat exchanger to overheat and fail, and cause the fan motor to heat up, increase electric consumption and reduce the life of the motor." He also looks for combustibles stored near the furnace or water heater, because the flame could cause an explosion.

Other common problems Erik has found include disconnected flue pipes, leaky ductwork, clogged condensation pipes, dirty burners and dirty fan blades. "I've found many furnaces missing the cover for the filter slot, and major leaks in the return-air ductwork. This causes depressurization in the furnace room and can draw dangerous exhaust gases out of the flue pipe and distribute these gases throughout the house," he says.

> *"Old boilers,* originally designed for coal, then converted to oil and then to natural gas, can be as low as 55 percent efficient—that's 45 percent waste! The best furnace designs feature variable-speed fan motors and modulating or multi-stage burners, which enable the furnace to match its Btu output to the home's temperature needs, thereby increasing the system's efficiency."

1 FURNACE EFFICIENCY TEST: The auditor tests the furnace exhaust with an electrical gas analyzer, which gives a combustion efficiency reading. It also measures draft pressure to determine if flue gases might leak into the house.

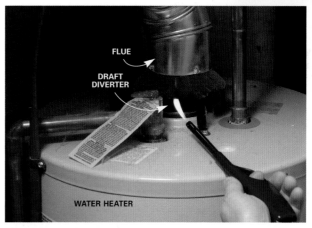

2 BACKDRAFT TEST: With all doors and windows closed and all combustion appliances turned on, the auditor tests for backdrafting at a natural-draft gas water heater. The flame, held next to the draft diverter, should be drawn up into the flue.

Testing for air leakage

Part two of the audit entails a "blower door" test, which measures the home's "tightness," or air infiltration rate. Erik first closes all doors and windows, then he sets an adjustable panel with a variable-speed fan in a doorway, completely sealing it. He turns on the fan to blow air out of the house, which reduces the indoor air pressure, and then measures airflow through the fan at predetermined pressure points (Photos 3 and 4). Outside air then enters through cracks and gaps in walls and ceilings.

With the fan running, you can feel air come in with your hand, especially around leaky windows and doors. Gauges connected to the fan measure the airflow rate needed to maintain a constant pressure, allowing the auditor to calculate the leakage rate.

Newer homes are built tighter under the most recent Minnesota building code. (Most other state codes have tighter rules too.) It even requires special ventilation fans to ensure adequate fresh air. Still, their leakage rate is often equivalent to a 6 x 6-in. hole in a wall. Older homes weren't built nearly as tight. They often have a leakage rate equivalent to a 19 x 19-in. hole, which is like having a window wide open all the time! The house we tested had leaks totaling .77 sq. ft. (about an 11 x 11-in. hole). Erik estimates that sealing air leaks alone will save 10 to 20 percent on this home's annual heating bills.

Erik pointed out several signs of air leaks: stains around exhaust fans and dirt on insulation. A batt of insulation between joists in the basement was dirty, meaning the insulation was serving as a filter for air leaking in through the foundation. "You can't fix these leaks with insulation because it won't stop the airflow," Erik says. "You have to seal them with caulk, expanding foam or some other sealant."

tip Have the audit performed in the spring, summer or fall. Auditors are usually busier in the winter, when homeowners see a spike in energy bills, and the wait for an audit can be two months or more.

"In my opinion, there's no limit to how tight you can make the ceiling. The less air that goes out the ceiling, the less that will come in around doors, windows and other leaky areas. When you're carrying water in a bucket, it doesn't matter if the top leaks, because no water is going to get out. What matters is the bottom. Think of your house like an upside-down bucket holding heat."

3 BLOWER DOOR TEST: With all doors and windows closed, the auditor inserts a blower door in the front or back doorway and starts the fan.

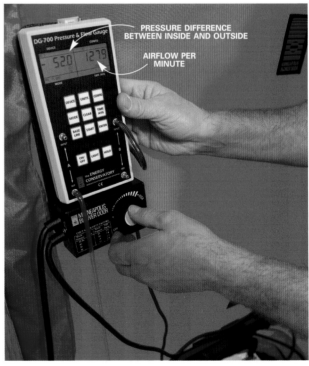

4 THE GAUGE shows the pressure difference between the inside and the outside and the airflow per minute. From these, the auditor calculates the leakage rate.

Pinpointing sources of energy loss

While the blower door test measures the overall leakiness of the house, infrared scanning (technically called "thermography") graphically identifies the precise locations of those leaks. Erik keeps the blower door fan running to draw in outside air. Then, using an infrared camera, he scans the walls and ceilings, photographing surface areas that show up as cooler (Photo 5).

Cold areas show up as blue, and warm areas as yellow (Photos 6 – 8). Today (a chilly day in March), the framing members showed up as blue, since they're cooler than the insulated portion of the walls. (The opposite would be true on a hot day when the indoors is air conditioned and the outside air is warmer.)

Air leaks in the ceiling typically cause the greatest energy losses. Openings made for light fixtures, plumbing vents, exhaust fans, attic access and smoke alarms will leak if the builder didn't make an extra effort to seal them. In this house, the area around the attic access panel and the exhaust fan in the upstairs bathroom showed extensive leaking (Photo 6), while a ceiling light fixture, which must have been sealed better, leaked very little.

Electrical outlets and light switches on outside walls also usually leak, unless the builder took extra pains to seal them. The infrared scan showed that four of these in the north kitchen wall leaked profusely (Photo 7). The homeowner confirmed this, noting that she often felt cold drafts when standing by this wall.

While some of these problems are easy to fix—foam weatherstripping on the attic access panel, spray foam or caulk around the exhaust fans, and foam seals under the outlet and switch cover plates—others are difficult to seal and may not be practical to go after. Leaks around exterior wall top plates and inadequate insulation in some wall cavities are common (Photo 8), but hard to access and therefore expensive to remedy.

Expect some air leakage around windows, sliding patio doors and exterior doors. "All doors will leak, especially since people step on the threshold as they enter and leave the house, wearing a gap between the door and sill," Erik explains. "The only doors that don't leak are the ones on submarines."

Infrared scanning can identify other hidden problems. It'll show cold spots where insulation is poor or missing. Erik has even found double-pane windows that have failed. Condensation between the layers of glass, which is the usual sign of failure, hadn't shown up yet. Yet the infrared image showed that the centers of the panes were cooler than the sides, which meant the special argon gas they had been filled with was completely gone.

Since infrared scanning works by identifying heat differences, it can also detect water leaks (not to mention warm-blooded critters in the walls). Erik once found an area in a basement floor that was inordinately warm. Turns out a hot water pipe was leaking under the concrete, which explained the homeowner's high energy bill.

"With my infrared scanner,

I've discovered missing batts of insulation, insulation that stops 2 ft. short of the top of the wall, and entire room additions—20 by 30-ft. rooms—with absolutely no insulation in the ceiling. I've also found broken ducts sending heat into uninsulated attics."

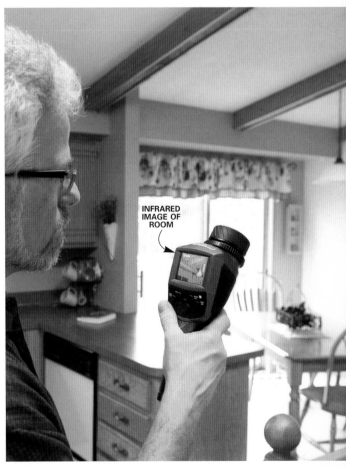

INFRARED IMAGE OF ROOM

5 THERMOGRAPHY: The auditor uses an infrared camera to scan walls and ceilings. The camera detects temperature differences and can pinpoint cold spots and air leaks.

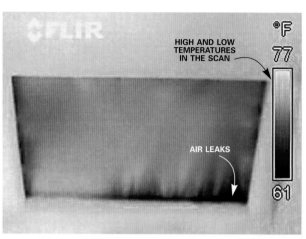

HIGH AND LOW
TEMPERATURES
IN THE SCAN

°F

77

AIR LEAKS

61

6 DARK BLUE AREAS around the perimeter of the attic access panel indicate air leakage. The overall blue tinge indicates poor insulation.

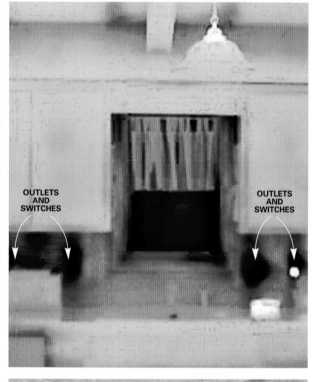

OUTLETS AND SWITCHES

OUTLETS AND SWITCHES

7 ELECTRICAL OUTLETS AND SWITCHES typically leak, but this is excessive. This kitchen wall feels cold and drafty in the winter.

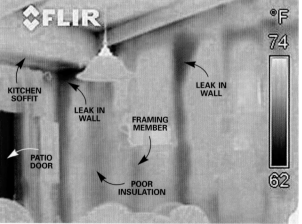

°F

74

KITCHEN SOFFIT

LEAK IN WALL

LEAK IN WALL

FRAMING MEMBER

PATIO DOOR

POOR INSULATION

62

8 INADEQUATE INSULATION in a wall cavity and gaps in the top plates (wall framing) cause most of the air leaks in this dining room.

Final report—what you can save

Once the testing is complete, the auditor prepares a comprehensive report detailing the amount of leakage, ways to improve efficiency, the cost of specific improvements and the time frame for recouping those investments (see below).

The report lists specific low-cost steps for reducing energy usage that you can usually do yourself. For this house, they include insulating the attic access panel, weatherstripping it with closed-cell foam tape, sealing ceiling penetrations at electrical fixtures, insulating kitchen soffits, adding attic insulation, insulating the rim joists and caulking around windows, doors and base trim. Erik estimates that these upgrades will cut annual energy bills by 15 to 20 percent. Adding insulation to exterior walls isn't worth the cost.

The furnace, installed when the house was built in 1979, had an "annual fuel utilization efficiency" (AFUE) of about 68 percent. This furnace is operating well below the current minimum standard specified by the building code and far below the efficiencies currently available. (ENERGY STAR furnaces must have at least a 90 percent AFUE. See p. 26 for more on ENERGY STAR.) Erik recommends replacing any old furnace (in Minnesota's cold climate) that's not at least 80 percent efficient since newer models use less energy and eventually pay for themselves (in this case, in nine years). Your energy auditor will make these calculations and recommendations based on your local climate. Furnaces that are at least 95 percent efficient may qualify for a federal tax credit.

Installing a programmable thermostat in this home will pay for itself in just two to three years. A new high-efficiency air conditioner isn't a priority, but it's likely to be a priority in warmer climates. You want to recoup your investment through predicted energy savings within seven to 10 years.

Recommended energy-saving tips

- Seal leaks in ductwork
- Clear space in front of heating units, registers and radiators
- Reduce water usage by using low-flow showerheads
- Insulate the water heater tank and water pipes
- Wash clothes in cold or warm water and rinse with cold
- Dry laundry loads consecutively to maximize dryer efficiency
- Replace incandescent bulbs with efficient compact fluorescent bulbs
- Use timers or motion detectors to turn off lights when not needed
- Install air-sealing gaskets behind switch/outlet cover plates
- Lock windows to create a better seal
- Add weatherstripping and caulking around doors and windows
- Seal around pipes and ducts that penetrate outer walls

< The final report lists energy-efficient upgrades, their cost (hiring a contractor vs. doing it yourself) and estimated annual savings. Upgrades that pay back in seven to 10 years are considered good investments.

Page 4

FINAL REPORT
Home performance and building diagnostic services

COMPONENT		CONTRACTOR		DIY		1st Year Savings
		Cost	Payback (years)	Cost	Payback (years)	
Exterior walls	OK	—	—	$2,024	46	$44
Attic floor/ceiling	Re insulate to R-44 after attic bypass sealing is done	—	—	$300	10	$30
Knee wall	Not applicable					
Side attic floor	Not applicable					
Slant walls	Not applicable					
Basement walls	Build 2x4 stud wall, R-15 fiberglass	$2,640	13	$845	4	$203
Foundation	Not applicable					
Rim Joist	Install icynene or spray polyurethane insulation	$385	7	$275	5	$58
Windows	Seal with 3M weatherizing tape and install plastic window insulator			$8	1	$13
Doors	Weather strip doors with Q-Lon; see examples in audit's extra folder	$90	*	$40	*	
Attic bypass	Seal plumbing, wiring, top plates and other air leaks into attic	$375	*	$75	*	
Attic access panel	Insulate and weather strip attic access panel; see examples in audit's extra folder	$55	*	$25	*	
Air sealing	Caulk window, door and base trim	$140	*	$28	*	$39
Programmable thermostat	Install programmable thermostat ; use 10° setback for 8 hours	$120	3	$60	2	
APPLIANCES						$317
Furnace/boiler	Install 95% AFUE "sealed combustion" furnace. Get $200 tax credit, plus rebates!	$2,500	8	—		$74
Water heater	Install high-efficiency/direct vent water heater	$600	8	—		$150
Air conditioner	Replace with 14 SEER model	$1,800	12	—		
Cost/benefit analysis notes	*Cost/benefit amounts are difficult to specify for small items, but savings are significant. Additional benefits are reducing drafts, reducing moisture intrusion into wall and ceiling cavities, and avoiding ice dams and other costly problems.					

Energy-saving projects and payback

Ballpark numbers on cost, do-it-yourself skill level and how long it'll take to recoup your investment

Deciding which energy-saving home improvements to make first (or at all) can be a daunting task. But knowing a few facts—especially regarding payback—can help uncomplicate matters.

The term *payback* refers to how many years it typically takes to recoup your investment in a product or project by way of utility bill savings. For instance, if a new energy-efficient water heater costs $200 more than a standard model, and saves you $20 per year, it will take you 10 years to recoup your investment. If it saves you $50 per year, that payback period drops to four years. After the payback period, you pocket the savings.

Inflation, utility costs, house age, living habits and other factors can greatly affect payback—but in general terms, the shorter the payback period, the smarter the investment.

Here are 15 of the top energy-saving home improvements, along with typical cost, payback period and skill level needed to tackle the job. The list is arranged from those with the shortest payback period to those with the longest. Best of all, we show you how to tackle nearly every project listed here in other parts of this book.

Rank: #1
Project: Install compact fluorescent bulbs
Difficulty level: Easy
Typical cost: $3 per bulb
Typical payback: 1/2 to 1 year

Rank: #2
Project: Install a programmable thermostat
Difficulty level: Intermediate
Typical cost: $30 to $100
Typical payback: 1/2 to 2 years

Rank: #3
Project: Seal large and small ceiling air leaks
Difficulty level: Easy to intermediate
Typical cost: less than $200
Typical payback: 1 to 2 years

Rank: #4
Project: Seal air duct leaks
Difficulty level: Easy
Typical cost: less than $25
Typical payback: 1 to 2 years

Rank: #5
Project: Install a water-saving showerhead
Difficulty level: Easy
Typical cost: $10 and up
Typical payback: 1 to 2 years

Rank: #6
Project: Insulate water heater
Difficulty level: Easy
Typical cost: $8 to $20
Typical payback: 1 to 2 years

Rank: #7
Project: Weatherstrip windows and doors
Difficulty level: Easy to intermediate
Typical cost: $10 to $20 per opening
Typical payback: 1 to 3 years

Rank: #8
Project: Tune up furnace or other heating equipment
Difficulty level: Professional
Typical cost: $100 and up
Typical payback: 1 to 3 years

Rank: #9
Project: Install ceiling insulation
Difficulty level: Intermediate
Typical cost: $.30 to .50/sq. ft. (based on 6-in. fiberglass batts)
Typical payback: 2 to 5 years

SOURCE: Data compiled from www.xcelenergy.com, www.energystar.gov and U.S. Department of Energy (www.energy.gov).

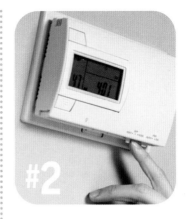

Rank: #10
Project: Install floor insulation (when space below floor is unheated)
Difficulty level: Intermediate
Typical cost: $.30 to .50/sq. ft. (based on 6-in. fiberglass batts)
Typical payback: 2 to 5 years

Rank: #11
Project: Install storm windows
Difficulty level: Intermediate
Typical cost: $30 per window and up
Typical payback: 4 to 10 years

Rank: #12
Project: Replace heating system
Difficulty level: Professional
Typical cost: varies greatly
Typical payback: 5 to 20 years

Rank: #13
Project: Blown-in wall insulation
Difficulty level: Advanced or professional
Typical cost: $1 to $2/sq. ft. of wall (includes material and labor)
Typical payback: 6 to 12 years

Rank: #14
Project: Landscaping (trees for windbreaks and sun screening)
Difficulty level: Intermediate
Typical cost: $30 and up per tree
Typical payback: 5 to 10 years (varies greatly)

Rank: #15
Project: Window replacement
Difficulty level: Advanced
Typical cost: $300 to $800 per window; higher for professional installation
Typical payback: 15 to 30 years

Prevent carbon monoxide poisoning

Follow these two steps to keep this silent killer at bay

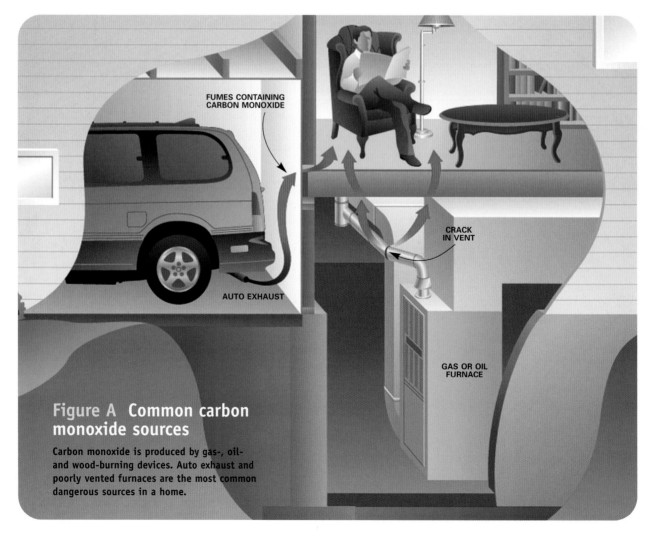

FUMES CONTAINING
CARBON MONOXIDE

CRACK
IN VENT

AUTO EXHAUST

GAS OR OIL
FURNACE

Figure A Common carbon monoxide sources

Carbon monoxide is produced by gas-, oil- and wood-burning devices. Auto exhaust and poorly vented furnaces are the most common dangerous sources in a home.

1 Install carbon monoxide (CO) alarms

What is CO?

CO is an invisible, odorless gas that's produced by fireplaces, furnaces, stoves, water heaters and heaters that burn natural gas, propane, oil or wood. Usually chimneys and flues safely carry these combustion by-products up and out of your home. But not always. Flue blockage, poor natural drafting, leaks and other problems sometimes cause CO and other combustion gases to spill out into your living space and pollute the air you breathe (Figure A). The CO is gradually absorbed into the bloodstream. Light doses cause flulike symptoms, and larger doses lead to unconsciousness and death.

Cars, lawn mowers and snow blowers also produce a lot of CO, especially at start-up. If you have an attached garage, natural drafts tend to pull that CO into your home, even if you have the garage door open! As a rule, never let a car engine idle in a garage.

Is the CO threat greater in an energy-efficient home?

Sometimes. Reducing air leaks in your home is one of the best ways to make your home more energy efficient. Air tightening includes such things as closing up attic bypasses, weatherstripping, caulking around doors and windows, and installing new windows. But as your home gets tighter, flues and chimneys can't vent CO and other combustion gases to the outside as easily, because they don't have as much makeup air (see Step 2, p. 24). CO alarms are simple, inexpensive insurance to warn you if CO spillage reaches a hazardous level ... even if your home is new or you haven't taken steps to improve energy efficiency.

How dangerous is CO?

Accidental carbon monoxide (CO) poisoning accounts for several hundred deaths in the United States every year. The deaths are particularly tragic because most could have been easily prevented with a warning from a $20 to $45 CO alarm.

Where do I put the alarms?

At a minimum, put an alarm near the sleeping rooms on each level in your home. CO accumulates in the bloodstream, and you're most vulnerable during long periods of sleep. Position alarms on ceilings or walls, away from drafts and solvents. (Read the directions that come with each alarm for more details.)

Plug-in alarm with digital display (about $45)

- PEAK CO LEVEL
- PEAK LEVEL BUTTON
- TEST/RESET BUTTON

Battery-powered alarm (about $20)

- TEST/RESET BUTTON

Both types of CO alarms sound an alarm when hazardous levels of CO are present. The type with a digital display will also show the peak CO level in your home when you push the peak level button. It will not record very low levels.

What's the best CO alarm to buy?

Look for a CO alarm with a UL (Underwriters Laboratories) listing on the package. It can be either battery-powered or a plug-in type (often with a battery backup; photos above). All alarms have a test/reset button that you should push weekly to make sure the alarm is operating.

We recommend the plug-in type with a digital readout that tells you the peak CO concentration whenever you push the peak level button. The CO level might not be high enough to trigger the alarm. But detecting a low level can alert you to a potential problem so you can trace the source before the CO reaches a higher level. This is particularly important if you have more vulnerable folks in your home such as young children, the elderly and those with certain illnesses.

What should I do if an alarm goes off?

Here are general guidelines taken from the more detailed instructions that come with your alarm:

1. Push the test/reset button. (This is easier with a wall-mounted CO alarm.)

2. Call an emergency number, such as 911 or your fire department in most areas.

3. Go outside or move to a well-ventilated area, like next to an open window or door. Make sure all family members are accounted for. Wait for emergency services to arrive; they'll make sure your house is well aired out.

4. If the alarm goes off again within 24 hours, follow steps 1 – 3 above and call in a qualified technician to test your fuel-burning equipment and find the problem. Be aware that furnace start-ups can set off the alarm under some conditions, as can starting cars in an attached garage.

WARNING: If an alarm sounds, you have a potentially lethal amount of CO in your home! Take the alarm seriously. Make every effort to find an explanation. You don't want any level of CO in your home, much less a lethal level. Unfortunately, CO sources can be difficult to pinpoint. Don't hesitate to call in a heating and ventilating technician experienced in CO issues to search out the probable causes and recommend corrections.

Also be aware of the symptoms of CO poisoning: slight headache, nausea, vomiting and fatigue (all flu-like symptoms) from mild exposures, and throbbing headache, drowsiness, confusion, fast heart rate or unconsciousness from heavier exposures.

2 Ask a heating service technician to conduct a complete backdrafting test at your annual heating equipment checkup

Backdrafting occurs when the combustion gases can't go up and out flues and chimneys because outdoor air is already flowing down them (Figure B). This often occurs when you run a clothes dryer, powerful range fan or any combination of venting fans. All suck air out of your home. If your house can't get enough makeup air leaking in around windows and doors and through cracks and gaps in walls, the makeup air may come down the flues or chimney. Then your furnace, water heater or wood-burning fireplace may not vent properly, and combustion gases, including CO, will spill into your living space. (Studies have shown that backdrafting is common even in homes that are not energy efficient or airtight, so this test is worthwhile regardless of any energy-efficiency improvements you've made.)

A complete backdraft test only takes about 10 minutes. The service technician should close all doors and windows and turn on your ventilating fans, creating a worst-case situation. The technician will then turn on your water heater and test it for combustion gas spillage, and test the furnace as well.

If you have significant spillage, the technician should inspect your venting system and recommend solutions.

DOWNDRAFT IN VENT/CHIMNEY

COMBUSTION FUMES

Figure B Backdrafting

Backdrafting is a condition in which air flows down a flue or chimney rather than up, and combustion fumes can't flow out. The fumes spill into your living spaces.

Permits, inspections and contractors

Permits

Many energy-saving home-improvement projects require you, or your contractor, to obtain a permit. Obtaining permits can be a hassle, but getting caught doing work without one, or using substandard building practices, can be much worse.

FREQUENTLY REQUIRED PERMITS

Permit requirements vary greatly from one community to the next. Some common projects requiring permits include:

- Projects involving structural alterations to your house, such as adding a larger window or removing a wall.
- Installing a deck, fence, outbuilding or pool.
- Finishing a basement or attic space.
- Adding an electrical branch circuit, outlet or fixture.
- Installing or replacing a water heater, furnace, air conditioner or fireplace.

Depending on the project, you may or may not be required to submit a blueprint or plan.

Inspections

Some small projects may require a single inspection, while larger ones may require a dozen or more. Make certain you know when and where inspections are required. Also remember you may not be able to move to the next step of your project until the inspection has been completed. Plan and schedule ahead.

FREQUENTLY REQUIRED INSPECTIONS

- Footing inspections (after the footings are formed, but before the concrete is poured).
- Framing inspections (after the framing materials and sheathing are in place).
- Rough plumbing/gas line inspection (while pipes are exposed).
- Final plumbing inspection (supply and drain-waste-vent pipes are pressure tested for leaks).
- Insulation inspection (sometimes after the vapor barrier is installed).
- Drywall inspection (often after drywall has been fastened, but before taping begins).
- Rough-in electrical inspection (rough wiring completed in electrical boxes but devices such as switches, outlets and light fixtures not installed).
- Final electrical inspection (all switches, outlets and lights in place and wiring at circuit panel complete).
- Final inspection (final check to make sure all codes have been followed).

Working with contractors

Though horror stories of unscrupulous contractors abound, most in the business are honest, hardworking folks. Most live and die by their reputations. Those who take the money and run or do substandard work don't stay in business long. Yet, there are things you should check out.

QUESTIONS TO ASK, THINGS TO CHECK

1. **Legal matters.** Do they have the proper licenses and insurance to work in your community? Ask to see the actual documents.

2. **Contract.** The more specific, the better. Specify the exact materials to be used, right down to the manufacturer, when necessary.

3. **References.** Will they provide names and contact information for their most recent clients? If the references are old or few-and-far-between, ask why. How long have they been in business? Check with the Better Business Bureau to see if any complaints have been filed.

4. **Down payment and money matters.** Determine at what points in the project payments will be made. One-third down for materials is common.

5. **Work schedule.** What date will the project start and what is a realistic date to expect completion?

6. **Changes.** Commonly, a change order spelling out the design and financial implications is drawn up and signed by the homeowner and contractor when there is a change in the initial contract.

7. **On the job.** Determine whom you'll speak with regarding the day-to-day operations. Who handles questions? How early in the day would work start and how long would it go on in the evening? What about a bathroom, smoking and eating? Who cleans up and when?

Understanding
ENERGY STAR

Shop smart, save energy, save money

CHANGE FOR THE BETTER WITH ENERGY STAR

As you can see, you don't have to sacrifice beauty and comfort for energy efficiency.

If you've been shopping recently for appliances, home electronics or building materials, chances are you've run across the blue ENERGY STAR logo. So just what does it mean?

Products that have earned the ENERGY STAR logo meet strict energy guidelines set by the U.S. Department of Energy and the U.S. Environmental Protection Agency. Products in over 50 categories are eligible for the rating. Items include the expected—furnaces, air conditioners and windows—as well as the unexpected—televisions, laptops, cordless tool chargers, vending machines, even entire new homes. The designation means you don't need to wade through

all the complicated specifications and abbreviations to find the most energy-efficient product; the legwork has been done for you. ENERGY STAR standards and products are also often used by manufacturers, utility companies and government agencies to grant rebates and tax credits.

Examples of ENERGY STAR products and qualifiers include:

- Televisions must consume 3 watts or less when switched off (most standard TVs consume 6 watts).
- Washing machines must use 50 percent less energy than standard washers.
- Furnaces must have an efficiency rating of 90 percent or greater.
- Computer monitors must consume 2 watts or less in SLEEP mode and 1 watt or less in OFF mode.

Descriptions of what it takes for a product to gain the ENERGY STAR, along with a manufacturer-by-manufacturer breakdown of qualifying products can be found at the ENERGY STAR Web site at www.energystar.gov. Other information on how to make your home more energy efficient, including interactive features such as the "Refrigerator Retirement Savings Calculator," the "Home Energy Yardstick" and store locators can also be found on the Web site. The ENERGY STAR Web site is refreshingly easy to navigate, and packed full of specific product and how-to information.

And is it working? You bet. Through the ENERGY STAR program, Americans saved $12 billion on their utility bill in one year alone.

Here are some general ENERGY STAR product categories, along with examples of the savings you might expect to see.

Lighting

ENERGY STAR-qualified bulbs—primarily compact fluorescent lights or CFLs—use two-thirds less energy than incandescent bulbs, while generating 70 percent less heat and lasting up to 10 times longer. ENERGY STAR light fixtures have been designed to easily accommodate energy-efficient bulbs and distribute light more efficiently, while using 33 percent less energy than standard fixtures. Many also contain extra energy-saving features, such as built-in dimmers, motion sensors and automatic daylight shutoffs.

When replacing bulbs and fixtures, start with the five most frequently used fixtures. Often they're the kitchen ceiling light, living-room table and floor lamps, bathroom vanity and outdoor porch or post lamps.

You can save $20 to $30 in energy costs over the lifetime of a single CFL. Save $60 per year by replacing your five most frequently used fixtures and/or the bulbs with ENERGY STAR-qualified models.

Appliances

When shopping for a new appliance, there are actually two price tags to look at: the one attached to the appliance and the one attached to your utility bill each month. In many cases, what initially looks like an expensive product can start looking like a smart investment when the utility bills roll in. ENERGY STAR-qualified appliances use anywhere from 10 to 50 percent less energy and/or water than standard models.

Here are laundry room and kitchen appliances that currently qualify for the ENERGY STAR:

Dishwashers. Heating the water is the most expensive part of running a dishwasher. Most ENERGY STAR-qualified units have built-in water temperature boosters that allow you to keep your water heater set at a lower temperature. Most also use less water. To qualify for the ENERGY STAR, a dishwasher must use 41 percent less energy than the federal minimum standards—which boils down to a savings of about $90 over the dishwasher's lifetime.

 tip You can reduce the amount of energy your refrigerator uses by positioning it away from heat-producing sources such as ovens, dishwashers or direct sunlight.

Refrigerators and freezers. In most homes, the refrigerator consumes more energy than any other kitchen appliance. ENERGY STAR-qualified models are better

insulated and have higher-efficiency compressors—the workhorse of any refrigerator. Qualifying refrigerators use 40 percent less energy than standard models sold in 2001, while freezers consume at least 10 percent less energy than federal standards. Check out the "Refrigerator Retirement Saving Calculator" on the ENERGY STAR Web site for a real eye opener. If your refrigerator was made prior to 1993, you may be able to save $100 or more a year by switching to a more energy-efficient model.

Clothes washers. Compared to a pre-1994 unit, an ENERGY STAR-qualified washer can save up to $110 per year on your utility bill. To qualify, a machine must use 50 percent less energy than a standard model. Most use half the amount of water as conventional older machines.

Ventilation and clean air

Clean, fresh air is something everyone appreciates—and using ENERGY STAR-qualified dehumidifiers, fans and ventilation fans can help save money at the same time.

Dehumidifiers. The lower the humidity, the cooler a body feels—meaning a dehumidifier may allow you to run your air conditioner less often. ENERGY STAR-qualified units use 10 to 20 percent less energy than conventional models, and in doing so, can save up to $20 per year in electricity costs.

Ceiling fans. Air movement from a ceiling fan can help make a room (and those in it) feel 2 to 8 degrees cooler, leading to lower air conditioning bills. ENERGY STAR-qualified ceiling fan/light units are 50 percent more efficient than standard units, which means you can save another $15-20 per year on utility bills by installing one.

Ventilating fans. Kitchen range hoods, as well as bathroom and other types of fans not only use 65 percent less energy than standard models, but are 50 percent quieter to boot.

Windows, doors, skylights and roofing

ENERGY STAR-qualified **windows, doors and skylights** are designed using new technologies to help keep your home warmer in winter and cooler in summer. Qualifying units also help reduce condensation and fading. Units qualify based on the climates in four geographic zones. Go to www.energystar.gov for more specific information. The Web site also includes tons of great information on purchasing products and on insulating and sealing your home.

Certain ENERGY STAR-qualified **reflective roofing materials** reflect more of the sun's rays, helping to lower roof surface temperature by as much as 100 degrees F. These lower temperatures mean cooling bills that are 10 to 15 percent lower.

Heating and cooling

Up to half your utility bill dollars go to heating and cooling your home. The older and less energy efficient your existing heating and cooling equipment, the greater your long-term savings with ENERGY STAR products. **Room and central air conditioners, furnaces, boilers, heat pumps and programmable thermostats** can all qualify for the ENERGY STAR. Qualifying furnaces are up to 15 percent more efficient than standard models.

One of the smartest places to put your money is in a programmable thermostat that can save you $150 or more per year depending on your utility costs, usage habits and house.

You can also save up to $25 per year by replacing a 10-year-old room air conditioner with an ENERGY STAR-qualified model.

The ENERGY STAR site also contains information on locating and hiring a dependable heating and cooling contractor.

Rebates, tax credits and incentives

Shop around for "free" money before you go shopping

Buying energy-efficient products can cost more initially, but save you money in the long run. In order to encourage people to make that bigger initial investment, government agencies, utility companies and, sometimes, even manufacturers and retailers offer rebates, assistance programs and tax incentives to help defray those upfront costs.

What, when, where, from whom and how much these incentives are worth varies greatly, but they're worth looking into. Here are a few tools to help you in your initial search.

Government incentives

One good starting place to look for both state and federal tax credits is the U.S. Department of Energy's Web site at www.energy.gov. Any current federal tax incentives will be prominently shown on the "Consumer" portion of the Web site.

For state incentives, click on the name of the state where you live, then look for relevant information and links. You may find listings under headings like "Incentives for Renewable Energy" or "Energy Assistance Programs." Or conduct a Web search by typing in "energy rebates" or "energy tax credits" along with the name of your state.

Utility company incentives

Utility companies often offer rebates or incentives to their customers for purchasing energy-efficient products; many use ENERGY STAR ratings as qualifiers. To find out about incentives, check the inserts that come with your monthly bill, call your utility companies or visit their Web sites.

A quick check of one Midwest utility company's Web site showed rebates of up to $100 to those installing tankless water heaters, and of more than $300 for those installing high-efficiency heat pumps.

While you're at it, check into "peak demand" energy conservation programs. One type involves the installation of a remote-controlled switch on your central air conditioner that the utility company can activate for brief periods during hot summer days when demand for electricity peaks. As an incentive, you'll receive some type of discount on your total electric bill; often in the 10 to 20 percent range.

Manufacturer and retailer incentives

When shopping for appliances, heating and cooling equipment or other products, check to see if manufacturers offer rebates. Some rebates are linked to energy efficiency, while others are linked to "package deals" or other scenarios.

Check manufacturers' individual Web sites, or check general information on Web sites such as www.myrebates.com for more information. The ENERGY STAR Web site at www.energystar.gov also lists special rebates and offers from thousands of their ENERGY STAR partners.

40 low-cost energy-saving tips

Save fuel, electricity and cold hard cash

ENERGY-SAVING
COMPACT
FLUORESCENT
BULB

Install and use an automatic setback thermostat
You can reduce your heating and cooling costs by 5 to 15 percent.

Replace worn-out thresholds
and weatherstripping around windows and doors.

DUCT SEALANT

Seal the joints
of heating and cooling ducts that run through attics and basements, and save 10 percent on your heating and cooling bills.

Replace lightbulbs
used more than two to three hours per day with compact fluorescent bulbs. Fluorescent bulbs last longer and use only one-third as much energy as standard bulbs.

Shade your windows
with trees, awnings, overhangs, shutters or other devices to keep direct sunlight from entering your home. Add window tint film.

Wrap the tank

of your gas-burning water heater in a special fiberglass blanket to decrease heat loss. Check your owner's manual to make sure that a blanket is a viable option for your model.

Change furnace filters

every month, more often if needed.

MOTION SENSOR

Install light controls

like motion sensors, photocell switches and timers to shut off lights automatically when they're not needed.

Clean the air conditioner condenser coils and fins when you see grass and airborne debris collected on them.

Insulate pipes,

especially if they pass through an area you don't want heated or cooled.

PIPE INSULATION

More tips

■ Reduce hot water usage by replacing high-volume shower-heads with low-flow heads (2 to 3 gallons per minute). Save up to $40 per year.

■ Have a furnace tune-up to clean and adjust burners and improve fuel-burning efficiency.

■ Fix leaky faucets; dripping hot water can cost $35 per year.

■ Buy gas stoves with electronic ignition rather than pilot lights.

■ Replace recessed light fixtures with air-tight models when you remodel.

■ Install a reflector (shiny aluminum foil over cardboard will do) behind radiators to reduce heat driven into and through the wall. Save 5 percent.

■ Have your air conditioner serviced to clean hard-to-reach evaporator coils and adjust coolant pressure to achieve maximum efficiency.

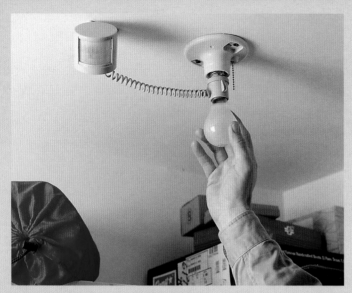

Finally—a light that turns itself off

Are your kids are always switching on the lights in the laundry room, storage room and pantry and never turning them off? Sometimes the lights burn all night, even for days, before you discover the light streaming under the closed doors. Here's a solution: buy a wireless motion-sensing light adapter ($20 at home centers) and aim the sensing unit straight down the wall inside the top of the door. The light automatically turns on when it senses that someone is after a can of tuna or wants that special T-shirt out of the wash, and then turns off.

Furnace filter reminder

Whenever you buy a new box of furnace filters, write the months of the year on the individual filters (and change them monthly). That way, you'll always know when you last changed the filter.

1 Lower the indoor temperature a few degrees in winter (you'll save about 2 percent per degree). Set it even lower at night and a full 10 degrees lower when you're on vacation.

2 Close the fireplace damper when the fireplace isn't in use. If it's never used, seal the flue with a plastic bag stuffed with insulation.

3 Open shades and blinds to let in sunlight during the day and close them to reduce heat loss at night. For cooling, close them during the day.

4 Close off unused rooms and lower the temperatures by adjusting the registers and dampers. You'll save up to $50 per year.

5 Clean your furnace's blower fan with a soft brush and vacuum cleaner.

6 Ventilate and cool your home with window or whole-house fans during the cooler hours of the day.

7 Fill clothes washers and dishwashers for more efficient energy use, rather than cleaning partial loads.

8 Skip the dishwasher's drying cycle (and cut the energy use by about half!).

9 Wash clothes in cool rather than hot water.

21 money- and energy-saving ideas
that don't cost a dime

15 Cook more efficiently using microwaves, Crock-Pots and pressure cookers.

16 Turn off room air conditioners when you leave for an hour or more. You can quickly cool the room later.

17 Recycle. Reuse. Take your bike instead of your car.

18 In warm weather, set the thermostat higher (75 to 78 degrees F) and rely more on ceiling and table fans for cooling, even when the air conditioner is running.

19 Reduce humidity in bathrooms and kitchens with exhaust fans. When dehumidifying a basement, keep basement doors and windows closed.

20 Consider higher-efficiency appliances when purchasing new refrigerators, freezers and dishwashers. The energy savings usually pays back the extra costs within a few years. The same goes for furnaces and water heaters.

21 Lower your water heater setting to 120 degrees F for both energy savings and safety. (Measure hot water temperature at a faucet with a cooking thermometer if the water heater setting isn't calibrated in degrees.)

10 Clean clothes washer and dryer lint screens after every use.

11 Turn off lights not in use. Reduce bulb wattage and use dimmers.

12 Clean refrigerator coils with a soft brush annually, or more often if you have pets that shed.

13 Run major appliances late in the evening or early in the morning when electric loads are less (off peak).

14 Flush your garbage disposer with cold water rather than hot. Grease solidifies in cold water and will wash away.

Energy-savings

Window film can be installed in about 30 minutes. The hazy appearance will disappear after 10 days.

FILM   NO FILM

Heat-reducing window film

Q My son's west-facing bedroom gets very hot in the spring and summer. Will a window film help, and if so, can I install it myself?

A A heat-control window film will help keep your son's room cooler, and yes, you can install it yourself. These films reflect the sun's heat and ultraviolet rays, and reduce glare without obscuring the view. Applying the film takes about 30 minutes per window. The film should last about 10 years. Prices vary with film size. A 3 x 15-ft. film (which can cover two to three windows) costs $30. The film is sold at home centers and hardware stores. Gila is one company that makes heat-control film (800-528-4481, www.gilafilms.com).

Different types of film are available, so get the one designed for heat control. The film can be applied to any window, including double-pane low-e windows, although they already reduce radiant heat loss and gain.

One drawback is that the film may void the manufacturer's warranty for the seal on double-pane windows. If the window warranty has already expired or reducing excessive heat is more important to you than a warranty, apply the film. Otherwise, consider options such as installing shades, awnings or shutters, or even planting a tree on the west side to block the sun.

Too-hot water heater

Q If I set my gas water heater temperature to 120 degrees F, it's often not hot enough. The water dispensed has been as low as 90 degrees. That's a 30-degree temperature swing. I don't want to raise the temperature setting, because the water at times will be scalding hot. Is this normal?

A No, the temperature range you're experiencing is not typical. A 17-degree swing is considered standard. The swing often occurs because the thermostat won't switch the heater on until the water cools a certain amount.

In an opposite situation, a water heater heats water beyond its temperature setting. This is usually caused by "stacking," which occurs when you use just enough water to switch on the burner but draw little off. Doing this repeatedly causes overheated water to rise to the top of the tank, where it could be drawn off extra hot.

Since you've tried adjusting your thermostat setting and you still get too large a temperature swing, you probably have a bad thermostat. Call a plumber. If you have a standard water heater that's more than five years old, buy a new unit. Gas water heaters cost about $400, and it would cost at least half that to have a plumber diagnose the problem and more for the fix.

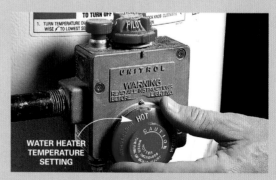

WATER HEATER TEMPERATURE SETTING

Q&A

Straight scoop on triple glazing

Q I'd like to replace the drafty single-pane windows in my house. Is upgrading to triple-pane windows a good idea in cold climates where it's often below zero in the winter?

A In cold regions, triple-glazed windows can save 2 to 3 percent of your heating bill, compared with double-glazed windows. From a cost standpoint, it'll take a few decades to recoup the 10 to 15 percent upcharge to go from low-e double-glazed windows to triple-glazed. For example, if you pay $1,000 per year in energy bills, have 20 windows in your house, and 22 percent of your energy is lost through your windows (which is average), then each window is losing $11 worth of energy per year. A triple-glazed window will reduce that loss by about $1, so it'll take 35 years to cover a $35 upcharge for triple-glazing. Of course, if your energy bills and energy loss are greater, you'll recoup the cost sooner.

However, the investment may be worth the cost in terms of comfort. Triple glazing will reduce condensation, which will allow you to maintain a higher indoor relative humidity in cold weather. These windows also reduce cold drafts. If you don't want to pay for triple-pane windows throughout the house, get them for the north- and east-facing rooms, where you'll get the biggest payoff.

Most of the major window manufacturers in the United States don't offer triple glazing. But here are two that do: Marvin (888-537-7828; www.marvin.com) and Weather Shield (800-222-2995; www.weathershield.com). Many Canadian window manufacturers offer triple glazing.

PHOTO COURTESY OF MARVIN

Marvin's triple-glazed window consists of three panes of glass, two of which have a low-e coating. The space between the panes is filled with krypton gas.

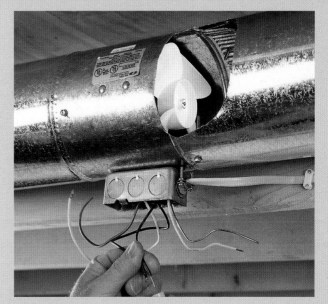

Duct booster for cold rooms

Q Our son's bedroom, located at the end of a long hallway, stays about 10 degrees cooler than the rest of the house. How can we direct more heat to just that room? We have forced-air heat.

A First check to make sure all the dampers controlling heat to that area are open; there can be as many as three. The damper in the floor- or wall-mounted register can be seen using a flashlight and can be adjusted by moving a lever or wheel on the register. Often there's another damper in the branch duct leading to the register. This is controlled by a wing nut on the side or bottom of the duct; when the wing nut is aligned parallel to the duct, the damper's open. In some cases there can even be a damper in the main trunk line, usually controlled by an L-shaped lever on the side of the vent.

If all the vents are wide open, consider installing an in-duct air boosting fan. This $25 part won't create more heat, but will pull more air to the trouble spot.

If you install the air-boosting fan, bear in mind:

■ Install it as near as possible to the cold room.
■ You can wire it to a manually controlled switch or to the furnace's blower fan, so the booster fan turns on every time the furnace blower fan kicks in. Follow the manufacturer's instructions and all applicable codes.
■ Installing it can be a pain. It's usually easiest to remove a few duct support brackets, drop down and remove one or two sections of round duct, install the booster fan, then reinstall the whole works.
■ These fans can also be used to improve the circulation of a gravity-type warm-air furnace.

Saving Energy:

Four out of every five homes built before 1980 have a less-than-recommended amount of insulation. Back when oil cost only a few dollars per barrel neither builders nor homeowners gave much thought to installing the stuff.

But insulating your home today can easily reduce both your heating and cooling bills by 20 percent to 40 percent. And with heating and cooling often accounting for nearly half the utility bill, insulating your home makes good economic sense. Adding attic insulation is by far the easiest and most cost-effective step you can take. Insulating walls with blown-in insulation will also save money in the long run, but it's nearly always a messier, more expensive proposition.

It is critical to remember that sealing up air leaks and insulating go hand in hand. For starters, it's much easier to seal attic air leaks before insulating. Secondly, your insulation will be much more effective when it doesn't have to fight air infiltration; after all, insulation is simply thousands of little pockets that trap air.

Insulation

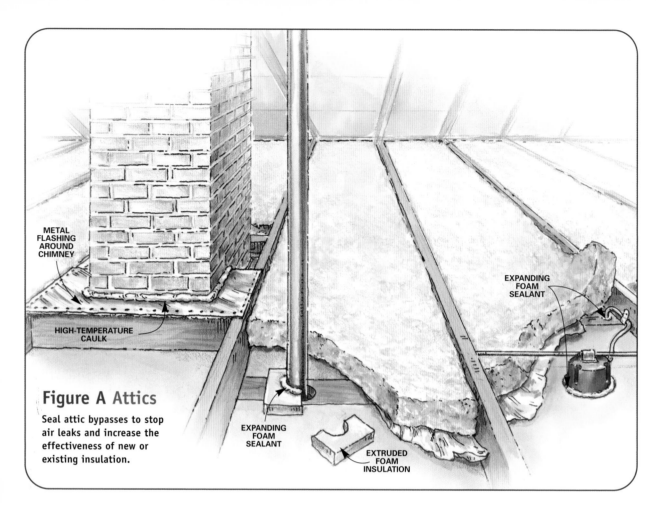

Figure A Attics

Seal attic bypasses to stop air leaks and increase the effectiveness of new or existing insulation.

METAL FLASHING AROUND CHIMNEY

HIGH-TEMPERATURE CAULK

EXPANDING FOAM SEALANT

EXPANDING FOAM SEALANT

EXTRUDED FOAM INSULATION

Insulating

Do it right to save $$, save energy and stay warm

Insulation—silently hidden in your walls, no moving parts to fix—is a material you probably spend precious little time thinking about. Then along comes subzero (or sweltering!) weather, a three-digit utility bill or chilly drafts, and you start thinking about it a lot! At home, you ponder whether it's worth the time and expense to add it to your ceilings, walls and basement. At the store, you ponder which type, thickness, width and density to buy. And when you install it, you wonder just how good is "good enough."

We asked insulation manufacturers and installers which questions they field most—and which blunders they see most. Following are six things they (and we) think you should know.

1 Seal up air bypasses before adding attic insulation (or you'll be wasting money).

Attics are one of the easiest and most cost-effective places to add insulation. But you'll increase the effectiveness of insulation substantially if you first seal up air bypasses (Figure A) around chimneys, plumbing vents, wires, interior walls and exhaust fans—places where warm, moist interior air escapes into the attic.

Heat has a natural inclination to both rise and migrate to colder areas. Combine these two tendencies and you can see why air bypasses can reduce the effectiveness of attic insulation by 30 to 70 percent. You can track down bypasses by lifting existing attic insulation and checking for dark patches of moisture or dust. Or head to the attic on a cold day and feel for pockets of warm air or use a stick of incense to check for drafts.

Before installing (or adding) attic insulation, take these steps:
- Use caulk and expanding foam sealant to close air gaps around pipes, ducts and electrical wires where they enter the attic.
- Cut and fit strips of 24-gauge sheet metal between the masonry chimney and the surrounding wood framing. Use high-temperature caulk to seal the flashing where it meets the chimney.
- Install weatherstripping around the perimeter of the attic access opening, then use screw hooks to pull the hatch tight against the weatherstripping. Glue rigid extruded foam insulation to the top of the hatch.

NOTE: After air-tightening your home, always test your carbon monoxide detectors, or install them if you don't have them ($20 to $40 at home centers and hardware stores).

2 Careful installation increases the insulation's R-value by over 20 percent.

Leaving 5 percent of a wall uninsulated will reduce the entire wall's R-value (resistance to heat flow) by 20 percent. It doesn't take much more time to install fiberglass insulation properly (Figure B). The most important steps you can take:
- Fill the stud cavity from top to bottom and side to side. To avoid guesswork when insulating walls built from standard 92-5/8-in.-long studs, purchase and install precut fiberglass batts that are 93 in. long and 15 in. wide. When you have to custom-cut batts at wall corners and other places, cut the batts 1 in. higher and wider than the cavity you're filling.
- Split your insulation so half goes in front of and half goes behind electrical wires. Compressing insulation reduces its R-value.

- Around electrical boxes, notch, rather than compress, the batt—then tuck the cutout behind the box. To help prevent frozen pipes, insulate only on the cold side.

3 You probably don't need kraft-faced insulation.

Kraft paper—the asphalt-impregnated brown paper facing available on insulation—is rarely called for these days. When insulation was first developed, it was only an inch or two thick and the attached kraft facing was stapled to studs to keep it from sagging. Insulation today is so "full-bodied" and fills stud and joist cavities so completely that it resists settling—even when walls have been purposely vibrated in tests.

Kraft paper does act as a vapor retarder to slow the movement of interior moisture through the wall cavity and insulation. But for a thorough job, especially in bathrooms and other high-moisture areas, a continuous 6-mil plastic sheeting vapor barrier is much more effective. Kraft paper still serves the purpose of temporarily holding insulation in place on horizontal or sloped surfaces. And when you're retrofitting insulation in the floor of a crawlspace (Figure D), installing the kraft-faced insulation paper-side-up provides an adequate vapor retarder. Kraft paper and its underlying asphalt adhesive are flammable and should always be covered with drywall or other fire-resistant material.

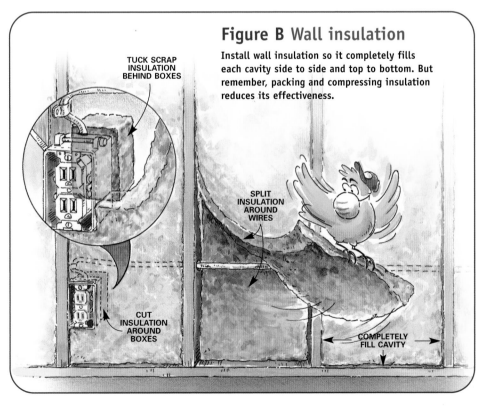

TUCK SCRAP INSULATION BEHIND BOXES

CUT INSULATION AROUND BOXES

Figure B Wall insulation

Install wall insulation so it completely fills each cavity side to side and top to bottom. But remember, packing and compressing insulation reduces its effectiveness.

SPLIT INSULATION AROUND WIRES

COMPLETELY FILL CAVITY

Another important point: Except in hot coastal regions, insulation should be installed with the kraft paper (or plastic vapor barrier) on the interior side of the wall. In hot regions, vapor barriers are often eliminated or positioned toward the outside of the stud wall. If in doubt, consult a local building inspector.

4 High-density insulation can pay off.

Insulation is rated according to its R-value, or resistance to heat loss: the higher the R-value, the higher the insulating value. Standard fiberglass insulation has an R-value of about 3.5 per inch of thickness (Figure C); this provides an insulating value of R-11 for 2x4 walls and R-19 for 2x6 walls. But if you're serious about energy savings, you can buy better-performing products. High-density types of fiberglass insulation, with more fibers and air spaces per square inch, offer R-values of up to 4.25 per inch. Some provide R-15 for 2x4 walls and R-21 for 2x6 walls. There's also high-density insulation for ceilings and attics. You'll wind up paying more, and in many cases you'll need to special-order it, but high-density insulation delivers up to 35 percent more insulating value per inch.

You can also pack 5-1/2-in.-thick insulation into a 3-1/2-in.-thick wall to increase its R-value, but the compressed R-19 batt will only yield an R-value of about 17.

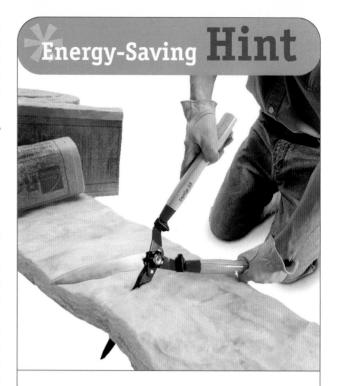

Energy-Saving Hint

Insulation trimmer

Here's a faster, cleaner way to cut fiberglass insulation. Use a hedge shears to slice through the insulation. Unlike a utility knife, the shears won't spread loose tufts of insulation all over, and the best part is, you stay itch free.

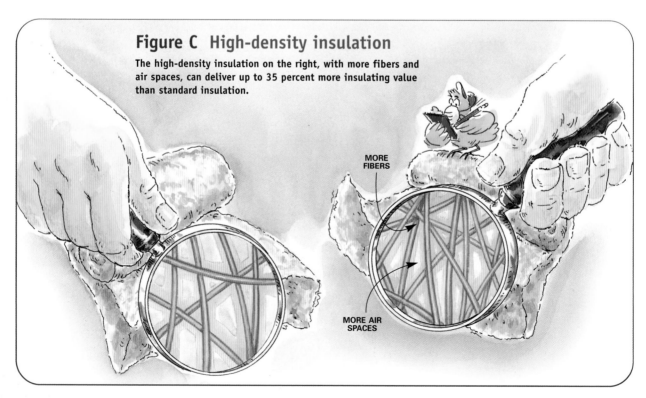

Figure C High-density insulation

The high-density insulation on the right, with more fibers and air spaces, can deliver up to 35 percent more insulating value than standard insulation.

MORE FIBERS

MORE AIR SPACES

Figure D Attic and crawlspace insulation

VENTING ATTICS AND CRAWLSPACES is critical to reduce moisture problems and allow the insulation to perform right.

RIDGE VENT

CHUTES TO MAINTAIN 1" AIR SPACE

SOFFIT VENT

5 How much insulation is enough?

The first 3 in. of insulation you add to a bare ceiling or wall will yield huge savings. Adding another 3 in. will increase energy savings, but not to as great a degree. For charts showing the Department of Energy's optimal amounts of insulation to install, go to www.certainteed.com or www.owenscorning.com. Their recommendations are based on climate, fuel costs and other factors. Adding more will give you a diminishing return on your investment.

The payback period for retrofitting insulation varies greatly, but studies show that added insulation usually pays for itself in saved energy costs within five to 10 years. One typical two-story Minnesota home was fitted with blown-in wall insulation, additional ceiling insulation and rim joist insulation at a cost of $1,890. The result was a $325 savings in yearly heating costs, which represents a payback period of slightly less than six years. Payback in more temperate areas takes longer, but remember that insulation reduces air-conditioning costs too.

6 When you insulate attics and crawlspaces, you've got to vent them too.

Since insulation changes the way attics and crawlspaces "breathe," it's critical that you maintain or install proper ventilation (Figure D). At first, it seems odd to add insulation for warmth and then purposely create ventilation "holes" for cold air to enter. But if you don't do this, you're setting yourself up for moisture problems.

When you add insulation to **attic rafters** and **attic floors**, it's important to maintain at least a 1-in. continuous air space between insulation and roof sheathing, from eaves to ridge. This air space flushes out moisture. It also helps maintain a "cold roof," which prevents ice dams from forming in the winter and excessive heat from damaging shingles and increasing cooling costs in the summer. The biggest mistake homeowners make with installation is to install it so it blocks the flow of air at the eaves. The best way to avoid this problem is to install inexpensive air chutes to keep the space open. See "Improve Attic Ventilation," p. 108.

Newly insulated **crawlspaces** also need proper ventilation. The standard procedure is to insulate the ceilings of unheated crawlspaces and the walls of heated crawlspaces. To reduce moisture migration if there's no slab, a 6-mil polyethylene vapor barrier should be laid on the ground in both cases. At least 1 sq. ft. of ventilation should be installed for each 1,500 sq. ft. of floor area.

There are regional differences and various codes and interpretations for insulating crawlspaces and attics. Contact a local building official to make sure your house stays code-compliant.

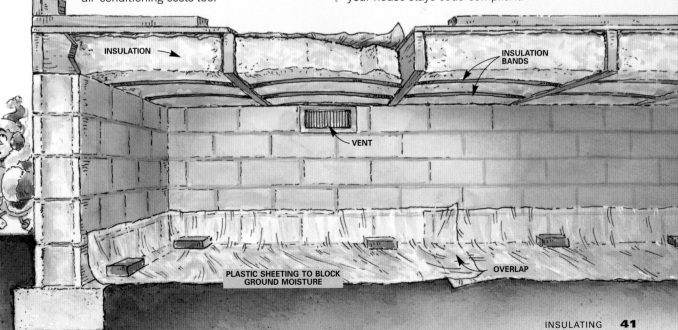

INSULATION

INSULATION BANDS

VENT

PLASTIC SHEETING TO BLOCK GROUND MOISTURE

OVERLAP

What is R-value?

The key to understanding insulation

The capacity of an insulating material to resist heat flow is called its R-value. The higher the material's R-value, the better it insulates. Recommended R-values differ for various parts of your home and vary by region. Check with your local utility company or read the insulation manufacturer's literature.

Type	R-Value per Inch	Cost	Pros & Cons
Fiberglass	R-3.0 to R-3.8	Low	**Pros:** Easy-to-install batts press into place; made in standard stud and joist widths; available with Kraft paper facing attached. **Cons:** Can be irritating to installer's skin and lungs; susceptible to air gaps during installation.
Loose fill	R-2.2 to R-4.0	Low	**Pros:** Better coverage in irregular spaces and over trusses; can be poured or blown into walls. **Cons:** Messy to work with; quality can vary; lower R-value; can shift or settle; may need to rent insulation blower.
Extruded foam	R-5.2	High	**Pros:** High compressive strength; great performance underground. **Cons:** Cover with drywall or other fireproof material.
Expanded foam	R-3.8 to R-4.3	Medium	**Pros:** Lowest cost among foams. **Cons:** Not for underground. Cover with drywall or fireproof material.
Sprayed urethane foam	R-6.0 to R-7.3	High	**Pros:** Makes a tough, seamless thermal and vapor barrier; covers irregular surfaces; adds structural strength. **Cons:** Must be professionally applied. Very expensive. Cover with drywall or other fireproof material.

SHARP UTILITY KNIFE

✳ Energy-Saving Hint

Easier fiberglass cutting

For easier cutting, temporarily flatten unruly fiberglass insulation with a piece of scrap plywood. Just cut a 1-1/2-in.-wide slot in the center of a 16 x 30-in. board, use the slot as a straightedge and get a clean cut every time.

Installing fiberglass batts

You have only one chance to do it right! Here's how.

Filling stud spaces with fiberglass batts is the cheapest, easiest way for you to insulate new walls. It's also the best way to upgrade wall insulation during remodeling. Installing the batts doesn't require any special skills, but it's slow, tedious, itchy work. It's often done poorly, and even small gaps can reduce efficiency as much as 25 percent. Here you'll discover how to cut and fit fiberglass batts and how to work around electrical outlets and cables to get the best job with the least hassle.

PRECUT FIBERGLASS BATTS

Push batts all the way to the back of each stud space and then pull out the front edges until they're flush with the face of the studs.

Fill all voids

The key to a quality insulating job is tight-fitting batts that completely fill the stud cavity with no voids or gaps. You can do top-quality work with only a few basic tools. You'll need a utility knife with a good supply of sharp blades, a tape measure and a straightedge, and a 3- or 4-in. putty knife for stuffing insulation around doors and windows. Fiberglass can irritate your throat and skin, so wear protective gear. Buy a two-strap mask rated for fiberglass insulation (3M No. 8210 is one example) and wear a hat, gloves, a long-sleeve shirt and goggles to keep fibers out of your eyes.

SPLIT BATT

Fit batts tightly around electrical cables and boxes

Running a full batt in front of electrical cables leaves an uninsulated space behind. Avoid this by splitting the batt as shown. Then when you come to an electrical box, trim the insulation to fit snugly around it. Run your knife blade against the outside of the box to guide the cut. But don't cut too deep or you risk nicking the wires. If you have plumbing pipes on an outside wall, insulate behind them, but leave the side facing the interior uncovered to allow heat from the house to keep the pipes warm.

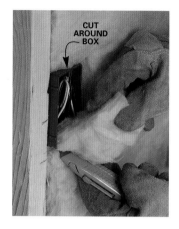

CUT AROUND BOX

Split batts to fit around electrical cables. Tear the batt in half, starting from the bottom. Slide one half behind the cable and lay the other half over the top.

Split and cut batts to fit behind and around electrical boxes. Slide half the batt behind the box. Then cut the front half to fit tightly around the box.

Fit first, then cut to length

We're using unfaced batts that are sized to friction-fit into standard stud spaces (either 16-in. or 24-in. on-center studs). They're also available precut to lengths that fit standard 8-ft. and 9-ft. walls. Buying precut batts eliminates some work, but you'll still have to cut some batts to length. You could measure the space and cut the batt to fit, but a quicker method that's just as accurate is shown below. Leave an extra 1/2 in. of length for a snug fit.

We're using unfaced batts because they're easier to cut and install. In most climates, you'll have to staple 4-mil plastic sheeting over the batts to form a vapor barrier. Check with your local building inspector for the recommended practice in your area.

Cut batts to length by setting the top of the batt into the space and cutting against the bottom plate with a sharp utility knife. Leave an extra 1/2 in. of length for a tighter fit.

UTILITY KNIFE

Trim batts in place

Accurate cutting is essential (actually, slightly oversized batts are best). A batt cut too small leaves gaps, and one cut too large bunches up and leaves voids.

The photos show two methods of cutting batts to width. If you're having trouble getting an accurate cut with the "eyeballing" technique, measure the width of the stud space and use the straightedge method instead. Add about 1/2 in. to the width to ensure a tight fit. It's better to compress the batts a little than to leave gaps. Don't worry if the batts bulge out a bit. The drywall will compress them tightly.

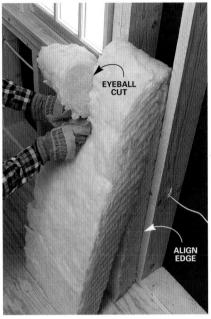

Leave the batt folded in half and hold one edge against the edge of the stud. Slice down the length while holding the top of the batt. Cut against the stud face.

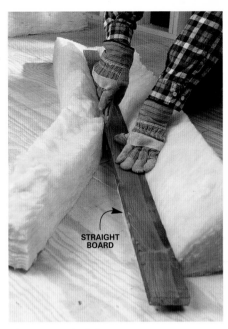

Alternate method: Press a straightedge down on the batt at the desired width and use it as a guide for the utility knife.

Fill gaps around windows and doors

The shim space around windows and doors is a prime spot for air leakage. Stop these leaks by reaching to the back of this space with the straw-type nozzle included with a can of expanding foam insulation and applying a bead around the perimeter. Let it cure at least an hour before stuffing the remaining space with a thin strip of fiberglass. Don't pack the fiberglass too tight or it will bow the jambs and cause trouble with the operation of the window.

Stuff skinny strips of batting into spaces around windows and doors with a 3-in.-wide putty knife. The insulation should fit snugly, but don't pack it.

Quick tip*

INSULATE RIGHT! When you insulate, do it right. Compressing fiberglass batts or leaving even small gaps can cut the efficiency of your new insulation in half.

Batt insulation

Buying the right stuff now helps you save big

Fiberglass insulation has a reputation for being itchy and irritating, but when it comes to convenience, price and installation ease, it can't be beat. You can buy it at almost any home center, toss it in your car and install it in a jiffy.

But it can be confusing to pick out the best type for your project. Fiberglass insulation varies not only in size, thickness and length but also in efficiency, type of vapor barrier and potential for skin irritation.

The following four steps show you how to sort through the many types of fiberglass insulation and choose the one that works best. Once you decide, call lumberyards and home centers to locate the product. And check for substitutes in case you can't find the type with the exact features you want.

1 Begin by selecting batts that completely fill the joist, rafter or stud space.

■ **Width.** Buy 15-in. widths for studs or joists 16 in. on center, or 23-in. widths for spacing 24 in. on center.
■ **Thickness.** Buy 3-1/2-in.-thick insulation to go between 2x4s, 6-in.-thick insulation (actual range between 5-1/2 and 6-1/4 in.) to go between 2x6s. (You can compress a 6-in. batt into a 3-1/2-in. space, but you won't gain much insulation value compared with a 3-1/2-in. batt.) Batts 8, 10 and 12 in. thick are also available for attics and deeper framing members.
■ **Length.** If installing insulation between studs at a standard wall height, buy batts precut in lengths that fit (usually about 93 in.). If the height isn't standard, buy whatever is readily available, from continuous rolls to standard precut 4-ft. lengths.
■ **Amount.** Measure and multiply to find the number of square feet you need to cover. The packaging for each bag, bundle or roll of insulation lists the square footage it covers.

CONTINUOUS ROLL

WIDTH

THICKNESS

2 Buy "faced" or "unfaced" depending on your installation method.

Faced batts have a brown kraft or shiny facing paper glued to one side. This special paper serves as a vapor barrier and has flaps so that you can staple the batt to studs and joists to keep it in place. The vapor barrier isn't necessary if you intend to cover the wall or ceiling with plastic. However, you'll need the paper facing for stud or joist spaces where unfaced batts might fall out. Faced batts cost about 2¢ more per sq. ft.

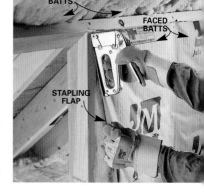

UNFACED BATTS

FACED BATTS

STAPLING FLAP

The vapor barrier should face the inside of the wall, except in hot coastal regions. If in doubt, call your local building inspector.

basics

bucks in the long run.

3 Select the thermal resistance value (R-11, for example) according to the insulation requirements of your region.

Manufacturers now produce batts with higher fiberglass densities, so you can buy 3-1/2-in.-thick batts with R-11, R-13 or R-15 thermal resistance values. The higher the number, the better the insulation. The high-density R-15 batts are best, but they cost more than twice as much as R-11 batts. (They also contain three times as much fiberglass!)

Balance the price with the insulation requirements of your local building codes. If you have to cram more insulation into a minimal wall space, high-density batts might be worth the price. But in most cases, low- or medium-density insulation is adequate. And where you have plenty of space, like in an attic, buy the least expensive. You can easily achieve adequate thermal resistance by piling it higher.

Because batts are sold in bundles of various sizes, cost comparisons are difficult. The best approach is to compare the cost per square foot for batts of the same thickness. You'll need a pocket calculator to do the math!

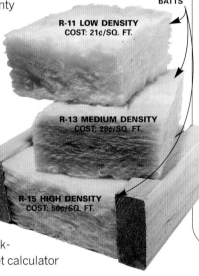

3-1/2" BATTS

R-11 LOW DENSITY
COST: 21¢/SQ. FT.

R-13 MEDIUM DENSITY
COST: 28¢/SQ. FT.

R-15 HIGH DENSITY
COST: 50¢/SQ. FT.

Energy-Saving Hint

DRAFTY GAP

GASKET

COVER PLATE

Stop a draft in 60 seconds

In exterior walls, electrical boxes that hold switches or outlets can let in a lot of cold air. Worse, they can let warm, moist indoor air into walls, causing problems like wood rot or peeling exterior paint. One way to stop the airflow is to seal the gaps around them and the holes inside them with caulk—messy and time consuming. But there's a much easier way: With foam gaskets, all you have to do is unscrew the cover plate, stick the gasket in place and put the plate back on. A pack of a dozen gaskets costs about $3 at home centers and hardware stores.

4 Look for wrapped or low-itch batts if the glass fibers cause skin irritation, coughing or any other discomfort.

Fiberglass dust is an irritant, so wear eye protection and a dust mask, as well as gloves and long sleeves and pants, when installing it (see top photo, opposite). Batts wrapped with perforated plastic or other materials reduce the dust and irritation while still letting moisture through. One brand, Miraflex (Owens Corning), is virtually dust-free.

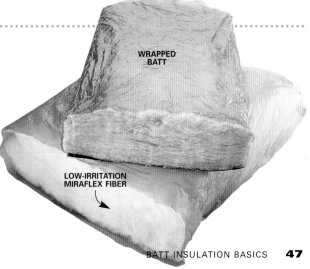

WRAPPED BATT

LOW-IRRITATION MIRAFLEX FIBER

Blowing in wall

Save energy, save money and feel more comfortable

STANDARD 16" O.C. STUD CAVITIES

PLUGGED HOLES

SOLID HEADER

ODD-SIZE STUD CAVITY

SHEATHING

FELT PAPER

ORIGINAL SIDING

BACKER BOARD

VINYL SIDING

INSULATION BLOWER

REMOTE CONTROL

REDUCER

BELOW WINDOW CAVITY

ELECTRICAL CABLE

About 65 percent of a home's heat loss occurs through the attic. Insulating and sealing up that, along with caulking around windows and doors, costs far less, saves far more, and is much easier than insulating the walls.

Serious DIYers can buy insulation and rent the blowing machine, but you need special tools and know-how to do the job right—and for a task you'll most likely undertake once in a lifetime, it may not be worth the hassle. Pros can often finish the job in a day. Some larger companies also provide before-and-after infrared pictures of your walls to show they did a complete job.

Installing blown-in insulation creates a huge mess, so most pros prefer to work from the outside. The procedure is to drill 2-1/2-in. holes in each stud cavity, fill the cavity with insulation, then plug the holes with tapered plugs. If the house has its original lap siding or has been re-sided, pros will remove rows of siding, do the work, then reinstall the siding. Some contractors (as in our example) remove a single strip of siding in the middle of each wall, blow the top half of the cavity first (the cellulose will stay put), then blow the bottom half. Others bore holes at the top or both midway and top, then blow insulation down through the holes. Odd-size cavities and spaces below

insulation

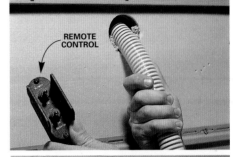

Step 1: Drill the hole

PLUG EJECTOR

2-1/2" HOLE SAW

SHEATHING
FELT PAPER
ORIGINAL SIDING
BACKER BOARD

Step 2: Fill the cavity

REMOTE CONTROL

Step 3: Install the plug

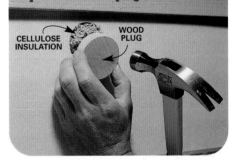

CELLULOSE INSULATION

WOOD PLUG

windows should also be insulated, though sometimes it's not cost effective to insulate every little nook and cranny.

Houses with brick exteriors must be insulated from the inside. Stucco homes can be insulated from the outside, but the dozens of plug holes can be an eyesore if the patches don't match perfectly. This is a challenge even for stucco experts. Working from the inside makes sense if the house is vacant or if remodeling is under way and the insulating holes will be painted, wallpapered, drywalled or paneled over.

Cellulose insulation is a popular choice because it's inexpensive, easy to blow, minimally irritating and good for packing around ducts, electrical boxes and wires. Fiberglass, mineral wool and foam insulation are also available.

Is it worth it? Many contractors charge $1 or more per sq. ft. of wall. The $1,500 job that saves $250 yearly on heating and cooling bills has a six-year payback. But there are other payoffs: Your house will be less drafty, the walls will feel warmer, your furnace and air conditioner won't work as hard, and you'll conserve natural resources.

Our advice? Get an energy audit that breaks out how much money each energy improvement will cost you—and save you—then make your decision. Also check with your utility company to see if it offers any special financing or testing programs. *[ALWAYS check your combustion appliances, especially the water heater and furnace, for backdrafting after making any energy improvement.]*

✳ Energy-Saving Goof

Insulation frustration

My wife and I rented an insulation blower to add insulation in our attic. When I got the unit home, I noticed it had remnants of tape on the hose connection. I checked it out, and it seemed to work fine. With my wife feeding bags into the hopper and me up in the attic with the hose, we proceeded to get the nasty job done. Working my way around the attic, I noticed that the hose seemed to be caught, so I gave it a tug. Then nothing was coming out, and finally I heard the machine stop. I squeezed back downstairs to discover the downstairs covered in insulation. After a whole day of cleaning, I figured out what all the tape was for!

The best way to insulate a foundation

Before beginning any work, you must determine whether your basement has any moisture problems. If your foundation walls are only damp on humid summer days, fine—you're good to go with the methods we recommend. But if you have any problems with standing or leaking water in the spring or during heavy rains, you've got some "prework" to do.

Fixes usually are as simple as adding or repairing gutters and downspouts or adjusting the grade to direct runoff water away from the house. But serious water problems may call for drastic measures, like interior or exterior drain tiling, or exterior waterproofing, which could mean digging around the house or tearing up part of the slab. You must solve all water problems or you'll risk boxing future water in behind a finished wall, thereby ruining it. You'll end up spending hundreds of bucks re-remodeling a recently finished lower level.

Just about every carpenter or building inspector has a different opinion on how to finish walls against masonry. The methods we'll demonstrate work well in most conditions, but consult with your building inspector before beginning any work to make sure you're meeting building codes in your area.

There are two methods of finishing against masonry: fiberglass-insulated 2x4 walls and foam-filled 2x2 walls. Both methods include a 3/4-in. foam moisture barrier between the framing and the foundation wall to eliminate condensation from interior humidity and to protect the walls from exterior moisture. Tack the foam to the foundation wall with a few blobs of foam construction adhesive to hold it while you frame the walls.

2x4 framing method

👍 Fast to build; lots of room for wiring and plumbing

👎 Gobbles up 38 sq. ft. of space in a 20 x 36-ft. basement

3" DRYWALL SCREWS

TOP PLATE SCREWED TO CEILING JOISTS

3-1/2" FIBERGLASS

3/4" RIGID INSULATION

2x4

PRESSURE-TREATED 2X4 BOTTOM PLATE

Method 1

Method 1: A conventional wall (R-16)

The easy finishing method is to simply frame conventional 2x4 stud walls with pressure-treated bottom plates (the 2x4s the wall rests on) and fill the walls with fiberglass insulation. Hands down, it's the way to go—if you have oodles of space in the room you're finishing. Two-by-four walls are quick to install, and there's plenty of space for electrical work. Plus, you don't have to hassle with fastening furring strips to concrete, and it's easier to cut fiberglass insulation than to fit foam. The downside is that each wall steals nearly 6 in. of floor space from the perimeter of the room.

Look at the photo above to see the details. Note that the wall is pushed against the foam and then anchored to the slab with concrete screws and to the ceiling with 3-in. drywall screws. Don't install a vapor barrier between the fiberglass and drywall, because moisture will be trapped in the wall.

wall

Two options for a warmer, more energy-efficient basement

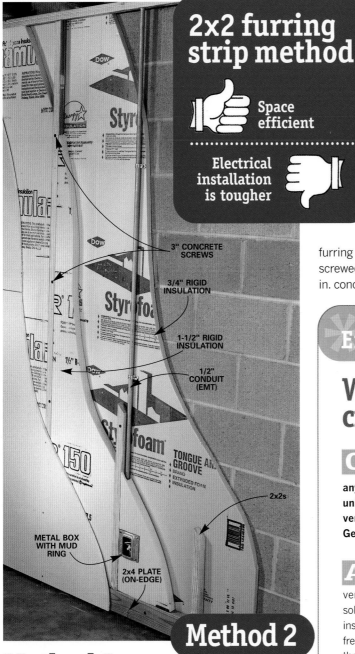

2x2 furring strip method

👍 Space efficient

....

Electrical installation is tougher 👎

3" CONCRETE SCREWS

3/4" RIGID INSULATION

1-1/2" RIGID INSULATION

1/2" CONDUIT (EMT)

2x2s

METAL BOX WITH MUD RING

2x4 PLATE (ON-EDGE)

Method 2

Method 2: 2x2 furring strips and foam (R-12)

To save precious floor space, use a thinner wall composed of 2x2s and foam insulation attached directly to the wall. Nail or screw a 2x2 to the bottom of the floor joists at the top of the wall, and screw a treated 2x4 flat against the bottom of the wall through the foam and into the concrete with 3-in. concrete screws. Then lay out the stud positions on the plates. Screw the treated 2x2s to the wall with three evenly spaced screws and fill in between with foam insulation ripped to fit. Hang the drywall with 1-1/4-in. drywall screws.

The downside is that electrical outlets and switches have special installation requirements. Cables must be at least 1-1/4 in. behind the front of the wood framing to prevent fasteners from accidentally piercing and damaging the cable. Use 1-1/4 in.-deep steel boxes and run cable through EMT (electrical metallic tubing) between the furring strips to the boxes. Boxes and conduit straps are screwed through the foam and into the masonry with 1-1/2-in. concrete screws.

Energy-Saving Q&A

Winterizing crawlspace vents

Q The crawlspace under my house has a vapor barrier and quite a few vents, so I don't have any moisture buildup. But the floor of my house is uninsulated. So, should I close off the crawlspace vents during the winter to save energy? I live in Georgia.

A In the South, where you're located, moisture in the crawlspace is a year-round problem, so the vents should stay open. To save energy, a better solution is to spend the money to add unfaced R-19 insulation between the floor joists. For the occasional freeze, you should also insulate any exposed pipes in the crawlspace.

In states where winters are moderate to hard, winter air tends to be much drier. So, closing crawlspace vents during the winter months is less likely to cause moisture problems and may slightly lower your energy bills. However, the walls of the crawlspace should be insulated (also with R-19), or closing the vents won't make much difference.

AIR
CHUTE

R-13 BATT
INSULATION

RAFTER
BAY

2" R-10
RIGID FOAM

STAPLER

Insulating a finished attic

The BEST way to save energy and headroom

If you need to insulate and ventilate your attic but don't want to lose headroom, use a combination of dense batt insulation, rigid foam sheeting and air chutes.

Most codes require a specified minimum amount of headroom, and it's tough to meet this requirement when insulating a finished attic, especially since most codes require insulation equal to R-38 or more. However, most inspectors we've spoken with will lower the insulation requirement if it means that the finished space won't otherwise have the required headroom. To get the most R-value with the least thickness, use batt insulation with a higher R-value per inch in combination with rigid foam insulation.

Rigid foam sheeting has an R-value ranging from R-5 to R-10 per inch of thickness. This means you can have a combined R-value ranging from R-23 to R-31 with only 5-1/2 in. of combined fiberglass and foam insulation.

Energy-Saving Hint

Duct tape wristbands

When you're working with fiberglass insulation, tape the cuffs of your long-sleeve shirts to gloves with duct tape. It'll keep the glass fibers from getting under sleeves and irritating your skin. Your wrists will thank you.

RIDGE VENT

CONTINUOUS SOFFIT VENT

AIR ENTERS the soffit vents, travels along the underside of the roof boards, then exits through the ridge vents to maintain a "healthy" roof.

To effectively ventilate your roof, create a 1-in. airspace from the soffit to the ridge by installing a continuous air chute in each rafter bay. To install the air chutes, staple them directly to the roof decking.

Air chutes, when combined with soffit vents and a ridge vent, will help prevent problems with condensation and ice dams. They come in 4-ft. lengths and 14-1/2 and 22-1/2-in. widths. They're readily available at home centers and cost 75¢ to $2 apiece.

(Air chutes work only when the rafter spaces run from the soffit to the ridge. This method won't work where rafter spaces stop short, such as in a valley or in the corner of a hip roof.)

Sealing attic air leaks

Sure, it's dusty, dirty work, but it's the quickest, cheapest way to save money on your energy bills

Chances are, your ceiling has the equivalent of a 2-ft.-square hole that's acting like a chimney, drafting expensive heated air into your attic and sucking cold air in around your windows and doors. You can't see the hole because it's the sum of many smaller openings. These gaps around plumbing pipes, light fixtures, chimneys and other attic bypasses are hidden under your insulation.

For less than $100 in materials and a day's labor, you can save lots of money on heating every year by sealing these holes. We'll show you where to find the bypasses in your attic and simple techniques for plugging and sealing them.

You'll find everything you need at any full-service hardware store, home center or lumberyard. If you can't find the reflective foil insulation (Photo 3, p. 56), substitute drywall or pieces cut from 4 x 8-ft. sheets of rigid foil-faced insulation. Fitting rigid material requires more precise measuring, but the result is the same.

1 Get your bearings from below

Before you crawl into the attic, make a quick sketch of the floor plan. Make note of dropped soffits over kitchen cabinets or bath vanities, slanted ceilings over stairways, and any other dropped-ceiling areas. These areas usually have open stud cavities leading directly into the attic that are huge sources of air leaks (Photos 1 – 3, p. 56). Locate the main plumbing stack, furnace flue or chimney and note this on your sketch for a reference point once you get into the attic.

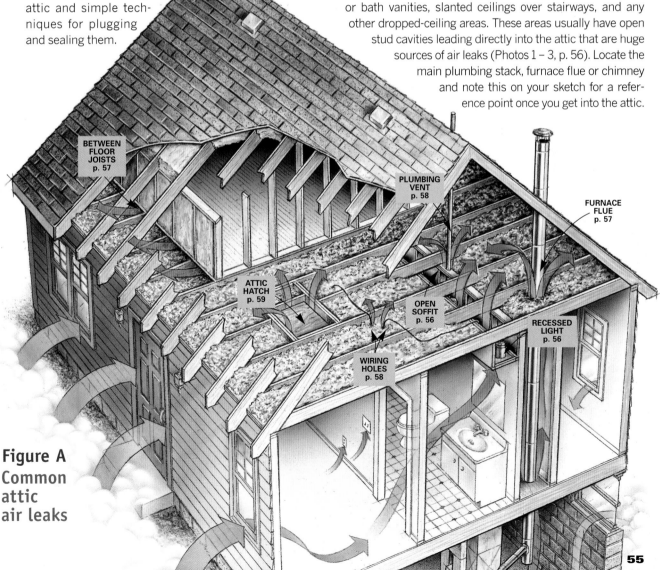

BETWEEN FLOOR JOISTS p. 57

PLUMBING VENT p. 58

FURNACE FLUE p. 57

ATTIC HATCH p. 59

OPEN SOFFIT p. 56

RECESSED LIGHT p. 56

WIRING HOLES p. 58

**Figure A
Common attic air leaks**

2 Pressurize your house

Before you crawl into the attic, place a box fan in a window so it's blowing air into the house and close all the remaining windows and doors. Tape cardboard around the fan to cover large gaps. When you turn the fan on high, the house will be pressurized, like an inflated balloon. And just as you can feel the air from a leaky balloon, you'll be able to confirm leaks in the attic by feeling the draft with your hand. You may even be able to locate bypasses visually by looking for insulation being blown about. Close the attic access door or hatch behind you to maximize the effect.

Gather your supplies and suit up. Attics are miserable places to work. Be sure to read the tips on p. 58 before you start.

3 Plug the big holes first

It's tempting to grab a can of expanding foam and squirt it into all the little holes, but your biggest savings will come from plugging the large holes. Find the plumbing stack or flue for a reference point. Then use your sketch to locate the soffits, stairwells or other dropped-ceiling areas. You'll probably have to dig around in the insulation to uncover them. Soffits may be filled with insulation or covered with cardboard or fiberglass batts. Push back the insulation and scoop it out of the soffits. Now plug the open stud spaces (Photos 1 and 2) and seal the top of the cavities with reflective foil (Photo 3). Cover the area with insulation again when you're done.

> **Caution:**
> Some attics have vermiculite insulation, which may contain asbestos, a health hazard. Vermiculite is a lightweight, pea-size, flaky gray mineral. Don't disturb vermiculite insulation unless you've had it tested by an approved lab to be sure it doesn't contain asbestos. Contact your local health department for the name of an approved lab.

1 CUT a 16-in.-long piece from a batt of unfaced fiberglass insulation and fold it at the bottom of a 13-gallon plastic garbage bag.

2 FOLD the bag over once and stuff it into the open stud cavity. Make sure there's enough insulation in the bag to form a tight fit in the cavity.

3 WITH a scissors, cut a length of foil insulation about 6 in. longer than the opening to be covered. Apply a bead of latex caulk around the opening. Embed the foil in the caulk and staple it in place.

4 Stuffed bags seal joist spaces too

Heated rooms built into attics often have open cavities in the floor framing under the walls. Even though insulation may be piled against or stuffed into these spaces, they can still leak air. Photo 4 shows how to stuff these spaces with the same type of garbage-bag plug we used to seal stud cavities.

4 PLUG all open joist spaces under insulated side walls. Cut a 24-in.-long piece from a batt of fiberglass insulation and place it at the bottom of a 13-gallon plastic garbage bag. Fold the bag over and stuff it into the joist space under the wall.

KNEE WALL

24" BATT ROLLED INSIDE GARBAGE BAG

FIBERGLASS BATT

OPEN JOIST CAVITY

13-GALLON PLASTIC GARBAGE BAGS

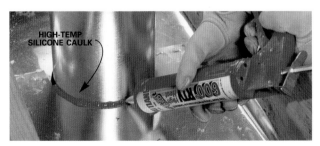

CLASS B FURNACE FLUE

STAPLE

HALF CIRCLE CUTOUT

GAP AROUND FLUE

14" ALUMINUM FLASHING

LATEX CAULK

5 CUT aluminum flashing to fit around the flue. For round flues like ours, cut half circles out of two pieces so they overlap about 3 in. in the middle. Press the flashing metal into a bead of latex caulk and staple it into place. If there's no wood, staple it right to the drywall.

HIGH-TEMP SILICONE CAULK

6 SEAL the gap between the flue and metal flashing with special high-temperature silicone caulk. Don't use spray foam here.

5 Furnace flues require special techniques

The opening around a furnace or water heater flue is a major source of warm air into the attic (Photo 5). Because the pipe gets hot, building codes require 1 in. of clearance from Class B flues (2 in. from masonry chimneys) to any combustible material, including insulation. Photos 5 and 6 show how to seal this gap with lightweight aluminum flashing and special high-temperature silicone caulk ($12 per tube). Before you push the insulation back into place, build a metal dam (Photo 7) to keep it away from the pipe. Use this same technique for masonry chimneys.

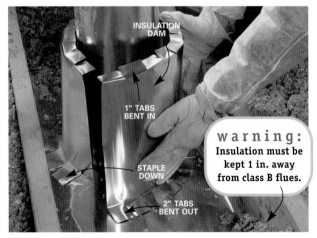

INSULATION DAM

1" TABS BENT IN

STAPLE DOWN

2" TABS BENT OUT

warning: Insulation must be kept 1 in. away from class B flues.

7 FORM an insulation dam to prevent insulation from contacting the flue pipe. Cut enough aluminum from the coil to wrap around the flue plus 6 in. Cut slots 1 in. deep and a few inches apart along the top and bend the tabs in. Cut slots about 2 in. deep along the bottom and bend out the tabs. Wrap the dam around the flue and secure the bottom by stapling through the tabs.

6 Use foam and caulk to seal small holes

Seal openings around plumbing vents and electrical wires with expanding foam (Photos 8 and 9). Be careful, though; this stuff is super sticky and almost impossible to get off your clothes and skin. Wear disposable gloves and eye protection. Seal around electrical boxes with caulk (Photo 9).

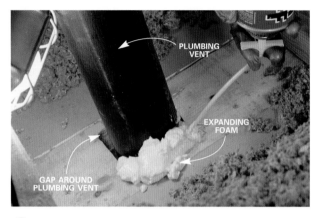

PLUMBING VENT

EXPANDING FOAM

GAP AROUND PLUMBING VENT

8 STUFF a small piece of fiberglass batt insulation into the space around the plumbing vent pipe as a backer for the expanding foam. Then follow the directions on the can to fill the space around the pipe with expanding foam insulation.

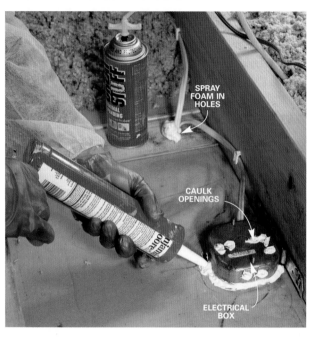

SPRAY FOAM IN HOLES

CAULK OPENINGS

ELECTRICAL BOX

9 FILL wiring and plumbing holes with expanding foam. Caulk around electrical junction boxes and fill holes in the box with caulk.

tip Telltale signs— finding attic bypasses

Even though most of the gaps spilling warm air into your attic are buried in insulation, you'll still see evidence of the escaping air. While in your attic, look for areas where the insulation is darkened (see photo), a result of filtering dusty air from the house. In cold weather, you may see frosty areas in the insulation caused by warm, moist air condensing and freezing as it hits the cold attic air. In warmer weather, you'll find water staining in these same areas. If you pressurize the house with a window fan (see "Pressurize your house," p. 56), you may be able to feel the leaks with your hand as the air finds its way into the attic.

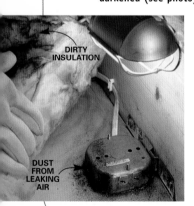

DIRTY INSULATION

DUST FROM LEAKING AIR

Materials checklist

- Roll of reflective foil insulation
- Bundle or roll of unfaced fiberglass batt insulation
- Acrylic latex caulk
- Special high-temperature silicone caulk
- Roll of 14-in.-wide aluminum flashing
- Roll of 13-gallon plastic garbage bags
- Can of expanding spray foam insulation

Tips for working in the attic

- Start in the morning when it's cool. Pick a cool, cloudy day if possible. Don't spend more than 15 or 20 minutes in a hot attic.

- Wear a lightweight disposable coverall (available in paint departments), gloves and a hat to keep itchy insulation off your clothes and skin.

- Always wear a double-strap dust mask or an OSHA-approved particulate respirator.

- Wear knee pads if you have them. Crawling around on joists gets painful. Use scraps of plywood to kneel on and as a platform for your supplies.

- Buy a rough-service lightbulb ($2.50) and a clamp-on light ($6), both available at hardware stores. Have a flashlight handy just in case.

- Minimize trips in and out of the attic by collecting all of your tools and supplies and placing them in the attic before you go up.

- Look out where you step. You must walk on ceiling joists or truss chords and carry a small piece of plywood to work from. Don't step on the ceiling drywall.

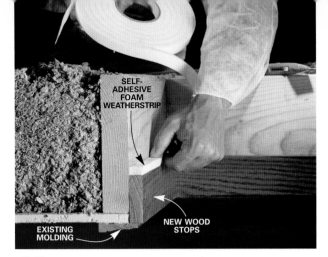

SELF-ADHESIVE FOAM WEATHERSTRIP

EXISTING MOLDING

NEW WOOD STOPS

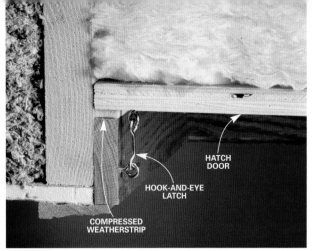

HATCH DOOR

HOOK-AND-EYE LATCH

COMPRESSED WEATHERSTRIP

10 WEATHERSTRIP the attic access hatch or door. Cut 1x3 boards to fit the perimeter of the opening and nail them on with 6d finish nails. Apply self-adhesive foam weatherstrip tape to the top edge of the stop.

11 ATTACH hook-and-eye fasteners to the door and stops. Position the eyes so that the weatherstrip is compressed when you latch the hooks.

7 Complete the job by sealing the hatch

When you're done sealing your attic bypasses, push the insulation back into place with an old broom handle or stick as you back out of the attic. Then finish up by sealing the access hatch with self-sticking foam weatherstrip (Photos 10 and 11). If your hatch rests directly on the moldings like ours did, add 2-1/2-in.-wide stops around the opening. The stops provide a wider surface for attaching the weatherstrip and a space to mount hook-and-eye fasteners. Position the screw eyes so the weatherstrip is slightly compressed when the hooks are latched.

Check for backdrafting

Whenever you make energy improvements—like sealing attic bypasses—that result in a tighter house, install carbon monoxide (CO) alarms if you don't already have them. Allow one per floor. Also have a pro check your combustion appliances for backdrafting at the next servicing.

Recessed can lights— no easy solution

Cut a 6-in. hole in your ceiling and add a 100-watt bulb—enough heat to bake cookies—and you have a recipe for huge heat loss as well as a major contributor to ice dams. That's what a recessed light does. Here are the solutions we recommend if you have recessed can lights protruding into your attic:

- Replace incandescent bulbs with cooler-operating compact fluorescent bulbs.
- Replace your old recessed lights with new airtight models available at some home centers and lighting

✳ Energy-Saving Goof

Insulation surprise attack

After moving into our new/old house, I decided to add 6 in. of insulation to our attic. Our attic is accessed through a small closet (36 x 30 in.) with a 30 x 14-in. opening at the top. I figured the best way to insulate the attic and keep the mess of fiberglass insulation out of the house would be to squeeze the tightly packaged rolls through the closet opening and open them in the attic.

Intending to pull them up after me, I climbed into the attic and proceeded to pull on the first roll of insulation. I found out very quickly that it wasn't going to fit. So rather than getting down from the attic, I decided to reach down and cut the plastic wrapping with the roll sitting on the closet shelf and pull up the pieces individually.

The roll exploded open and engulfed the small closet with insulation, leaving me trapped in the attic. (Attics sure are quiet and HOT.) The insulation was so tightly bound in the closet that I couldn't push it out of the closet or pull it up. I finally had to use a utility knife to cut the insulation into smaller pieces so I could make my itchy, scratchy escape!

stores. This is the best solution for those with electrical skills. New cans are relatively inexpensive—about $20 apiece plus decorative trim and bulb—and can usually be installed in a few hours each.

Saving Energy:

J ust as tuning up your car will help you save at the gas pump, tuning up your furnace or boiler and fireplace before winter will help you save on your monthly utility bill. Some tasks—like tuning up your furnace or boiler—can be complex enough to require professional help. But there are simple steps anyone can take. Just replacing the dirty filter on your forced-air furnace can reduce your gas or electric bill by 10 percent. Sealing up leaky air ducts can reduce it by another 10 percent. And installing (and actually using) a $50 setback thermostat can save you hundreds of dollars over the course of a winter.

Don't overlook the obvious. Make sure the glass panels of your storm windows and storm doors are shut tight. Keep south-facing shades open during the day to harvest free solar heat. Make sure your fireplace damper is closed when not in use. And when it does come time to replace that old 60 percent-efficient furnace or boiler, look into one of the high-efficiency units available; some of the newer, ENERGY STAR-qualified furnaces and boilers are 90 percent or more efficient.

Heating Season

Warm up a cold room

16 common problems & 16 (sometimes) simple solutions

Bugged by a chilly room in the winter? If you have to wear an extra pair of heavy socks in the family room or huddle under the covers at night, you're not alone. A chilly room is as common as, well, a common cold.

It's not always easy or cheap, but there's always a way to chase those chills. Here you'll find the causes (Figure A) and the solutions (Figure B, p. 65). Plus, you'll discover the least expensive options, what you can do yourself and when to call in a heating expert. The focus here is on homes with forced-air heating systems—that is, homes with blowers and ductwork. However, many of these solutions will work in homes heated by other systems.

Problems in the duct system

Obstructions. It may seem obvious, but you might have forgotten that you closed the register during the cooling season (**1**). Embarrassing! But more often the culprit is at the furnace in the form of a clogged filter or dirty air-conditioning coil that's blocking the airflow (**2**). It's easy to change the filter, but you can't clean the coil yourself, and on many furnaces you can't see it well enough to tell if it's dirty. Rely on professional service every year or two to detect a dirty coil.

Sofas, desks and chairs as well as drapes can block the airflow at registers (**3**). Plastic deflectors or registers with different "throw" patterns aren't always attractive, but they offer partial solutions. Or move the furniture; it's simpler than moving the register.

Sometimes construction debris falls into the ducts, and the builders forget to fish it out (**4**). Unscrew the register and look down with a flashlight, or reach into the duct with a gloved hand to retrieve anything you can feel. With any luck, it won't have fur or feathers!

Badly balanced dampers. Every duct system is supposed to have dampers to balance the heat flow to each room (**5**). In fact, some systems require that you adjust the dampers twice a year, when you go from

Figure A Common causes of cold rooms

Insulation inflation

My husband and I bought a big bundle of insulation to insulate our shop. The huge bundle was actually five bundles wrapped together. I could barely lift it into the truck, so we decided to cut the bundle and load the individual bundles one at a time onto the truck bed. As soon as we cut it, it expanded to about four times its original size, much too large to fit into the truck. We had to buy some rope and spend a half hour wrestling the stuff into a manageable size.

PROBLEMS

1. Closed register
2. Furnace filter or air-conditioning coil dirty and clogged
3. Drapes and furniture block heat flow
4. Clogged ducts
5. Dampers closed down
6. Thermostat located in a warm area
7. Duct has too many bends or is too small
8. No cool-air return
9. Drafty windows
10. Addition has many windows
11. Poor attic or wall insulation
12. Cold floor over crawlspace
13. Cold basement
14. No air chutes or poorly installed chutes
15. Heat loss due to leaks
16. Uninsulated floor

air-conditioning mode to the heating mode and back again. Look for the dampers near the main trunk lines. Contractors usually label the correct position. But not always. Open the damper farther for the duct serving the cold room. Unfortunately, dampers are often covered during remodeling, or hidden under insulation in the attic. You might have to call in a heating contractor to help out.

"Hot" thermostat. If the thermostat area heats up fast, it'll shut off the furnace before other rooms warm up (**6**). Close nearby registers to lessen the warm airflow near the thermostat, and adjust the register louvers in other rooms to help balance the heat flow. A $3 room thermometer is handy for comparing temperatures from room to room.

Bad duct design. Design problems can include too many bends in a run (**7**) and inadequate cool-air returns (**8**). While Figure B suggests design solutions, be sure to consult a heating contractor for advice on the best methods and materials. But go through the rest of this list first. You might find a simpler, less expensive solution.

Bad windows

Leaky, inefficient windows are notorious heat drains, especially in older homes (**9**). Stop drafts with caulk and weatherstripping and add heavy drapes if necessary. Replacing worn-out windows with new, energy-efficient windows often solves the cold room problem.

But even good windows can't always make up for the heat loss in a room with a lot of glass (**10**). For these rooms, you may have to consider additional ducts, or an additional heater with a separate thermostat. Both are expensive and require the advice of a heating pro.

Bad insulation

Finding out you have poor insulation is frustrating, because insulation was easy to install when your house was built, but it's difficult and expensive

to add it now (**11**). Attic insulation is an exception. If your attic has 6 in. or less, add at least another 6 in. of fiberglass or cellulose to warm up cold rooms directly below. Other exceptions include crawlspace or floor insulation for cold floors over a crawlspace (**12**), and rim joist insulation for basements (**13**).

While you're up in your attic, make sure you have vent chutes and that they're properly positioned (**14**). Cold air blowing through the insulation can chill the ceiling of the room below.

Insulation installers often fail to close up ceiling gaps, and warm air leaks out (**15**). Seal areas around light

Figure B Ways to warm up a cold room

fixtures, plumbing pipes, ducts and other gaps into attics with caulk or expanding foam. Usually you can reach these only from the attic.

Bad mixing & cold slabs

Without good mixing, warm air rises and cool air falls, chilling your feet, especially in rooms with tall ceilings and on uninsulated concrete floors (**16**). If the airflow from the registers doesn't do the job, slow-moving ceiling fans can get the warm air down to the floor where you need it.

SOLUTIONS

1. Open the register.

2. Change furnace filter and check for dirty air-conditioning coil with flashlight; call a pro to clean the coil.

3. Add plastic deflector ($5 at home centers or heating-supply dealers) and rearrange furniture.

4. Clean out debris as far as you can reach.

5. Adjust dampers for higher airflow.

6. Close registers around thermostat; use thermometer to compare room temperatures.

7. Install larger ducts where possible; add more runs if possible.

8. Undercut door 3/4 in. or add louvers; adding new return ducts is difficult.

9. Caulk and weatherstrip windows or replace with tighter, higher-efficiency units.

10. Increase heat flow if possible; add supplemental heat (gas fireplace, electric).

11. Increase attic and wall insulation if possible.

12. Insulate floor if crawlspace is vented, or insulate crawlspace perimeter and ground if closed off.

13. Insulate rim joists and basement; add more registers in basement.

14. Install attic vent chutes.

15. Seal leaks to attic at plumbing stacks, around lights and chimneys.

16. Increase heat flow, add supplemental heat or encourage better mixing with ceiling fan.

Save energy with a
programmable
Invest $75 now and save hundreds

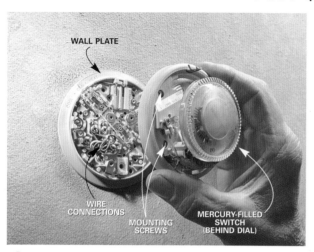

WALL PLATE

WIRE CONNECTIONS

MOUNTING SCREWS

MERCURY-FILLED SWITCH (BEHIND DIAL)

1 TURN OFF power to heating/cooling systems at the main panel. Mark wires with a tab (or tape) and letter that represents the terminal; unscrew them. Remove and discard the old thermostat.

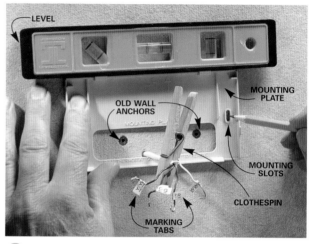

LEVEL

OLD WALL ANCHORS

MOUNTING PLATE

MOUNTING SLOTS

CLOTHESPIN

MARKING TABS

2 LEVEL the new mounting plate in position and mark the mounting screw holes. Drill 3/16-in. holes, insert drywall anchors and screw the plate to the wall.

You can reduce your home's heating and cooling costs by about 15 percent with a programmable thermostat. It automatically keeps the temperature at a comfortable level when you're home, but switches to an energy-saving level when you're away or asleep. Programmable thermostats are available from home centers and hardware stores for $25 to $100. The higher-priced models provide more programming options.

Programmable thermostats will work with most gas or oil furnaces, and central air conditioners. However, heat pumps, electric baseboards and a few other systems require special features. Read the package to make sure the programmable thermostat you buy is compatible with your heating and cooling system. If you're unsure, call your local utility or a heating and cooling contractor listed in your yellow pages.

Quick tip*

PROGRAMMABLE THERMOSTAT OPTIONS. When shopping for a programmable thermostat, select one with the options that are right for you. Some contain a time-to-change-the-filter light or low-battery indicator. Others have keypad lock features to prevent tampering, or contain mechanisms that automatically reset your temperature settings when moving between heating and cooling seasons.

Energy-Saving Q&A

Setback thermostats save money

Q We've always used a setback thermostat to lower the temperature at night and during the day while we're gone. My son-in-law says we're not saving anything, claiming the amount of energy used to reheat the house is far greater than if we left the thermostat set at a constant temperature. Who's right?

A You're right. Your son-in-law holds a common misconception, which has been dispelled by years of research and numerous studies. The fuel required to reheat a building to a comfortable temperature is roughly equal to the fuel saved as the building temperature drops to the lower setting. You save fuel between the time that the temperature stabilizes at the lower level and the next time the heat is needed. So, the longer your house remains at the lower temperature, the more energy you save.

Studies show you can cut costs by as much as 20 percent by lowering your thermostat 5 degrees F at night and 10 degrees during the day when no one is home. The same goes for raising the temperatures by that same amount when using air-conditioning in warmer climates.

thermostat
in the years to come

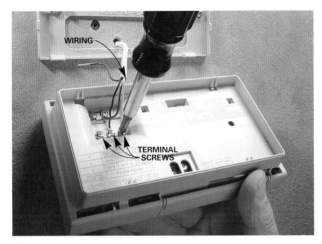

WIRING

TERMINAL SCREWS

3 SCREW wiring to terminals on new thermostat using labels as reference (strip wires back if needed). Hook wires up to same terminals on new thermostat. Snap thermostat to mounting plate.

Quick tip*

DON'T USE DUCT TAPE ON DUCTS. Studies have shown that cloth-backed duct tape is one of the worst materials you can use for sealing leaky ducts; it degrades quickly. Use aluminum tape, mastic or other adhesive specially approved for sealing ducts.

Remove the old thermostat as shown in Photo 1. If your old thermostat contains mercury, you'll see a small glass tube with a shiny silver ball inside. Mercury is toxic. Take this type of thermostat to a hazardous-waste disposal site.

There will be anywhere from two to five wires hooked up to the old thermostat. Label the thermostat wiring with marking tabs using the letters on the old screw terminals as reference. If your new thermostat doesn't come with marking tabs, use masking tape.

Clip a clothespin to the cable so it doesn't slide down inside the wall cavity, and mount the new wall plate (Photo 2). If the thermostat has back-up batteries, insert them before wiring the new thermostat (Photo 3).

The thermostat may need to be configured to your heating system. It may come preprogrammed, but to maximize savings, set it up according to your schedule. Consult the instructions that come with the thermostat for system adjustments and programming. You won't save energy if the thermostat isn't programmed correctly.

Energy-Saving Q&A

Duct tape: not for ducts

Q What's the best way to seal leaks in my ductwork? Duct tape seems to deteriorate pretty quickly.

A It's one of those goofy ironies that duct tape really doesn't work well on ducts. In fact, the Model Energy Code bans the use of duct tape for sealing ducts. Instead, use the aluminum tape you'll find with the vents and ducting at home centers. This tape, which costs about $20 for a large roll, works on most ductwork connections as long as the metal is fairly clean.

Aluminum tape won't work where a round trunk line connects to rectangular ductwork. For these joints, use either pure silicone ($3 to $4 a tube) or a sealant specifically designed for ducts.

Aluminum tape for straight seams

ALUMINUM TAPE

Silicone for curved seams

GRAY

SILICONE OR DUCT SEALANT

Fall furnace tune-up

Simple maintenance pays big dividends for comfort, efficiency and safety

AIR INTAKE

BURNER COVER

COMBUSTION CHAMBER DOOR

Caution: Turn off power switch

1 FLIP the electrical power switch to OFF. Remove the combustion chamber door by lifting up and pulling it out, and remove the burner cover (if you have one). It's usually held in place by two screws.

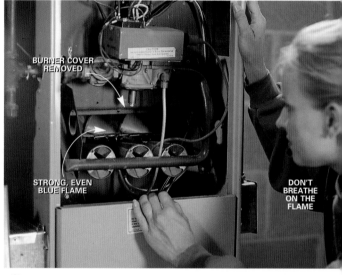

BURNER COVER REMOVED

STRONG, EVEN BLUE FLAME

DON'T BREATHE ON THE FLAME

2 TURN the power switch on and activate the burners by turning up your thermostat. Inspect the burner flames. The flames should be fairly even and blue. Yellow flames indicate dirty burners. (Don't breathe on the flames because the extra oxygen will also make them turn yellow.) Don't adjust the burners yourself. Call in a pro.

When it comes to furnaces, an ounce of prevention truly is worth a pound of cure. To help you avert the hassle of your furnace dying or simply not putting out enough heat—just when you need it most—we'll walk you through a series of simple steps that will keep it in tip-top shape. The entire maintenance operation takes less than three hours and costs only a few dollars—pretty cheap insurance.

Here, the focus is on natural gas and propane-fueled furnaces. The maintenance tasks involving the blower chamber also apply to oil furnaces; however, oil furnace combustion chambers are very different and should only be worked on by professionals.

(Heat pumps, on the other hand, work more like a central air conditioner than like a furnace, so we won't deal with them here.)

Routine furnace maintenance and cleaning don't require special skills. If you're handy with a few basic

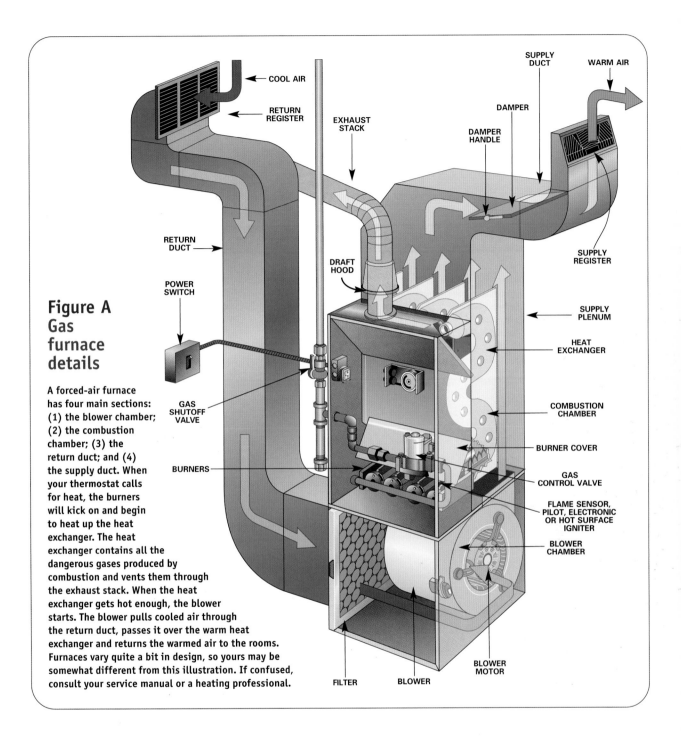

COOL AIR

RETURN REGISTER

EXHAUST STACK

SUPPLY DUCT

WARM AIR

DAMPER

DAMPER HANDLE

RETURN DUCT

DRAFT HOOD

SUPPLY REGISTER

POWER SWITCH

SUPPLY PLENUM

Figure A Gas furnace details

HEAT EXCHANGER

A forced-air furnace has four main sections: (1) the blower chamber; (2) the combustion chamber; (3) the return duct; and (4) the supply duct. When your thermostat calls for heat, the burners will kick on and begin to heat up the heat exchanger. The heat exchanger contains all the dangerous gases produced by combustion and vents them through the exhaust stack. When the heat exchanger gets hot enough, the blower starts. The blower pulls cooled air through the return duct, passes it over the warm heat exchanger and returns the warmed air to the rooms. Furnaces vary quite a bit in design, so yours may be somewhat different from this illustration. If confused, consult your service manual or a heating professional.

GAS SHUTOFF VALVE

BURNERS

COMBUSTION CHAMBER

BURNER COVER

GAS CONTROL VALVE

FLAME SENSOR, PILOT, ELECTRONIC OR HOT SURFACE IGNITER

BLOWER CHAMBER

BLOWER MOTOR

FILTER

BLOWER

hand tools, you can do it. You won't be doing tricky or potentially dangerous stuff like adjusting the gas burners. Leave that for a pro. See "Symptoms That Call for a Heating Professional," p. 72, for more details.

We should warn you that your furnace may look somewhat different than the one we show here. If you don't feel confident about taking some of the steps shown, skip

them. And pay close attention to the safety precautions in this article, in your furnace service manual (if you can find it!) and posted on your furnace.

Even if you follow our maintenance steps, call in a heating professional for a thorough furnace checkup at least every three years. (Look under "Heating" in your yellow pages.)

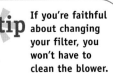 **tip** If you're faithful about changing your filter, you won't have to clean the blower.

1/2" DRAIN LINE

TAPE

VACUUM HOSE

Caution:
Turn off power switch

BLOWER COMPARTMENT

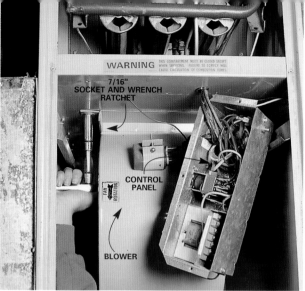

WARNING THIS COMPARTMENT MUST BE CLOSED EXCEPT WHEN SERVICING. FAILURE TO COMPLY WILL CAUSE CIRCULATION OF COMBUSTION FUMES.

7/16" SOCKET AND WRENCH RATCHET

CONTROL PANEL

FAN ROTATION

BLOWER

3 TURN OFF the power switch again and shut off the gas by giving the valve a one-quarter turn (see Figure A for approximate gas shutoff valve location). Vacuum the burners and the furnace base. To get at the back of the burners, tape a 20-in. length of 1/2-in. drain line to your vacuum hose. Vacuum everywhere you see dust. While everything is open, use a flashlight to look for signs of soot (fine black powder), which often indicates poor combustion (see Symptom 5, p. 72). Lift off the lower door (blower door) and vacuum the blower compartment.

4 REMOVE the blower (also called a squirrel cage) in order to clean it. If you have a control panel in front of the blower, two screws will loosen it and you can let it hang. Next, using a 7/16-in. socket and ratchet, remove the two bolts that hold the blower in place, then gently lift it out.

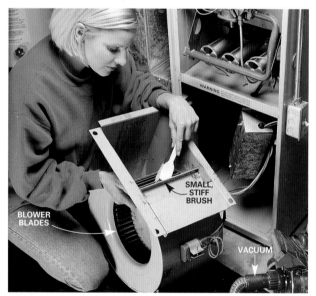

SMALL, STIFF BRUSH

BLOWER BLADES

VACUUM

WARNING

FIBERGLASS FILTER

HIGH-EFFICIENCY FILTER (DIRTY)

5 CLEAN the blower blades thoroughly with a vacuum and small brush. Take care not to stress the wiring or disturb the counterweights that will be on the fan blades. If you can't clean the blower thoroughly, don't clean it at all; you could throw it off balance.

6 CHANGE the furnace filter every one to three months. A $1 fiberglass filter will adequately protect the blower and blower motor. If you want to install a more expensive, high-efficiency filter, check the owner's manual for the manufacturer recommendations. High-efficiency filters can restrict the airflow, strain the blower motor and make your furnace less efficient. If you want cleaner air, the best option is a separate air-cleaning system.

Carbon monoxide alarm

INSTALL A CARBON MONOXIDE ALARM on each floor. If you already have these alarms, test them. Carbon monoxide is an odorless, colorless gas sometimes produced by oil-, gas- and wood-burning appliances (furnaces, stoves, fireplaces, etc.). If this gas spills into your home in high enough concentra- tions, it can be fatal. Plug carbon monoxide alarms into electrical outlets or directly wire them to the electrical system. They cost about $40. Do not install them in utility rooms, garages, kitchens or bathrooms.

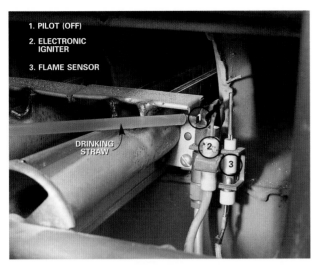

1. PILOT (OFF)
2. ELECTRONIC IGNITER
3. FLAME SENSOR

DRINKING STRAW

7 BLOW dust off the pilot. Direct air to the exact spot by blowing through a drinking straw. A dirty pilot can cause the flame sensor (or thermocouple) to get a false reading that the pilot isn't lit. Some newer furnaces have hot surface igniters instead of pilots and electronic igniters (Photo 9). (Note: One burner was removed for clarity.)

> **Caution:**
> While working on your furnace, do not remove burners, stick anything into the pilot orifice or make adjustments. Misaligned burners can pose a serious hazard by allowing gas to build up before the burner ignites, causing a flash fire. Poking a sharp object into a pilot can widen the orifice, turning the pilot into a flamethrower.

tip If your furnace has a standing pilot (a pilot that burns all the time), turning off the gas to the furnace when the heating season is over will save you as much as 5 percent per year on your gas bill. To relight the pilot, consult the instructions on your furnace's gas valve.

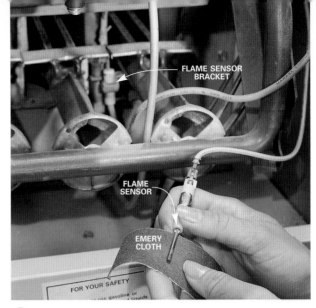

FLAME SENSOR BRACKET

FLAME SENSOR

EMERY CLOTH

FOR YOUR SAFETY

8 THE FLAME SENSOR occasionally becomes coated with residue and will prevent your furnace from lighting. Remove it by pulling it down out of its bracket. Lightly clean the surface with fine emery cloth and slip the sensor back into its bracket.

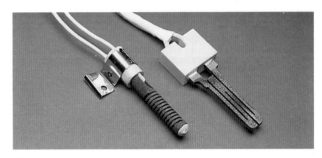

9 HOT SURFACE IGNITERS are the most common ignition system on furnaces being manufactured today. They take the place of standing pilot lights and electronic igniters. Clean the dust off the hot surface igniter by leaving the igniter in place and blowing air through a straw. This part breaks very easily; don't even touch it. In fact, when you replace the furnace doors, do so gently to avoid breaking the igniter.

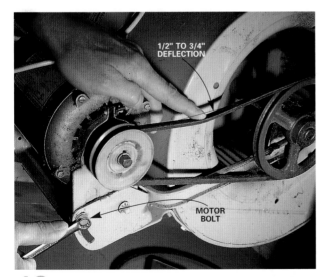

1/2" TO 3/4" DEFLECTION

MOTOR BOLT

10 THE BELTS on belt-driven blowers need occasional adjustment or replacement. Inspect the drive belt for cracks or frayed areas. A new belt costs about $5. When you install the new belt, tension it so it deflects 1/2 to 3/4 in.

OIL HOLE

11 SOME OLDER FURNACES have two motor bearings and two blower shaft bearings that require annual oiling. Clean around the oil caps and remove the caps. Apply two to three drops of lightweight machine oil and replace the caps. Don't overlubricate!

12 IF YOUR FURNACE heating ducts also serve as air-conditioning ducts, they may have dampers that require adjusting for seasonal changes. The seasonal settings should be marked. Two-story homes often have separate supply trunks to serve the upstairs and downstairs. To send more warm air downstairs (winter setting) or more cold air upstairs (summer setting), adjust the damper handle on each supply trunk.

13 SEAL leaky ducts, especially return-air ducts, with special metal tape (available at home centers for $12) or high-temperature silicone. Then conduct the following backdrafting test to make sure the combustion gases go up the flue: Adjust the thermostat so the burners come on. Hold a smoking stick of incense beside the draft hood (Photo 14). The smoke should be drawn into the hood. Also inspect the exhaust vent pipes on your furnace and water heater (while they're cool). White powdery residue can indicate corrosion. Gently squeeze the exhaust stack with your hand. It should be firm but slightly flexible. Call a heating professional or plumber to fix all these types of problems.

Symptoms that call for a heating professional

Symptom 1: Short cycling

When your furnace runs for only short periods (less than three minutes) before shutting off, the problem is called short cycling. This happens when the thermostat is out of adjustment or when the heat exchanger overheats and the burner automatically shuts off to prevent damage.

Symptom 2: Irregular flame

Properly functioning burners have fairly even rows of flames. If the flames are uneven or lean toward the back of the furnace, call in a pro. It could be a sign of dirty burners or a cracked heat exchanger.

Symptom 3: Odd noises or rumbling

While rumbling and popping aren't cause for concern in a hot water or steam heating system, they shouldn't be present if you have forced-air heat.

Symptom 4: Chronic illness

Frequent headaches or flulike symptoms can be a sign of combustion gases leaking from a cracked heat exchanger or carbon monoxide leaking from an exhaust stack. With these symptoms, have your heating system checked out even if your carbon monoxide alarm remains silent.

Symptom 5: Soot deposits

Soot is a fine black powder that collects when combustion is incomplete. Its presence may indicate that your burners need adjusting or that you have a cracked heat exchanger that needs replacing.

14 TEST your gas water heater for backdrafting while your furnace is off. Turn up the water heater thermostat until the water heater burner comes on. After a minute or more, hold a smoking stick of incense or match up to the exhaust stack. The smoke should be pulled into the stack. Conduct the test with all exterior doors and windows closed and bath and kitchen fans running. If the vent doesn't draw, call in a heating specialist or plumber to find the problem. Turn the thermostat back down.

Cheap vs. expensive
furnace filters

When you purchase higher-cost filters, you're getting a filter that requires less changing and captures more, and smaller, particles. The $1 woven fiberglass filters do one thing—screen out dirt and debris that could damage your furnace blower motor, though they do take out some pollen and mold spores. If you can remember to swap them out every month and air quality isn't an issue, these will do the job.

But if you're the kind of person who forgets to change the oil in your car, buy $4 pleated filters, which require changing only every three months. If you stretched out the accordion-like material in these filters, you'd find two, three or four times the amount of surface area. This means they can capture smaller particles for longer periods of time without impeding the airflow of your furnace.

If members of your household smoke or have allergies or asthma, or if you have pets, look

into the more expensive, high-efficiency electrostatic filters—ones that both filter and magnetically attract contaminants. Some are effective for up to a year. They can filter out bacteria, dander, odors and smoke particles. But health experts warn that you may be wasting your money on these $20 to $40 filters unless you take the following steps: Use them in conjunction with a high-efficiency vacuum cleaner, install a dedicated air purifier, wash or vacuum the filter monthly and take other steps to clean up your air and house as well.

Many filters carry a MERV (minimum efficiency reporting value) rating, which indicates their effectiveness. The higher the MERV rating, the more effective. Most spun filters have a MERV rating of 4. Standard pleated filters average MERV 6. Electrostatic pleated versions start at MERV 8, with the highest quality ones hitting MERV 12.

WOVEN FIBERGLASS FILTERS

PLEATED FILTERS

Bleed a hot-water radiator

If some fins on your radiator stay cold while others are hot, don't despair! The only thing that's clogging your hot-water radiator is trapped air, and getting rid of it is simple. At the top or bottom of your radiator, look for a small valve like the one shown. Use a radiator key, 1/4-in. 12-point socket, or a flat screwdriver (depending on your valve type) and slowly turn the valve counterclockwise until water starts dripping out. This will release trapped air and let hot water into the cold fins. While you're at it, you should repeat the process with your other radiators.

Bleeding the radiators will lower the pressure in your system, so you might have to slowly add water to increase the pressure. Do this by opening, then closing, the valve on the water pipe above the boiler. In fact, you may need to add water while bleeding the radiator in order to purge the air from the system. This is where a helper will save on trips up and down the stairs. If you're unfamiliar with your system, call a pro.

How much pressure you need depends on how high the water has to rise. The basic rule is 1 lb. of pressure for every 2 ft. of rise. Your gauge may read in pounds, feet or both. A basic two-story house, with the boiler and expansion tank in the basement, needs 12 to 15 lbs., or 25 to 30 ft., of pressure.

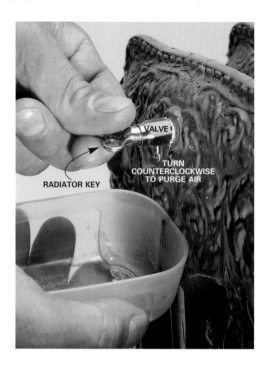

VALVE

TURN COUNTERCLOCKWISE TO PURGE AIR

RADIATOR KEY

Clear a steam-radiator vent

AIR VENT

Don't confuse a hot-water system with a steam system. Steam radiators have an air vent, like the one shown, about halfway down the side. Unfortunately, many of these air vents get painted over, plugging the air hole. Clear the air hole in the top of the vent with a small wire or a sewing needle. If you're still worried about the air vents working, consult a hot-water/steam-heat specialist. Replacing these vents costs $16 to $20 per radiator.

Flip a Switch,
Save $200

Look for simple solutions first

A furnace can be intimidating—especially when it's not working. However, there is good news from furnace repair pros. Roughly a quarter of all service calls could be avoided with easy fixes that cost little or nothing.

Here, you'll learn about the common culprits and what to do about them.

C a u t i o n :
Always turn off the shutoff switch (see No. 2 on p. 77) and turn the thermostat off or all the way down before changing the filter or working on the thermostat or furnace.

8 quick furnace fixes you can do yourself

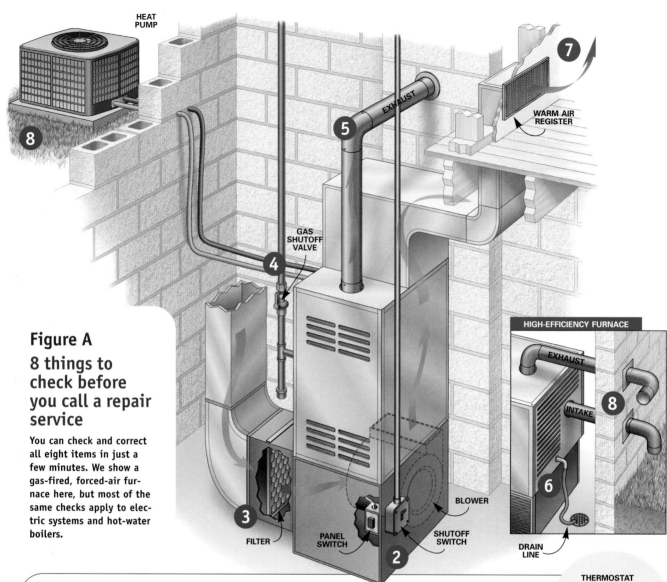

HEAT PUMP

8

GAS SHUTOFF VALVE

4

EXHAUST

5

7

WARM AIR REGISTER

HIGH-EFFICIENCY FURNACE

EXHAUST

INTAKE

8

6

DRAIN LINE

Figure A
8 things to check before you call a repair service

You can check and correct all eight items in just a few minutes. We show a gas-fired, forced-air furnace here, but most of the same checks apply to electric systems and hot-water boilers.

3

FILTER

PANEL SWITCH

2

BLOWER

SHUTOFF SWITCH

THERMOSTAT

HEAT · OFF · · COOL · AUTO · · ON · FAN

1 Check the thermostat to make sure it's on

Before you assume you have a furnace problem, check the thermostat to make sure it's actually telling the furnace to turn on. Thermostats, especially programmable ones, can be complicated, and the more options a thermostat has, the more that can go wrong.

- Make sure the switch is on "Heat" rather than on "Cool."
- Check the temperature setting.
- Compare the temperature setting to the room temperature. Set the temperature five degrees higher than the room temperature and see if the furnace kicks on.
- Make sure the program is displaying the right day and time, as well as A.M. and P.M. settings.

- Trace the thermostat wires back to the furnace to check for breaks, especially if you've done any remodeling recently. If you find a break in one of the thin wires, splice the line back together and wrap it with electrical tape.
- Replace the battery. If you have a power outage with a dead battery, you'll lose your settings and the thermostat will revert to the default program.
- Open the thermostat and gently blow out any dust or debris. Make sure it's level and firmly attached on the wall, and that none of the wires coming into it are loose.
- If you can't make the program settings work, you can bypass them altogether. Simply punch in the temperature you want with the up/down control and then press the "Hold" button. That will switch on the furnace if the thermostat programming is the problem.

tip Lost your owner's manual? Most major-brand manuals are listed on the Web—just go to the manufacturer's Web site.

2 Check shutoff switches and breakers

It sounds unbelievable, but furnace technicians often find that the only "repair" a furnace needs is to be turned on. Look for a standard wall switch on or near the furnace—all furnaces, no matter what age or type, have one somewhere. Check the circuit breaker or fuse for the furnace as well. Make sure the front panel covering the blower motor is securely fastened—there's a push-in switch under it that must be fully depressed for the furnace to operate.

3 Change filters

Dirty filters are the most common cause of furnace problems. Dust and dirt restrict airflow—and if the filter gets too clogged, the heat exchanger will overheat and shut off too quickly, and your house won't warm up. If the blower is running but no heat is coming out, replace the filter. A dirty filter also causes soot buildup on the heat exchanger, reducing the efficiency of the furnace and shortening its life.

The owner's manual shows where the filter is and how to remove it. Change inexpensive flat filters at least once a month. Make sure that the arrow points toward the furnace. Inspect pleated filters once a month. Hold them up to the light, and if you can't see the light clearly through them, replace them. Manufacturers say pleated filters are good for three months, but change them more frequently if you have pets, kids or generate lots of dust.

NEW FURNACE FILTERS

4 Make sure the gas is on

Just as with switches, someone may have turned off a gas valve and then forgotten to turn it back on. Trace the gas line back from the furnace to the meter, and if you see a handle that's perpendicular to the gas pipe, turn it so it's parallel.

If you have an old furnace or boiler, you may have a pilot light. Remove the front panel and the burner cover and check to make sure it's lit.

5 Make sure the chimney exhaust flue is clear

Drawn by the warmth, birds sometimes fall into the chimney exhaust flue. Turn the furnace off and the thermostat all the way down, then dismantle the duct where it exits the furnace and check for debris. Be sure to reassemble the sections in the same order and direction that you took them out.

6 Flush out drain lines

High-efficiency furnaces can drain off several gallons of water a day in heating season. If the drain lines become restricted by sediment or mold growth, the furnace will shut down. If the drain hose looks dirty, remove the hose, fill it with a mixture of bleach and water (25 percent bleach), then flush it after several minutes.

7 Look for blocked or leaky ducts that can restrict airflow

If your furnace comes on but one or two rooms are cold, first make sure all the room registers are open. Then examine any ductwork you can get access to and look for gaps between sections or branching points. Seal any gaps between sections of duct with special metal duct tape. Don't use standard cloth duct tape—it quickly deteriorates, and it may also cause ducts to leak if it was used to seal sections in the past.

Also check for handles protruding from the ductwork. These are dampers or air-conditioner bypasses—make sure they're open.

8 Clean away leaves and debris from heat pumps or intake and exhaust vents

If you have a furnace that vents out the side of the house, make sure nothing is blocking the intake or exhaust. If either of the pipes is covered with screen mesh (like window screen), replace it with 1/2-in.-mesh hardware cloth. If ice is clogging one of the pipes, you have a bigger problem somewhere in the system. Clear it off and call a technician to find out why it's happening.

If you have a heat pump, clear away grass and leaves from the fins of the outdoor compressor unit. Before heating season starts, hose it down gently from the top to rinse dirt and debris out of the housing.

Warming up fireplaces

Dampers, glass fronts, inserts & "good habits" make for better efficiency

Many people have a love-hate relationship with their fireplace. There are an estimated 35 million fireplaces in the United States, which means nearly 1 billion fireplace fires burn each year. Most of your neighbors have fireplaces. And if your home lacked a fireplace and you installed one, you'd recoup more than 75 percent of your investment at resale.

All of this, despite the fact that your fireplace is by far the least efficient piece of equipment in your home; 90 percent of the heat it creates goes—literally—up the chimney. It pulls four to 10 times more air out of a room than what's required to keep the fire going. Even when the fireplace is not operating, the chimney sucks warm air from your home. Furthermore, the smoke from your fireplace contains methane, carcinogens, carbon monoxide and other toxic gases. When conditions aren't right, the fireplace backdrafts, sending that sooty smoke into your house, blackening a wall and stinking up the place for days. Plus you have to cut, split, haul and store all that wood.

Still, you wouldn't give up your fireplace for anything. Why this twisted love affair?

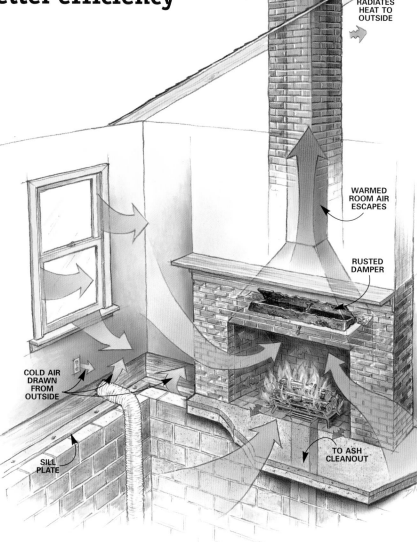

CHIMNEY RADIATES HEAT TO OUTSIDE

WARMED ROOM AIR ESCAPES

RUSTED DAMPER

COLD AIR DRAWN FROM OUTSIDE

TO ASH CLEANOUT

SILL PLATE

Figure A Standard masonry fireplace

Fireplaces provide "heat highways" for the warm air of your home to escape. When the fire is burning, cold air drawn in from around windows, doors, vents and outlets is heated and then propelled up and out the chimney. When not in use, rusted or loose-fitting dampers still allow warm air to escape.

Quick tip*

CLOSE THAT DAMPER. Keep the flue damper tightly closed when the fireplace isn't in use. An open damper is an open escape path for warm air—whether it's generated by your fireplace or furnace.

A brief history of the fireplace

By the 1200s, fireplaces roughly resembling yours were being built. These fireplaces, grossly inefficient, would warm the front sides of those huddled about them—while their back sides and the rest of the room froze.

Despite the fireplace's crucial role in both cooking and heating, improvements came slowly. In the 1400s, firebacks—metal sheets that reflected heat back into the room—came into use. In the 1600s, metal doors were added to prevent room air from escaping up the chimney, baffles for circulating heated air into the room were experimented with, and coal came into use. In the early 1700s, someone by the name of Count Rumford designed a fireplace with a sloping back, angled sides and an improved chimney that greatly increased efficiency. Still, in the mid-1700s Ben Franklin bemoaned, "In common chimneys the strongest heat from the fire, which is upwards, goes directly up the chimney and is lost—five-sixths of the heat is wasted."

And truth be told, your 20th-century masonry fireplace still burns at about the same efficiency as one built 200 years ago.

Why are fireplaces such losers?

Let's look at what happens when you fire up your fireplace on a winter night that's a brisk 10 degrees F.

Place crumpled newspaper, kindling and logs on the grate. As you open the damper, heavy, cold outside air pushes its way down the chimney and into the room—creating a reverse draft. You light the newspaper and stand back. One of two things may happen: The fire could create a strong enough updraft and pull smoke up the chimney. But not only is your house built fairly tight, your daughter is cooking in the kitchen with the range hood on, your son just finished a shower and left the bath fan running; and the gas furnace and water heater are sucking up air for combustion. There's simply not enough air to go around, and the house becomes a vacuum. The fireplace loses this air tug-of-war, and smoke is pulled into the room. You crack a window to let in more air. (If your house was built in the '70s or later, building codes require a fresh-air intake for combustion air to the fireplace.)

Eventually a strong draft is created. Your fire begins pulling and exhausting air from the surrounding room at a rate of about 450 cubic feet per minute. The house, still unable to provide enough air, sucks in air from around windows and doors, through dryer vents and electrical outlets and along sill plates. This 10-degree-F outside air mixes with heated room air, is drawn past the fire, and then is exhausted up the chimney.

When the fire is well established, you—if you remember—will close that open window and partially shut the damper to slow the rate of burn. Now is when your fire will burn most efficiently, returning a whopping 20 percent of the heat it generates back into the room. However, if you place a spark screen in front of the opening, this number will drop to about 12 percent.

As the fire dies down, you turn in for the night. As you sleep, the dying fire generates little heat—but the draft up the chimney creates a virtual freeway for heated house air to escape. The net result? You reached your main objective of spending a comfy hour or two reading in front of the fire. But all in all, the fire drew more heat out of your house than it generated. A working knowledge of why your fireplace performs so poorly offers clues as to how to make it perform better.

Good fire-building habits

You can improve the efficiency of your fireplace by simply improving your habits. You should burn hot, blazing fires because the combustion of wood and gases is more complete and the fire and surrounding bricks radiate more heat more efficiently. You should also get rid of your raised grate and use good old-fashioned andirons. These metal stands allow the burning logs to fall into the hot bed of coals, where they burn more efficiently.

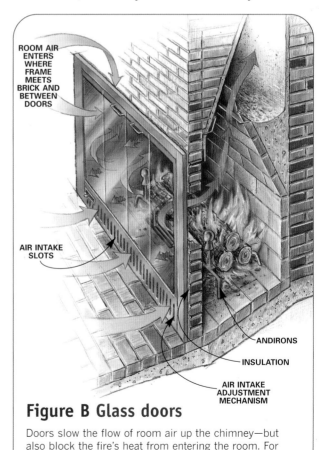

ROOM AIR ENTERS WHERE FRAME MEETS BRICK AND BETWEEN DOORS

AIR INTAKE SLOTS

ANDIRONS

INSULATION

AIR INTAKE ADJUSTMENT MECHANISM

Figure B Glass doors

Doors slow the flow of room air up the chimney—but also block the fire's heat from entering the room. For best results, keep the doors open while the fire is burning hot; close them in the waning stages of the fire.

Caution: Highly foolhardy

I came home early one spring afternoon to find it was a bit cool in the house, so I decided to build a fire in the fireplace. I hate to admit it, but sometimes we use a little charcoal lighter fluid to get the fire started. This time, however, the can was empty. I went to the garage to find a substitute and spotted a can of starting fluid that said "highly flammable." Just what I wanted, or so I thought. I brought it into the house and sprayed some onto the logs. Big mistake. I lit a match, and before I could even get it into the kindling, there was a thunderous explosion. Blue flames shot out of the lower vent, hitting my shins just above my shoes and scorching my socks. Luckily I escaped without injury or any major damage to my house. I never told anyone, not until now. My advice: Start your kindling only with a little newspaper and a match!

Dampers and glass fronts

When a fire is burning, adjust your damper to the smallest opening that's possible without smoke spilling back into the house. And shut it completely when the fireplace isn't in use. Still, your built-in damper—like most—is notoriously leaky. If the masons who built your fireplace never put a cap over it, years of rain and condensation may have rusted and pitted the damper. And high heat may have slightly distorted it. To fix this, you could install a chimney-top damper—a spring-loaded cap that seals off the top of the chimney to block air leakage when the fireplace isn't in use. It can be opened to varying degrees when the fireplace is in use.

You could also install tempered glass doors (around $500) with adjustable air intake slots (Figure B). They'll help prevent room air from escaping up the chimney when the fireplace isn't in use, and slow the mass exodus of room air up the chimney in the waning stages of a fire. But if you leave the doors closed during a fire, they'll block over half the heat from entering the room.

Wood-burning inserts

You can increase the output of your fireplace up to five-fold with a wood-burning insert (Figure C). This metal unit sits inside the fireplace and uses the old chimney as a chase for a new metal liner. Faceplates cover the space between the insert and fireplace opening. The unit's heat-exchange chamber, which warms and circulates room air, is part of what makes these so efficient. Their other advantage is you can adjust the air intakes to closely control the amount of room air allowed into the fire chamber during combustion and close it off completely when not in use. Some inserts come with glass doors for fire viewing; others have metal doors.

If you go this route, you'll need to go through some

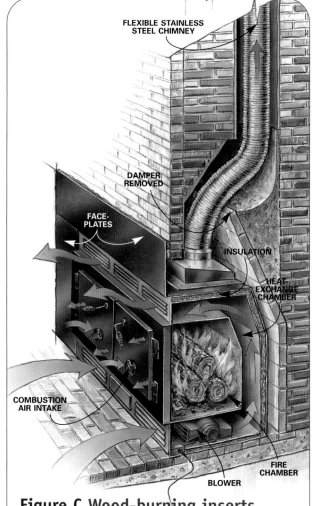

FLEXIBLE STAINLESS STEEL CHIMNEY

DAMPER REMOVED

FACE-PLATES

INSULATION

HEAT EXCHANGE CHAMBER

COMBUSTION AIR INTAKE

BLOWER

FIRE CHAMBER

Figure C Wood-burning inserts

These inserts allow you to control the amount of room air entering the fire chamber. Air circulated and warmed through the outer heat-exchange chamber makes efficient use of the fire's heat.

serious contortions, snaking the 25-ft., flexible stainless steel liner through the existing chimney and attaching it to the insert. Most damper openings are only about 6 in. wide, so you may need to use several different connectors and elbows.

A less complicated insert you could install is a tubular grate/glass door variety. C-shaped hollow tubes, the ends of each protruding above and below the glass doors, sit in the firebox. Room air enters the bottom of the C, is heated as it flows past the fire, then exits through the top of the C as heated air. Tubular grates alone—not used in conjunction with glass doors or blowers—won't appreciably increase the efficiency of a fireplace. The warmed air is apparently sucked back into the fireplace and up the chimney.

Gas-fired inserts

If you were building a house today, you'd have the option of installing an enclosed, gas fireplace (Figure D). These sealed units are airtight, meaning combustion air is brought in, heat is created, and exhaust gas is exhausted, all within the confines of the firebox. Blowers circulate air up and around the units, expelling warmed air into the room. No room air is used for combustion or escapes up the chimney.

True, you couldn't burn wood or roast marshmallows in your gas fireplace, but neither would you have to haul in wood, haul out ashes or lose massive amounts of heat. If you installed a direct vent unit—one that vents directly through the wall behind the unit—your gas fireplace could be 75 percent efficient. If you really wanted to go first class, you could operate it by remote control.

But even with your existing house and masonry fireplace, you can make use of this technology. You can slide a top-venting gas fireplace insert into your old fireplace—and still have the brick hearth, mantel and fairly natural-looking flame—and 50 percent efficiency. The fresh-air intake and exhaust pipes would run up through your existing chimney.

You would pay at least $1,500 for the insert and pipes. You'd have to remove the existing damper or permanently clamp it in place for safety. And you'd be wise to hire a licensed plumber to install the gas line to the unit and tie into the existing gas lines—but the rest of the installation you could do yourself.

Making sure

Before you get too excited about any changes, have a professional chimney sweep come out to clean and inspect your fireplace. Some chimneys are so encrusted with creosote deposits, they present a fire danger.

Also, consult your local building inspector. He or she may require the installation of an outside air intake near your wood-burning insert. Or, if you go the gas insert route, you'll have to abide by the many regulations regarding the distance between the outside vents and windows, the ground and the gas meter.

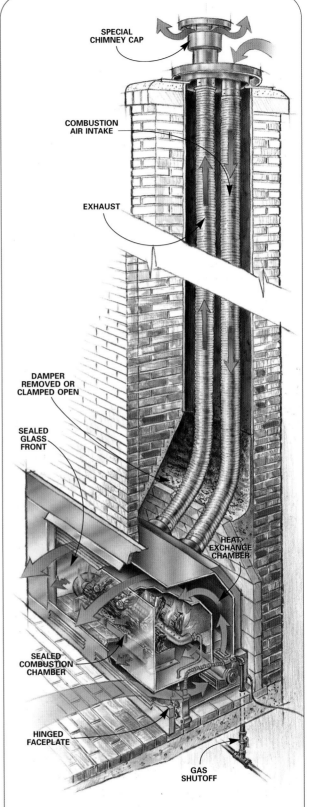

SPECIAL CHIMNEY CAP

COMBUSTION AIR INTAKE

EXHAUST

DAMPER REMOVED OR CLAMPED OPEN

SEALED GLASS FRONT

HEAT-EXCHANGE CHAMBER

SEALED COMBUSTION CHAMBER

HINGED FACEPLATE

GAS SHUTOFF

Figure D Gas-fired inserts

These inserts use the existing chimney to draw in fresh air and exhaust spent gases. The combustion chamber is sealed off from the room, and the outer heat-exchange chamber makes these units up to 75 percent efficient.

Understanding

Escaping heat creates higher energy bills

A picturesque array of icicles might make a nice image for a holiday card, but there's nothing charming about the damage that built-up roof ice can do to your home, especially the continuous chunks called ice dams. Several conditions are required for their formation (see "How ice dams form," below), but the factors you can control are heat loss through your roof and proper ventilation to maintain a cold roof.

Spot problem roofs by observing them during the few days following a snowfall. If significant heat loss occurs, the blanket of snow will rapidly develop thin areas or holes from melting. Icicles will soon appear at the eaves, then thicker layers of ice will form above them.

The only effective strategy against ice dams is this: Keep the attic cold by preventing upward heat loss from the living areas of the house, and keep the roof cold by providing a clear path for cold air to move from eave to ridge. Attic insulation between and above the ceiling joists is essential; most modern codes specify as much as 1 ft. of insulation with a heat retention value above R-32. Equally critical is sealing off ceiling penetrations—from a small electrical box to a large access hatch—that allow warm air to leak past the insulation.

How ice dams form

Ice dams can't form from snow and cold weather alone; they need a warm roof too. This is how they're created:

1. Heat rises through ceiling penetrations and into an attic.
2. The snow on the shingles melts, and the water runoff travels down the roof slope until it gets to the edges.
3. Because the heat loss stops at the eaves, they are typically cold enough to refreeze the melted water, forming icicles and ice dams. Gutters magnify the problem by providing a platform for the ice to accumulate on and are often damaged by the added weight.
4. As the dams accumulate ice, they form an obstacle to the melted water that's still making its way down the roof.
5. With nowhere else to go, the water backs up under the shingles and eventually finds its way through the sheathing and into the house.

Quick tip*

FREE HEAT FROM THE SUN. During the winter and other cold months, keep the curtains on the south side of your house open during the day to let in free solar heat. Close those curtains at night to help prevent heat loss.

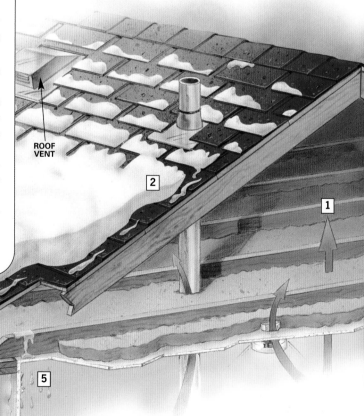

ROOF VENT

SOFFIT VENT CLOGGED WITH INSULATION

ice dams

and harmful ice dams

Ice dam solutions

When ice dams occur on a roof, it's usually not long before the symptoms move inside. Rust spots from drywall fasteners might show up on the ceilings, paint will peel and water stains will appear around windows and exterior doors. Even under the best conditions, some ice dam formation is often unavoidable; the daytime sun can melt snow on sections of a roof, but as night falls, temperatures drop and the water refreezes. You can't prevent this melting-refreezing cycle completely, but you can reduce the attic heat loss that aggravates it, and you can also protect your roof sheathing and house from the inevitable ice dams that will form from normal climatic changes.

Above all, stop or at least minimize the heat loss through your attic. Air leaks can occur wherever a ceiling or wall penetration isn't sealed properly. Light fixture boxes, access hatches and open pipe or duct chases can all be routes for warm air to migrate up into your attic, so use caulk, expanding foam insulation or other sealants to close them. This requires a trip to the attic to pull away the insulation and apply a sealant from the top side of the drywall or plaster, so this is a good project to tackle in the fall, when the attic will be reasonably cool. Aside from reducing the ice dams' severity, these measures should lower your energy bills. Upgrading insulation also helps; it's likely the attic already has some—probably fiberglass batting nested between the joists—but additional blown-in cellulose or fiberglass helps seal gaps and improve the R-rating.

Also important is maintaining a cold roof by installing or improving ventilation with soffit vents and roof or ridge vents that keep cold air circulating freely. Even with some attic heat loss, this will reduce the melting rate. Also, the next time you reroof, install a self-sealing membrane along the roof edges.

Keeping a cold roof

Insulate and seal every ceiling penetration so heat intended for living areas can't migrate into the attic and warm the roof. Add an extra layer of insulation across the entire attic, if necessary. Make sure there's adequate vent area along the soffits and eaves so cold air from outside can flow freely under the roof sheathing and out through vents on or near the ridge.

Installing ice-and-water barrier

Even if ice dams do form, you can prevent damage to the roof sheathing and interior by installing an ice-and-water membrane along the roof edges before shingling or reshingling. These 3-ft.-wide adhesive membranes are waterproof and self-seal around nail and staple holes. The membrane should run at least 2 to 3 ft. up the roof beyond the exterior wall plane.

Using secondary measures

If there's no snow on the roof, it can't melt to form ice dams at the edge. You can remove snow manually using a snow rake on an extension handle, although you'll have some cleanup to do on the ground afterward. Beware of overhead power lines. For a surefire preventive measure, place heating cable intended for this purpose along the roof edges and all the way out the downspout to melt the ice and snow. Always follow all manufacturer's instructions.

Keeping a Cold Roof

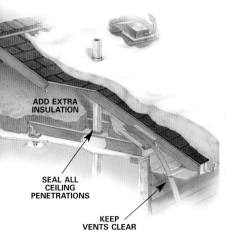

ADD EXTRA INSULATION

SEAL ALL CEILING PENETRATIONS

KEEP VENTS CLEAR

Installing Ice-and-Water Barrier

SELF-SEALING MEMBRANE

WALL PLANE

Using Secondary Measures

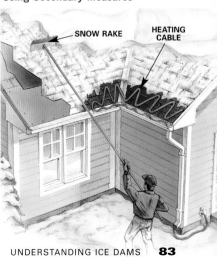

SNOW RAKE

HEATING CABLE

Saving Energy:

You can take a clue from the chapter on saving energy during heating season to help you save energy during cooling season, too. Clean furnace filters, well-sealed air ducts and programmable thermostats can go a long way in lowering your cooling bill. And other things, like insulating, caulking and sealing up attic bypasses—things normally associated with keeping cold air out in the winter—will also help lower your cooling bill by keeping warm air out in the summer.

Keeping your ceiling fans on and air conditioner tuned up will obviously help save on your electric bill, but one of the smartest ways to save energy during the summer is to keep the heat out to begin with. Trees, window shades, tint film and awnings are all passive forms of cooling that will deliver active forms of savings.

Cooling Season

TALL DECIDUOUS TREES

ROOF OVERHANG

INTERIOR SHADES

VINE-COVERED ARBOR

EXTERIOR SHADE

SMALL TREES AND BUSHES

AWNINGS

CURTAINS

SHADE CLOTH SCREENING

VINE-COVERED TRELLIS

Figure A
Natural Cooling

Cool your home with shade to supplement or eliminate air-conditioning. Window shading devices include awnings, interior and exterior shades, shade screens, dark films and tinted glass. Other shading features, like roof overhangs, covered porches, arbors, trellises and trees, shade the roof and walls of your house as well as the windows.

Cooling with shade

Use Mother Nature and window shading to lower your energy bill

Summer heat. It makes tomato plants droop, barefoot kids hotfoot it across paved sidewalks, and your ice-cream cone drip before you can give it a lick.

It's hard to imagine that only two generations ago, before air-conditioning, shade was the best defense against summertime heat. In those days, everyone worked inside if they could, near open windows. After work, they headed for the nearest covered porch, where they sat and fanned themselves, waiting for a cool breeze or simply sweating it out. Indoors, electric fans worked overtime. And once commercial air-conditioning arrived, they escaped to the air-conditioned theater for the afternoon matinee or shopped in an air-conditioned department store on weekends.

Today, about 60 years later, shade has taken a back seat to air-conditioning, which has become standard in homes, workplaces and cars. But don't dismiss shading strategies as outdated. Although porches are no longer so common, good shading still provides comfort and energy savings. Shade can reduce your air-conditioning bill by as much as a third. And it will make your yard cooler and more pleasant too.

Here you'll see how shading can help you and your house escape the sun's heat. If other front-line cooling strategies, like insulation and ventilation, are already in place, consider shading as a secondary strategy.

To begin, we'll follow the sun through a typical summer day and describe how it heats your house.

Following the sun's path

Morning

As every gardener, construction worker and farmer knows, sunrise is the coolest time of the day and the best time to get heavy work done. All night long, while the sun bakes folks on the other side of the globe, air temperatures drop around your home. At sunrise, the process reverses and the air begins to heat up again.

While the heat might not bother you, it does affect your house. Morning sunlight directly strikes the east wall of your house and begins a daylong warming process. The massive walls and roof slowly but steadily absorb the sun's rays on the outside, then warm up and radiate heat to the inside. Houses don't sweat, so once this heating begins, there's almost no way to reverse the process until sundown, except by turning on an air conditioner.

In most homes, good wall and attic insulation provides at least one built-in defense against heat buildup. The same insulation that keeps your home warm in winter keeps it cool in summer, trapping most of the heat in the exterior part of a wall. As long as the interior surfaces of the walls and ceilings remain cool, your house will feel cool. However, even a well-insulated house has weak spots—the windows. Morning sunlight that pours through the eastern windows bypasses the insulation and rapidly accelerates the heat buildup inside. To keep cool without turning on the air conditioner, it's critical that you shade these east-facing windows. (See more on shading methods on p. 88.)

Noon

By noontime, the sun's rays reach maximum intensity, beating down from directly overhead. Your roof and attic catch the brunt of the noontime heat. Roof temperatures can soar beyond 160 degrees F (egg-frying temperatures!), and attics become ovens. Fortunately, most homes have a

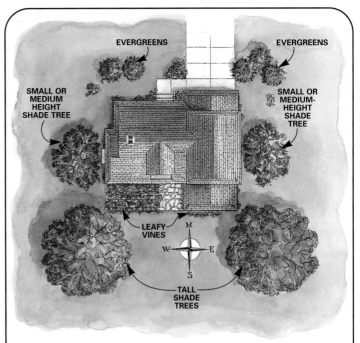

Figure B Shade

Shade with foliage by planting trees to shade the east- and west-facing walls of your home. Leave the south side open to receive the sun's warmth in winter. In regions with cold winters, plant dense evergreens on the north side to block the wind.

thick blanket of insulation on the attic floor, usually twice as much as in walls. Good attic ventilation helps too, but insulation is the main defense to keep the heat from reaching the rooms below. Before the widespread use of ceiling insulation, hot weather sometimes forced entire families to cook, eat and sleep on the covered back porch so they could escape the stifling heat indoors.

The walls and windows of your house absorb much less heat during this period because the sun hits them at such a sharp angle during the summer months (Figure C, p. 88). Actually, the noontime sun perches slightly to the south side of your house. Good roof design should include overhangs or porch roofs to shade the south walls and windows during the middle of the day.

Afternoon

The sun continues to heat the roof and begins to hit the west walls. On most hot summer days, your air conditioner will switch on by now to counteract the heat buildup from the morning and noon hours. The outside air temperature usually peaks about 4 p.m., then begins to drop.

Evening

In most regions, a summer day feels hottest about 6 p.m. By now, the air temperature has dropped slightly, but rising humidity in the early evening intensifies the sensation of heat. So the evening sun can feel especially hot. If your kids are going to grumble, they'll probably do it now, and you can

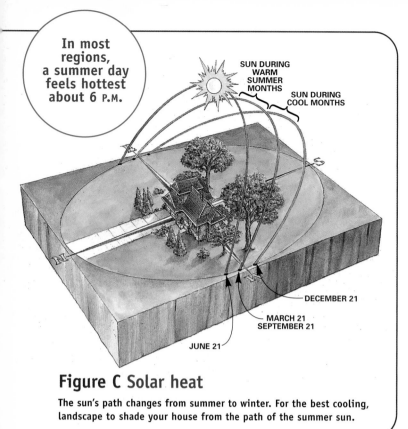

In most regions, a summer day feels hottest about 6 P.M.

SUN DURING WARM SUMMER MONTHS

SUN DURING COOL MONTHS

DECEMBER 21

MARCH 21 SEPTEMBER 21

JUNE 21

Figure C Solar heat

The sun's path changes from summer to winter. For the best cooling, landscape to shade your house from the path of the summer sun.

bet that the evening shade will feel especially welcome.

The evening sun heats your home just like the morning sun, except that it strikes the west wall instead of the east wall. However, its effect feels hotter than the morning sun's because the inside of your house has been heating up all day. In fact, unless your air conditioner is running, the inside temperature will continue to rise even after sunset, because the heat already absorbed by the exterior walls and ceiling slowly continues to work its way inside, where it radiates off the walls. You can sweat it out inside, but it's more pleasant to relax outdoors or on a screened porch in the evening and into the night.

After sunset, your house slowly cools down until morning, when sunrise begins the process all over again.

Window-shading devices

The path of the sun dictates the best placement for shading devices. Figure A, on p. 86, shows a variety of ways to shade windows, especially those east- and west-facing windows that catch direct sunlight. Blinds and curtains are perhaps the most popular because they also provide privacy. The side facing out should be light-colored so it reflects heat away from the window. Dark-colored shades absorb heat and draw it inside. Outside blinds work better than inside blinds because they block the heat before it gets into the house. But few people use them because it's so inconvenient to run outside every time you want to raise and lower them.

On the downside, blinds, curtains and shades block your view as well as the cooling breezes if you keep your windows open.

One shading product particularly popular in the South is a densely woven insect screening, sometimes called shade cloth. This screening, made from fiberglass or aluminum, blocks up to 75 percent of sunlight. Another option is tinted plastic film in various densities that you apply to your window glass to reflect or filter out some of the heat. These films are particularly useful if you want to prevent rugs and upholstery from fading. Don't apply these films to double-pane windows, however, because they can cause a temperature imbalance that could crack the glass.

If you have to replace your windows, buy double-pane glass with tinted or "low-E" coatings. Low-E windows, which are specifically designed for cooling, block much of the sun's heat without darkening the view through the window (a weakness of tinted glass). These are good choices for east-, west- and south-facing windows if you spend more for air-conditioning than for heating.

All of these shading methods (except buying new windows) are relatively inexpensive and can do a good job. You can install most of them yourself, using materials from well-stocked lumberyards and home centers.

Awnings are a good alternative if you want to catch cooling breezes, because they shade without blocking the wind. And they only partially block the view. They're semipermanent, you don't have to open and close them, and you can leave them up until cooler weather arrives in the fall. If you have a good sewing machine, you can make them yourself from canvas or reinforced nylon and inexpensive hardware parts purchased from an awning dealer. Awnings should extend about halfway down the window and have fabric sides to block the sun at all but extremely low angles.

No matter which ideas you use, remember to shade your east-facing windows to block the morning sun, and your west-facing windows to block the evening sun. Shading can also be effective over south-facing windows. In all regions except Florida and the extreme southern United States, you'll save on heating costs if you remove the shading devices during cold winter weather to allow maximum heat gain from the sun.

Shading with landscaping

Landscape shading blocks the sun before it ever hits your house. So it's a great house-cooling strategy, plus it'll make your yard cooler and more attractive too.

For maximum energy savings, place trees and other foliage so that the house is shaded in summer but not in winter. Figures A, B and C show low foliage positioned on the east and west sides to block the early morning and late evening sun. Moderate-size trees block late morning and early evening sun, and tall trees placed fairly close to the house cast shade over the roof during midday hours. These are all broadleaf deciduous trees, which conveniently lose their leaves in winter, allowing more sunlight to hit the house when you welcome the heat. (In stormy areas with frequent high winds, you might not want to plant trees close to your house. Ask experts at your local nursery for advice about which trees to plant and where to plant them.)

However, even the branches of leafless trees can block 30 to 40 percent of the sunlight. Because the winter sun hangs so low in the southern sky (Figure C), the south-facing windows are by far the most important to keep as unobstructed as possible for winter heating.

Landscaping with trees is a long-term proposition, and an ideal plan might run afoul of other hazards. Large, south-facing exposures are ideal, but your house might face the east or west. Electrical and underground utility lines might limit tree positioning. Your yard might be too small, and established trees might be growing in the wrong spot. You won't want to cut down a beautiful tree just because it's in the wrong place. So use Figures A and B as models and pick the parts that apply to your situation.

Landscaping by region

A good shading strategy has to take account of the local climate. (Suitable shade trees and plants vary too, so rely on your local nursery to help you choose.) Figure D illustrates four zones, all of which have somewhat different cooling requirements.

In Zone 1, summer cooling isn't nearly as important, or as expensive, as winter heating. If you live in this zone, gear your landscaping plan to winter rather than to summer. Position trees and evergreens on the northwest side, the direction of cold north winds, and keep the south side completely clear to gain as much heat through the windows as possible in winter. Even broadleaf shade trees that lose their leaves block considerable sun in the winter. You'll also want to shift the shading arbor out into the yard away from the south wall and build your screen porch on a different wall as well. In Figure A, both shade the south wall.

Without modifications, the landscape plan in Figure A works best in Zone 2. This zone is a region of hot and cold extremes, so the cooling shade of the arbor against the house makes sense. The arbor also shades the patio, which would otherwise reflect sunlight and heat into the house. Closely spaced trees and shrubs on the north side still block the cold north wind, but foliage on the other three sides should be open enough to channel cooling summer breezes around the house.

The design in Figure A also works well in Zone 3, except that you don't have to worry about blocking a cold north wind.

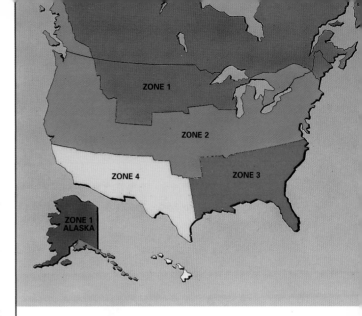

Figure D Zones

Climates vary, so plan shading strategy according to local conditions. Zone 1 has warm summers but cold winters. Zone 2 has hot summers, cold winters and sometimes high humidity. Zone 3 has hot summers, mild winters and high humidity. Zone 4 has clear, hot, dry summers and mild winters. Hawaii's climate is moderate year-round.

Shade trees with high canopies (leaves and branches) work best here because they allow the breezes to circulate easily beneath them. (Obviously you can't grow tall trees overnight, so keep them if you have them and get them started if you don't!)

The high humidity in this zone will make you feel hotter and stickier. Since dense foliage produces a lot of humidity, move vines and arbors away from the house and rely more on awnings, porches, roof overhangs and other architectural devices for window shading.

In Zone 4, the hot, arid region, you can plant the shading vines, arbors and other foliage right near the house, because the extra moisture these plants produce helps cool the air in this dry region. Your plant choice will be more limited in an arid climate, so you might have to rely on awnings, window shades, porches and other architectural features to shade the east, west and south walls and windows.

Quick tip *

PASSIVE COOLING = ENERGY SAVINGS

Shading your home with trees, awnings and shades can lower the indoor temperature by as much as 20 degrees F on a hot day.

The payoff

No one shading device or landscaping idea is best for every home. But basic shading principles will help you choose what fits your home's style, your local climate (sometimes different from the regional climate) and certainly your budget. The main payoff is the comfort of not having to rely on your air-conditioning as much. The bonus is that your home will look better and be more energy-efficient.

How to plant a
shade tree

A natural way to lower your summer utility bills

Fall is the ideal time of year to plant a shade tree—or any other tree, for that matter. The cool weather of fall gives roots a chance to grow, develop and get established without the stress of developing new leaves or fruit. Don't be surprised to find that you'll have to wait for a whole growing season to see significant growth. In fact, with fruit trees, it's a good idea to pinch off any blossoms or fruit the first year so the tree can channel its energy into establishing its root system instead of developing fruit.

The basic planting techniques are the same for all trees. For starters, pick a well-drained area (one where water doesn't pond after rain) in a sunny location so the tree will get the light it needs to thrive. Keep in mind the mature size of the species you're planting and consider whether nearby trees, buildings and power lines could cause problems later.

When you've picked your planting spot, first dig a 1-ft.-square, 1-ft.-deep drainage test hole, fill it with water and go have a cup of coffee. If there's still water in the hole after about an hour, you have heavy, poorly drained soil. If so, use the same directions as for well-drained areas, but dig the hole only as deep as two-thirds the height of the root ball. Then heap dirt over the root ball before mulching. That way, some water is directed away from the hole so the root ball won't drown in trapped water.

For well-drained areas, dig a hole 1 to 2 ft. wider than the root ball and as deep as the height of the root ball of the tree. Your tree will be sold either in a plastic container or bundled in burlap. Rough up the sides of the hole with the tip of the shovel, especially when planting in heavy soil. It'll make it easier for roots to penetrate the surrounding soil. Carry the tree by picking up the container or the burlapped root ball. Never carry the tree by the trunk; you could damage delicate roots.

If you have a burlapped tree, lower the burlapped root ball into the hole. Burlapped trees have a wire basket to hold the root ball together. You can leave the wire basket in place; the roots will grow through it and the rotting burlap. If your tree has synthetic burlap, or if you're planting in heavy clay or sand, remove the wire and burlap first. If you have a container-grown tree, cut away the sides of the container and peel them back to expose the root ball. Lift the ball from the container and lower it into the hole.

Hold the tree straight while you fill the hole with soil. Tamp the soil down around the ball with the end of a 4x4 until the soil level is about three-fourths the depth of the hole (but be careful not to damage roots). Cut away the exposed burlap in the top one-fourth of the hole. Fill the hole with water to allow the soil to settle and to remove trapped air. After the water drains, finish filling the hole with soil and lay a 3- to 6-in. bed of mulch around the base of the trunk to help retain soil moisture.

Always use native soil to fill around the root ball. Filling with enriched soil will pamper the roots and they'll refuse to penetrate poorer surrounding soil to establish a good root base.

Don't fertilize your tree right after planting. Instead, apply a 10-10-10 fertilizer the following spring and every year thereafter.

CUT OFF TOP
QUARTER OF
BURLAP

3" TO 6" DEEP MULCH

ABRADE SIDES OF
HOLE WITH SHOVEL

HOLE SAME DEPTH AS
ROOT BALL

LEAVE ON WIRE
AND BURLAP

HOLE 1' TO 2' WIDER THAN ROOT BALL

Window air conditioner spring cleaning

Easy steps to make it work more efficiently

Follow these steps to get a window-mounted air conditioner ready for summer.

The secret is simply a good cleaning. Room air conditioners, like central air conditioners, have two sets of coils (a "coil" is an arrangement of fins and tubes for efficient heat transfer). The condenser coil is on the outside and the evaporator coil on the inside (Figure A). Keeping them clean is 90 percent of the battle in keeping your air conditioner operating efficiently.

The most important maintenance steps are easy, but if this is the first time you've cleaned the unit, allow about a half day to pull things apart and put them back together. A professional (look under "Heating and Air-Conditioning" or "Air-Conditioning Service" in your yellow pages) will service an air conditioner for about $75. But don't expect quick service in the spring when everyone has the same idea.

You really can't clean your window air conditioner unless you unplug it and remove it from the window. Hold on to it when you remove the window support. It can weigh 100 lbs. or more. Have a strong helper standing

Figure A Window Air Conditioner

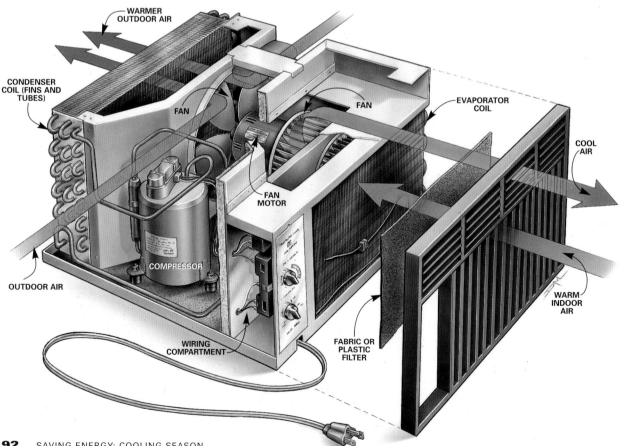

WARMER OUTDOOR AIR

CONDENSER COIL (FINS AND TUBES)

FAN

FAN

EVAPORATOR COIL

COOL AIR

FAN MOTOR

OUTDOOR AIR

COMPRESSOR

WIRING COMPARTMENT

FABRIC OR PLASTIC FILTER

WARM INDOOR AIR

Quick tip *

SAVE $$$ BY INSTALLING YOUR AC UNIT IN THE SHADE

A window or central air conditioner located in the shade can use up to 10 percent less energy than one located in the sun. Install units on the north side of your house or shield them with shrubbery (but don't block the airflow).

by to help you lift it out. The cleaning process shown in the photos applies to most air conditioners, but refer to your owner's manual for more details about your brand and model.

When the air conditioner doesn't seem to cool well, most folks assume that the coolant needs recharging (a job for pros only). But most often the culprit is dirt, a problem solved by cleaning the coils. The evaporator coil (Photo 2) is protected by a filter. Rinse it out or replace it ($1 from appliance stores), and vacuum the fins if they're dusty.

The dirtiest side of the condenser coil, the fan side, is harder to get at (Figure A). Since you usually can't vacuum the fins from the fan side, spray water back through the fins from the outside (Photo 5). Do this outdoors or inside near a floor drain. Wrap plastic around the fan motor to protect it and keep the wiring compartment dry (Figure A). Let the unit dry for 24 hours before setting it in the window and plugging it in again.

It's important to use the correct oil for fan motor lubrication. Don't use all-purpose or penetrating oils. Buy oil made specifically for electric motors (usually nondetergent SAE 20 motor oil) unless otherwise specified in

1 UNPLUG the unit and lift it from the window. Remove the front cover, then unscrew and lift off the case to expose the compressor, fan motor and evaporator coils.

Quick tip *

COOL TIPS FOR BUYING AN AIR CONDITIONER

Central air-conditioning systems carry a SEER rating (Seasonal Energy Efficiency Rating), which typically ranges from 10 to 17. The higher the SEER rating, the more efficient the unit. Before you go air-conditioner shopping, check with your utility company to see if it offers rebates for AC units with a high SEER rating.

2 VACUUM the evaporator fins (the inside coil) with a soft brush attachment. Replace the filter or wash and reuse the old one.

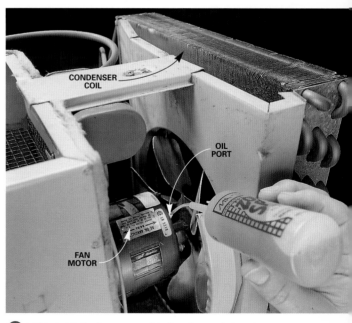

3 LUBRICATE the fan motor with five drops of electric motor oil if you can find oil ports. Check the owner's manual for help. Don't apply too much oil—more is not better.

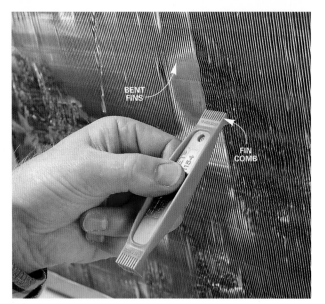

BENT FINS

FIN COMB

4 STRAIGHTEN bent fins with a special plastic fin comb to improve air circulation.

CONDENSER COIL

PLASTIC AROUND FAN MOTOR

5 WASH the condenser coil with a spray of water from the outside inward. Cover the fan motor with plastic to keep it dry. Then rinse and wipe up as much dirt and crud as possible from the bottom pan, making sure drain holes and overflows are open.

your owner's manual. The oil bottle in Photo 3 has a handy plastic tube that reaches fittings in tight areas. It costs $1.50 at appliance parts or repair dealers.

Another handy tool is the fin comb we show in Photo 4. Fins are delicate and can easily bend when you're handling the unit. You'll be amazed at how fast and easily a fin comb can straighten them. It costs only $3–$5, but you might have to buy a whole set to get the right size.

You can use them on the outdoor units of central air conditioners too. Finally, inspect the cord for cracks in the insulation, especially around the plug. Replace the entire cord if it's damaged.

*Energy-Saving Goof

A/C on the loose

At the end of the summer, I decided to beat the fall to-do list and remove the window air-conditioner units at my law office. I proceeded to remove the screws from the window sash of the first unit and muscle it out myself. Well, it slipped and fell out the window a few feet into a mulched flower bed. My secretary asked if I could use some help with the next one. Stubbornly I forged ahead by myself. The second unit was much larger, and my plan of attack failed even more miserably as the unit slipped from my hands and went crashing to the sidewalk 10 ft. below. Luckily, no one was in its path. I promised my secretary that next time I'd ask for help!

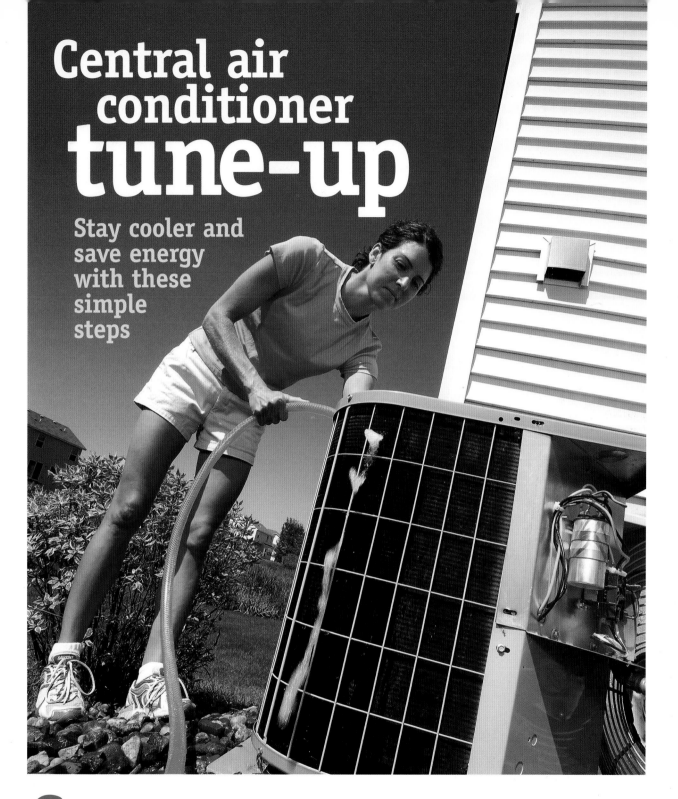

Central air conditioner
tune-up

Stay cooler and save energy with these simple steps

Chances are that if you've neglected a spring checkup, your air conditioner isn't cooling nearly as well as it could. A year's worth of dirt and debris clogging the cooling fins, a low coolant level, a dirty blower fan filter and a number of other simple problems can significantly reduce the efficiency of your air conditioner and wear it out faster.

You can't do everything; only a pro can check the coolant level. But you can easily handle most of the routine cleaning chores and save the extra $120 that it would cost to have a pro do them.

Here you'll see how to clean the outdoor unit (called the condenser) and the accessible parts of the indoor unit (called the evaporator). All the steps are simple and straightforward and will take you only a few hours, total. You don't need any special skills, tools or experience. If you aren't familiar with air conditioners and furnaces/blowers, don't worry. See Figure A "Parts of a central air conditioner,"

1 TURN OFF the electrical power to the condenser unit at the outdoor shutoff. Either pull out a block or move a switch to the "Off" position. If uncertain, turn off the power to the AC at the main electrical panel.

BLOCK SHUTOFF

2 VACUUM grass clippings, leaves and other debris from the exterior fins with a soft brush attachment. Clear away all bushes, weeds and grass within 2 ft. of the condenser.

3 REALIGN bent or crushed fins with gentle pressure from a dinner knife. Don't insert the knife more than 1/2 in.

FAN

ELECTRICAL WIRES

4 UNSCREW the top grille. Lift out the fan and carefully set it aside without stressing the electrical wires. Pull out any leaves and wipe the interior surfaces clean with a damp cloth.

p. 97, to become familiar with how an air conditioner works and the parts of the system.

You may have a different type of central air conditioner than we show here—a heat pump system, for example, or a unit mounted horizontally in the attic. However, you can still carry out most maintenance procedures because each system will have a condenser outside and an evaporator inside.

Use the owner's manual for your particular model to help navigate around any differences from the one shown in our photos. And call in a pro every two or three years to check electrical parts and the coolant level ($150).

> **tip** Call for service before the first heat wave, when the pros become swamped with repair calls!

Cleaning the condenser

Clean your outdoor unit on a day that's at least 60 degrees F. That's about the minimum temperature at which you can test your air conditioner to make sure it's working. The condenser usually sits in an inconspicuous spot next to your house. You'll see two copper tubes running to it, one bare and the other encased in a foam sleeve. If you have a heat pump, both tubes will be covered by foam sleeves.

Your primary job here is to clean the condenser fins, which are fine metallic blades that surround the unit. They get dirty because a central fan sucks air through them, pulling in dust, dead leaves, dead grass and the worst culprit—floating

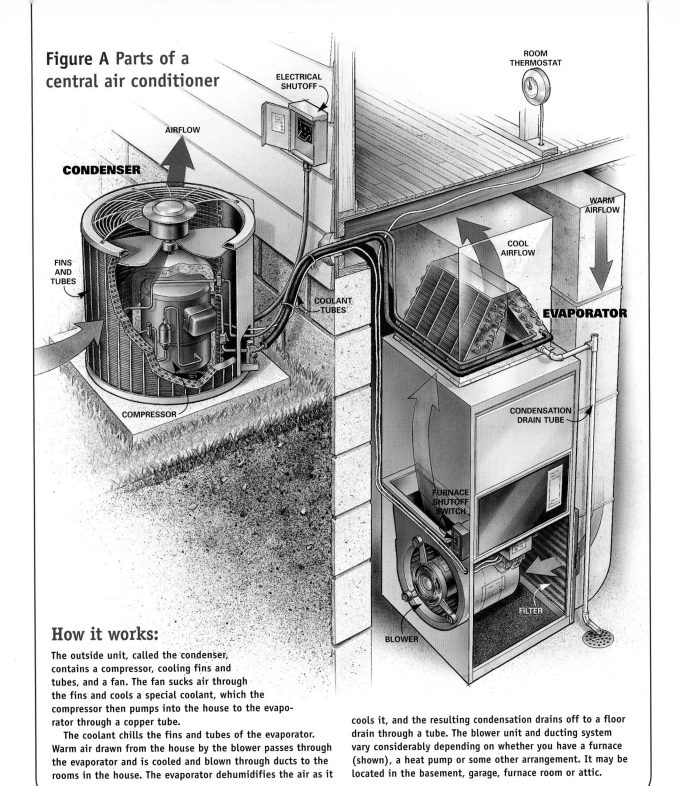

Figure A Parts of a central air conditioner

ELECTRICAL SHUTOFF

AIRFLOW

CONDENSER

ROOM THERMOSTAT

FINS AND TUBES

COOLANT TUBES

WARM AIRFLOW

COOL AIRFLOW

EVAPORATOR

COMPRESSOR

CONDENSATION DRAIN TUBE

FURNACE SHUTOFF SWITCH

FILTER

BLOWER

How it works:

The outside unit, called the condenser, contains a compressor, cooling fins and tubes, and a fan. The fan sucks air through the fins and cools a special coolant, which the compressor then pumps into the house to the evaporator through a copper tube.

The coolant chills the fins and tubes of the evaporator. Warm air drawn from the house by the blower passes through the evaporator and is cooled and blown through ducts to the rooms in the house. The evaporator dehumidifies the air as it cools it, and the resulting condensation drains off to a floor drain through a tube. The blower unit and ducting system vary considerably depending on whether you have a furnace (shown), a heat pump or some other arrangement. It may be located in the basement, garage, furnace room or attic.

"cotton" from cottonwood trees and dandelions. The debris blocks the airflow and reduces the unit's cooling ability.

Always begin by shutting off the electrical power to the unit. Normally you'll find a shutoff nearby. It may be a switch in a box, a pull lever or a fuse block that you pull out (Photo 1). Look for the "On-Off" markings.

Vacuum the fins clean with a soft brush (Photo 2); they're fragile and cann be easily bent or crushed. On many units you'll have to unscrew and lift off a metal box to get at them. Check your owner's manual for directions and lift off the box carefully to avoid bumping the fins. Occasionally you'll find fins that have been bent. You can buy a special set of fin combs ($10 at an appliance parts store) to straighten them. Minor straightening can be done with a blunt dinner knife (Photo 3). If large areas of fins are crushed, have a pro straighten them during a routine serv-

5 SPRAY the fins using moderate water pressure from a hose nozzle. Direct the spray from the inside out. Reinstall the fan.

6 TURN the power back on, then set the house thermostat to "Cool" so the compressor comes on. After 10 minutes, feel the insulated tube. It should feel cool. The uninsulated tube should feel warm.

7 TURN OFF the power to the furnace at a nearby switch or at the main panel. Then pull out the furnace filter and check it for dirt buildup. Change it if necessary.

8 OPEN the blower compartment and vacuum up the dust. Check the motor for lubrication ports. If it has them, squeeze five drops of electric motor oil into each.

ice call.

Then unscrew the fan to gain access to the interior of the condenser. You can't completely remove it because its wiring is connected to the unit. Depending on how much play the wires give you, you might need a helper to hold it while you vacuum debris from the inside. (Sometimes mice like to overwinter there!)

After you hose off the fins (Photo 5), check the fan motor for lubrication ports. Most newer motors have sealed bearings (the one shown does) and can't be lubricated. Check your owner's manual to be sure. If you find ports, add five drops of electric motor oil ($5 at hardware stores or appliance parts stores). Don't use penetrating oil or all-purpose oil. They're not designed for long-term lubrication and can actually harm the bearings.

If you have an old air conditioner, you might have a belt-driven compressor in the bottom of the unit. Look for lubrication ports on this as well. The compressors on newer air conditioners are completely enclosed and won't need lubrication (Figure A, p. 97).

Restarting procedure

In most cases, you can simply restore power to the outside unit and move inside to finish the maintenance. However, the compressors are surprisingly fragile and some require special start-up procedures under two conditions. (Others have built-in electronic controls that handle the start-up, but unless you know that yours has these controls, follow these procedures.)

1. If the power to your unit has been off for more than four hours:
   - Move the switch from "Cool" to "Off" at your inside thermostat.
   - Turn the power back on and let the unit sit for 24 hours. (The compressor has a heating element that warms the internal lubricant.)
   - Switch the thermostat back to "Cool."
2. If you switched the unit off while the compressor was running:
   - Wait at least five minutes before switching it back on. (The compressor needs to decompress before restarting.)

With the air conditioner running, make sure it's actually working by touching the coolant tubes (Photo 6). This is a crude test. Only a pro with proper instruments can tell if the coolant is at the level for peak efficiency. But keep a sharp eye out for dark drip marks on the bottom of the case and beneath the tube joints. This indicates an oil leak and a potential coolant leak as well. Call in a pro if you spot this problem. Don't tighten a joint to try to stop a leak yourself. Overtightening can make the problem worse.

Clean the indoor unit

The evaporator usually sits in an inaccessible spot inside a metal duct downstream from the blower (Figure A). If you can get to it, gently vacuum its fins (from the blower side) with a soft brush as you did with the condenser. However, the best way to keep it clean is to keep the airstream from the blower clean. This means annually vacuuming out the blower compartment and changing the filter whenever it's dirty (Photos 7 and 8).

Begin by turning off the power to the furnace or blower. Usually you'll find a simple toggle switch nearby in a metal box (Photo 7); otherwise turn the power off at the main panel. If you have trouble opening the blower unit or finding the filter, check your owner's manual for help. The manual will also list the filter type, but if it's your first time, take the old one with you when buying a new one to make sure you get the right size. Be sure to keep the power to the blower off whenever you remove the filter. Otherwise you'll blow dust into the evaporator fins.

The manual will also tell you where to find the oil ports on the blower, if it has any. The blower compartments on newer furnaces and heat pumps are so tight that you often can't lubricate the blower without removing it. If that's the case, have a pro do it during a routine maintenance checkup.

The evaporator fins dehumidify the air as they cool it, so you'll find a tube to drain the condensation. The water collects in a pan and drains out the side (Figure A). Most tubes are flexible plastic and are easy to pull off and clean (Photos 9 and 10). But if they're rigid plastic, you'll probably have to unscrew or cut off with a saw to check. Reglue rigid tubes

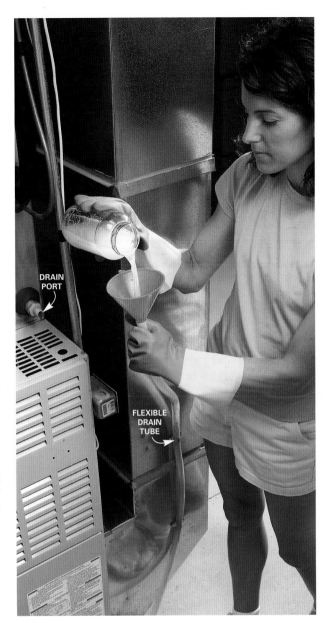

9 PULL OFF the plastic condensation drain tube and check it for algae growth. Clean it by pouring a bleach/water solution (1:16 ratio) through the tube to flush the line. Or simply replace the tube.

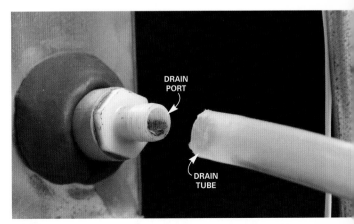

10 POKE a pipe cleaner into the drain port and clean out any debris. Reinstall the drain tube and turn the power back on.

Split air-conditioning system

WARM AIR INTAKE

INSIDE UNIT

COOL AIR EXHAUST

COOL REFRIGERANT TO INSIDE UNIT

WARM REFRIGERANT TO COMPRESSOR

CONDENSER AND COMPRESSOR

SPLIT AIR-CONDITIONING REMOTE CONTROL

More
to top-
Strategies for

If your upper floors are too hot and lower floors too cold in the summer, try this: In the summer, almost completely close down the first-floor heating and cooling vents (there's usually a lever on the grate) and completely open the ones on the second floor. That may force more cool air upstairs. The cool air will sink to the lower floor naturally. Reverse the procedure during the heating season.

If that doesn't work, contact an air-conditioning company to have a pro look over your home and see if it's possible to convert your heating and cooling system to a "zone"-type system. Each floor is then treated as an independent zone—complete with its own thermostat and helper fans that force heated or cooled air to where it's needed. Depending on the existing ductwork and structural considerations, it may be next to impossible to convert an existing home, but a pro can help you decide.

If a zone system isn't feasible, ask the company about installing a "split," or "ductless," air conditioner that will be solely dedicated to cooling the upper floor. A split air conditioner is similar to a conventional window air conditioner except that it's split in half. The unit that contains the

cool air
floor bedrooms
efficient and quieter whole-house cooling

noisy compressor is usually on the ground outside the house. Refrigerant lines connect it to an indoor air handler that's typically mounted to a wall or ceiling in the area you wish to cool. A very quiet fan blows room air over cool coils to distribute the conditioned air. Installation costs start at $2,000, including parts and labor.

Quick tip*

RAISE YOUR THERMOSTAT, SAVE $$. You can save up to $100 in a summer by raising your air conditioner's thermostat to 78 degrees F.

*Energy-Saving Product

Portable air conditioner for cool rooms

When you want to stay cool without the expense of firing up your central air and cooling the entire house, plug in a portable air conditioner. They cool up to 400 sq. ft., and you can roll them from room to room—wherever you want to cool. We tried a $500 unit (DeLonghi, www.delonghi.com) and were impressed. It made little noise when running and quickly cooled the room.

Most portable air conditioners have an exhaust hose that goes out the window. The exhaust also drains condensation water, so there's no drip pan to empty. Air intake can come from the room (for higher efficiency) or from outside through an intake hose (for fresher air).

Hanging a ceiling fan

Ceiling fans keep you cool for a few cents a day

A high-efficiency ceiling fan can cost as little as $1 a month when run eight hours a day; a window air conditioner can cost 50 times as much to run. And you can enjoy a fan all year long, as it circulates warm air in the winter.

Ceiling fans (technically called "paddle fans") used to be frustrating to install, to say the least. Most of the time you had to wing it because specialty hanging systems were poorly developed or nonexistent. Now, most manufacturers have designed versatile mounting systems that take the hassle out of installation. When you add in the improved, stronger ceiling boxes, you'll find that just about any ceiling

fan can go up quick and easy on any ceiling, sloped or flat.

Here you'll find crystal-clear instructions that go beyond the basic set included with the fan. Also, see how to avoid common pitfalls like putting on parts in the wrong order and forgetting to slip shrouds on ahead of time. Some mistakes are more serious than these. Standard electrical boxes or blades hung too low can be downright dangerous.

Expect to spend at least $150 for a high-quality fan (see "Buying a ceiling fan," opposite) and a bit more for accessories like electronic controls, fancy light packages and furniture-grade paddles.

DIVIDE MEASUREMENT BY 2

6"

12"

12"

2' LEVEL

3/12 SLOPE

1 DETERMINE the ceiling slope by holding a 2-ft. level against the ceiling and measuring the vertical distance from the level to the ceiling. Divide that number by 2 to get the drop over 12 in. of horizontal run, 3/12 slope in our case. See the chart on p. 107 to determine the minimum downrod length for the blade diameter you'd like.

2 SHUT OFF the power at the main panel and remove the light fixture. Knock the existing electrical box free of the framing with a hammer and a block of wood, then pull the electrical cable free of the old box and through the ceiling hole. Leave the old box in the ceiling cavity unless you can easily remove it through the hole.

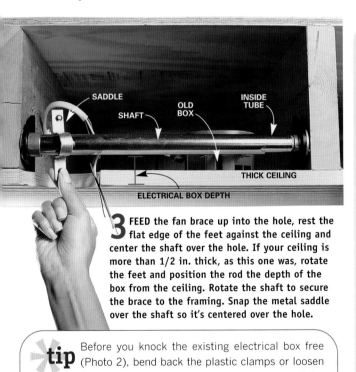

SADDLE

SHAFT

OLD BOX

INSIDE TUBE

THICK CEILING

ELECTRICAL BOX DEPTH

3 FEED the fan brace up into the hole, rest the flat edge of the feet against the ceiling and center the shaft over the hole. If your ceiling is more than 1/2 in. thick, as this one was, rotate the feet and position the rod the depth of the box from the ceiling. Rotate the shaft to secure the brace to the framing. Snap the metal saddle over the shaft so it's centered over the hole.

tip Before you knock the existing electrical box free (Photo 2), bend back the plastic clamps or loosen the metal cable clamps so it'll be easier to pull the electrical cable free after the box is loosened.

Put up a new fan in a leisurely Saturday afternoon

If everything goes well, you can put up a ceiling fan in a couple of hours, including cleanup. In most cases, the whole job will take only a hammer, a screwdriver, a 3/8-in. nut driver and a wire stripper.

Buying a ceiling fan

IF YOU HAVEN'T WALKED UNDER A LARGE FAN display yet, hold on to your hat. You'll be overwhelmed by the selection of colors, styles and accessories, especially if you visit a ceiling fan store. If you intend to use your fan regularly, invest in a model in the $150-plus category. You'll get a quieter, more efficient, more durable unit. If you spend beyond that amount, you're usually paying for light packages, radio-actuated remote and wall controls, style and design (fancier motor castings, inlays, blade adornments or glasswork). If you spend less, you're likely to get a less efficient, less durable, noisier unit with fewer color, blade and electronic choices.

Choose the blade diameter that best suits the room visually and make sure the unit will fit under the ceiling without jeopardizing the foreheads of your tallest friends. (See p. 107 for height requirements.) Bigger rooms call for wider fan blade diameters. The bigger fan will not only look better but also move more air.

Most ceiling fans are designed for heated, enclosed spaces. If you're putting a fan in a screen room, a gazebo or other damp area, the building code requires you to use a "damp-rated" fan. These fans have corrosion-resistant stainless steel or plastic parts that can stand up to high humidity and condensation. If you live in a coastal area with corrosive sea air, or if you're putting a fan in a particularly wet environment like a greenhouse or an enclosed pool area, you should choose a "wet-rated" fan.

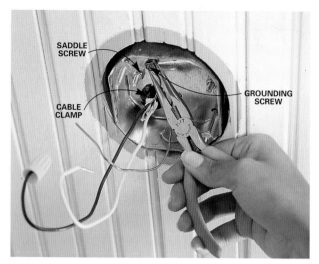

4 FEED the existing wire through the cable clamp in the top of the new metal box, slip the box over the saddle screws, and tighten the nuts to clamp the box to the shaft with a nut driver or a deep-well socket. Crimp a loop of grounding wire three-quarters around the grounding screw and tighten the screw.

5 POSITION the hanger bracket so that the opening in the bracket is on the uphill side of the sloped ceiling. Then screw it into the box with the special screws provided with the fan brace.

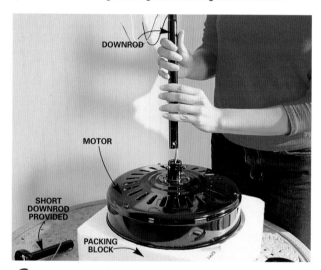

6 PLACE the motor right side up, thread the wire through the downrod and insert the downrod into the mounting collar.

7 SLIP the downrod pin through the collar and tube, lock it into place with the cotter pin, and tighten the screws and locknuts.

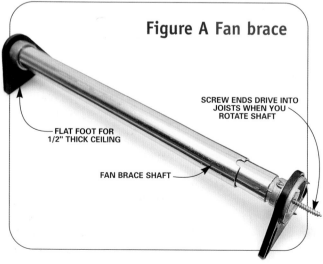

Figure A Fan brace

Most of the time, the wires that fed a previous ceiling light fixture are adequate for hooking up a new fan. If you have a wiring arrangement that's different from the one shown here and you are unfamiliar with wiring techniques, consult an electrician or building inspector for help.

Follow the photo series for basic installation steps that apply to more than 95 percent of all fans. There may be small variations, particularly when it comes to the light and blade mountings, so you'll still need to consult the instructions provided with your fan. As with any other electrical work, you may need an electrical permit from your local building department before starting the job. The inspector will tell you when to call for an inspection.

tip Tighten the locknuts firmly. Loose locknuts are the most common cause of wobbly fans.

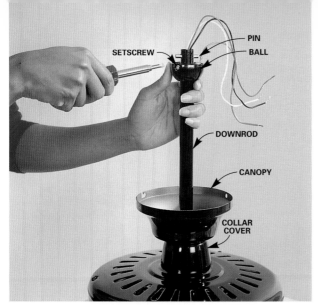

SETSCREW · PIN · BALL · DOWNROD · CANOPY · COLLAR COVER

8 SLIP the collar cover, then the canopy, over the downrod. Slide the ball over the downrod and push the pin through both sets of holes, then lift the ball over the pin and tighten the setscrew.

TAB · SLOT

9 LIFT the assembly over the open side of the bracket and lower it into place. Rotate the motor until the ball slot locks into place over the tab on the bracket.

10 CONNECT the bare ground wire from the box to the green ground wire on the bracket with a wire connector. Connect the white neutral wire from the motor to the neutral wire from the box. Connect the blue and black wires from the motor to the black hot wire from the box and neatly fold them into the box.

Replace electrical boxes with specially designed paddle fan braces

Before starting any work, shut off the circuit breaker that feeds the switch and light fixture. If there's a working bulb in the fixture, turn it on. Then you'll know you have the right breaker when the bulb goes out. Check the wires with a voltage tester to make sure they're off after removing the fixture and when changing the wall switch.

The next step is to remove the existing plastic or metal electrical box and install a "fan brace" that's designed to hold ceiling fans. Few conventional boxes are strong enough to support a ceiling fan, so don't even think about trying to hang your fan from an existing box.

✳ Energy-Saving Q&A

Sizing a ceiling fan

Q I understand ceiling fans can save energy and money for heating and cooling. Is there a rule of thumb for what size fan I need?

A Yes, a quick rule of thumb matches the diameter of the fan with the largest dimension of a room. For 12 ft. or less, use a 36-in. fan. For 12 to 16 ft., use a 48-in. fan. For 16 to 18 ft., use a 52-in. fan. And for dimensions larger than 18 ft., install two fans.

Placement of a ceiling fan for adequate air circulation is 7 ft. above the floor with the blades 8 to 10 in. from the ceiling. And to move more air at low speed, a fan with five blades is best.

Regarding energy savings, research has proven that ceiling fans can save energy during the cooling season by creating a gentle breeze. You get your savings then by raising your thermostat by a minimum of 2 degrees. This decreases air conditioning energy used by 10 to 15 percent, or 5 to 8 percent per degree.

By reversing your fan (so it runs clockwise) during winter, you pull heat from the ceiling and push it down to the floor for more even heating.

Instead, buy a fan brace (about $15) when you purchase your fan. You can choose braces that fasten with screws if the framing is accessible from the attic or if it's new construction. Otherwise, pick a brace that's designed to slip through the ceiling hole and through the electrical box.

11 SCREW the fan blades to their brackets and screw the brackets to the bottom of the motor. It's easiest to hold the screw in the bracket with the screwdriver while you lift the blade assembly into position. Then drive in the screw.

12 PLACE the radio receiver into the switch housing/light pod assembly and connect the light pod wires according to the manufacturer's instructions. Note the settings on the receiver's code toggles so you can dial in the same settings on the electronic controls at the wall switch. Now loosen the screws in the switch-housing hub halfway. Plug the motor wiring into the receptacle on the receiver and twist the switch housing into place on the hub. Retighten the screws.

These braces (Photo 3) adjust to fit between the framing members in your ceiling; you simply rotate the shaft to anchor them to the framing.

Most existing electrical boxes are fastened to the framing with nails, making them easy to pound out with a hammer and a block of wood (Photo 2). After you free the cable, just leave the old box in the cavity (Photo 3) rather than struggling to work the box through the ceiling hole. Then pull the cable through the hole and slip the fan brace through the opening and secure it, following the directions that came with the brace. Little feet on the ends of braces keep them the correct distance from the back side of 1/2-in.- thick ceilings so the new electrical box will be flush with the surface. If you have a thicker ceiling, rotate the ends to achieve the correct spacing.

OPTIONAL REMOTE CONTROL

New electronic controls save you from running additional wiring

Since most fan installations are retrofits into existing electrical boxes, there's usually a single electrical cable connecting the fixture to a single wall switch. You can leave the switch and use it to turn the fan on and off, then use the pull chains on the fan to control fan speed and lights. A second option is to install electronic controls. Higher-quality fans give you the option of adding a radio receiver kit for about $75. The receiver accepts signals from a special wall switch (included in the kit) to control the fan and light separately without additional wiring. The receiver also accepts signals from a handheld remote, so you can operate multiple fans and fine-tune fan speed and light intensity from your easy chair. Electronic switches are matched to fans by flipping code toggles in the controls and the fan, just like with your garage door opener. Installing an electronic switch (Photo 12) is a snap. The receiver drops right into the fan housing and plugs into the bottom of the motor.

If the old light is fed by two three-way switches instead of a single switch, the control options are a little more complicated. You have three choices:

1. Leave the existing switches in place and turn one of them on. Then use a remote (see photo, opposite) to control the fan and lights.

2. Use the existing switches and control the fan and lights independently with pull chains.

3. Disable one of the three-way switches and rewire the other one to receive a wall-mounted electronic control. Sorting out all the wires is complex. You'll need an electrician's help for this.

Fan height requirements

Manufacturers generally require that fan blades be at least 7 ft. above the floor. Since most fan and motor assemblies are less than 12 in. high, they'll fit under a standard 8-ft. ceiling with the proper clearance.

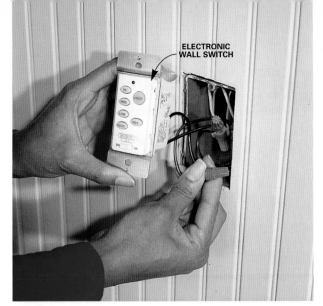

ELECTRONIC WALL SWITCH

13 CHECK and reset (if necessary) the code toggles on the wall-mounted electronic switch to match the ones on the receiver. Remove the existing wall switch and connect the two black wires on the new switch to the ones that were connected to the old switch with wire connectors. Screw the switch into the box and install the cover plate.

Quick tip*

CEILING FANS HELP ALL YEAR LONG
In the summer, set your fan so the blades are pushing air downward to create a breezy, cooling effect. In the winter, reverse the direction so the blades push hot air that accumulates near the ceiling out toward the edges of the room, then down the walls.

Angled ceilings require that you install "downrods" (also called extension tubes or downtubes) that will lower the motor and fan blades so they'll clear a sloped ceiling surface. The more space between the ceiling and the fan, the better. The fan will have more air to draw from, and you'll feel more air movement because the blades are closer to you.

Most fans come with a short downrod designed for mounting on 8-ft. ceilings. If your ceiling's less than 8 ft., you'll need to remove the rod provided and flush-mount the fan. But if you have a higher or sloped ceiling, purchase a longer downrod.

Minimum downrod length (in inches) for angled ceilings

Blade Dia.	Ceiling Slope						
	3/12	4/12	5/12	6/12	8/12*	10/12*	12/12*
27 in.	6	6	6	12	18	24	36
36 in.	6	6	6	12	18	24	36
44 in.	6	6	12	12	24	30	42
52 in.	6	12	18	18	24	30	42
56 in.	12	12	18	24	30	36	48

* Also requires slope adapting kit.

*Energy-Saving Goof

Fan-tabulous job!

When my son turned seven, I decided to build a special bed/shelving/desk project to fit into his small bedroom. Having read previous goofs in your magazine, I was careful to use knockdown hardware so I could get this sizable project in and out of the room. When the big day arrived to install this 6-ft.-high beauty, my son climbed up the ladder to the bunk. My wife turned on the light to admire the project and the ceiling fan nearly took my son's head off. I'd completely forgotten about the fan in the middle of the room. We moved the project into every conceivable configuration and still the fan spun over the bed. The fan just wasn't in the plan!

Improving attic
ventilation

A well-ventilated attic makes for a cooler house. Here's how to keep the air moving.

PLUMBING DRAIN VENT PIPE

AIRFLOW   STAPLE

LONG-SLEEVED SHIRT

AIR CHUTE

DUST MASK AND GOGGLES

AIRFLOW

SOFFIT VENT

A well-ventilated attic offers four benefits:

1. It reduces cooling costs in the warm season. The savings will be slight if you have a well-insulated attic space, greater if you have little insulation.
2. It prevents mildew growth and rot on your roof's framing and sheathing by reducing moisture buildup.
3. It helps prevent ice dams in winter by keeping your roof colder. (See p. 82 for details on ice dams.)
4. It extends the life of your shingles by keeping the roof cooler in hot weather. (The manufacturer's shingle warranty requires ventilation.)

Here you'll learn when to add ventilation, how to install several types of passive roof vents and soffit (eave) vents, and how to keep your ventilation system working. We won't cover fan-powered ventilation, since this type is usually not necessary.

As you will see, improving attic ventilation isn't expensive, time-consuming or difficult, even for the novice. You only need basic hand and power tools. However, when you climb up on your roof, be sure to follow safety precautions. If your roof is steep or you don't feel confident up there, hire a pro. (Look under "Roofing" in your yellow pages.)

1 INSTALL air chutes ($1 each at home centers) in each rafter space to keep the air path clear between the rafters and the roof sheathing. Staple the chutes in place. Be sure to wear long sleeves, goggles and a dust mask. Tip: Coat your arms, face and neck with talcum powder to reduce the itching from insulation.

Does your house need more vents?

Before you go out and start poking holes in your roof and soffits, check to see if you have the type of problem that attic ventilation can solve.

One common problem is caused by ice buildup along the edges of a roof. These ice dams form when warm attic air melts the snow on the roof and the water refreezes along the colder edge of the roof. The ice traps water behind it, allowing the water to seep back under the shingles and leak through the roof. Increased ventilation will make the entire roof cold and reduce or eliminate ice dams. (For more details, see "Understanding ice dams," p. 82.)

Another common problem is moisture buildup. After cold weather arrives, grab a flashlight and inspect your attic. Cover all your skin to protect it from the itchy insulation, and wear a dust mask. If your attic doesn't have a walkway, take two small (2 x 4-ft.) sheets of 1/2-in. plywood to move around on. Here are the signs to look for:

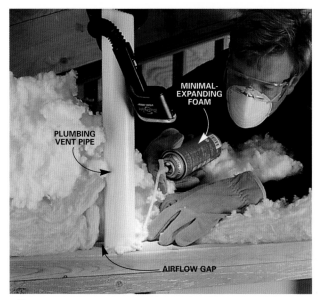

2 SEAL gaps around plumbing drain vent pipes, ductwork and electrical boxes with minimal-expanding foam or caulk. This helps keep warm, moist air out of the attic.

3 CLEAR your soffit vents every few years with blasts of compressed air. Always do this after you install air chutes because you'll probably knock insulation down into the soffit.

Roof safety tips

TIP 1: Use a safety harness (see Photo 9), especially if your roof has a slope steeper than 6:12.

TIP 2: Work only when the roof is dry. Wet shingles can be slippery.

TIP 3: Keep your shoe soles flat on the roof, rather than digging in with the edges.

TIP 4: After making cuts with your circular saw, sweep away the sawdust to avoid slipping.

TIP 5: Don't step on power cords or ropes. They'll roll under your feet and cause a fall.

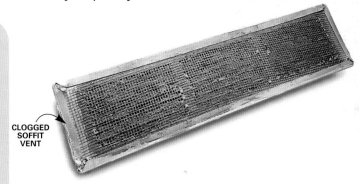

1. Frost on the underside of the roof or rafters. Warm, moist air trapped in the attic condenses and freezes on the wood.
2. Water-stained or blackened wood. A sign of mildew or rot. You can also spot this in the summer.
3. Heavily rusted nails. A sign that condensation is forming on metal surfaces.
4. Matted-down insulation. A sign of roof leaks from ice damming or other causes.

If you have either ice dams or moisture buildup, improve your attic ventilation. Begin by making sure your existing system works (Photos 1 and 3), plugging major air leaks into the attic (Photo 2) and correcting any other of the "Five common causes of poor attic venting" (at right). If those steps don't solve the problem, add more vents, following the techniques shown in Photos 4 – 17. For help figuring how much venting you need, see "Minimum venting requirements," p. 110.

Even if you aren't having problems, bring your attic venting up to code when (1) you install new shingles and (2) you add attic insulation.

Five common causes of poor attic venting

PROBLEM 1 Insulation often clogs the space between the rafters, blocking air from traveling to and from the soffit area. **Solution:** Install air chutes or clear them if they're clogged (Photo 1).

PROBLEM 2 Aluminum or vinyl soffits (eaves) installed over plywood soffits that don't have venting holes. **Solution:** Cut holes in plywood soffits as needed.

PROBLEM 3 Gaps to the attic around plumbing pipes, ducting and electrical boxes. Many experts consider plugging these holes to be more important than ventilation. **Solution:** See Photo 2.

PROBLEM 4 Rectangular roof vents installed on one side of the roof only. Rectangular roof vents work best when the wind blows over the top of them, rather than into them. **Solution:** Install rectangular roof vents on both sides of the roof.

PROBLEM 5 Kitchen and bath fans vented into the attic. **Solution:** Vent these fans through the roof or soffit.

Rectangular Soffit Vents

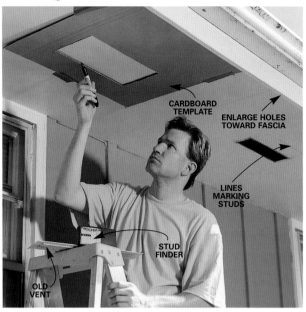

4 ADHERE template against fascia and mark soffit hole locations. Make vent hole 1/2 in. smaller on each side than the new vent. If you widen existing holes, widen them toward the fascia, but no closer than 3 in. from the fascia to avoid ripples in the soffit plywood. Position holes between rafters at equal intervals. You can find rafters by locating nailheads or using a stud finder.

5 DRILL 3/8-in. starter holes at opposite corners of the vent hole. Then cut out the hole with a jigsaw. If the soffit plywood begins to tear and splinter in the crosscut, use a utility knife to score the cutting line.

6 INSTALL the soffit vent with self-tapping screws. Angle the vent louvers toward the house wall. (This prevents blowing snow from entering the vent, and it looks better from the ground.)

Add soffit vents first

You can gain the most airflow with the least amount of trouble by installing soffit vents. The two most common are rectangular vents (Photo 9) and continuous strip vents (Photo 7). Continuous strip vents allow perfectly even ventilation along the eaves (Photos 7 and 8), but they're difficult to retrofit in an existing soffit.

Rectangular vents are easiest to install (Photos 4 – 6). Here all 4 x 16-in. vents (28 sq. in. of net free vent area, or NFVA) with 8 x 16-in. vents (56 sq. in. NFVA) were replaced and more were added. This increased soffit ventilation almost five times. An 8 x 16-in. vent costs less than $2 and takes less than 10 minutes to install.

Minimum venting requirements

MOST BUILDING CODES REQUIRE 1 sq. ft. of venting (technically, "net free vent area," or NFVA) for each 150 sq. ft. of attic. In some circumstances you can have less, but we recommend the 1:150 ratio. So a house with a 1,500-sq.-ft. attic will need 10 sq. ft. of venting, ideally about half placed high on the roof and half in the soffits. Look for the NFVA of each vent you buy stamped somewhere on the metal.

Caution:

Asbestos has been found in some types of vermiculite insulation. Vermiculite, a lightweight material resembling gravel, was used as attic insulation in perhaps as many as a million homes. If you have vermiculite in your attic, don't disturb it unless you have a sample checked by an accredited laboratory. Disturbing it can release the asbestos fibers, which, once airborne, can enter your lungs and eventually cause lung disease. For a list of accredited testing labs, call your local department of public health. For more vermiculite details, go to the Environmental Protection Agency (EPA) Region 1 Web site (www.epa.gov.region01) or call your regional EPA office.

Soffit Strip Vents

FASCIA

2" X 8' CONTINUOUS
SOFFIT STRIP VENT

3" MINIMUM

7 INSTALL a 2-in. continuous-strip soffit vent so that it's closer to the fascia than to the house wall. Loosely nail one side of the soffit, then slide the strip vent's flange underneath the plywood.

8 FINISH nailing up the strips. The narrowest soffit plywood strip should be at least 3 in. wide.

✳ Energy-Saving Q&A

Flat roof vents vs. wind-driven turbine vents

Q I've hired a roofer to replace my shingles. He's planning to tear off all the shingles and replace all the roof vents and flashing. Here's my question. He wants to replace the wind-driven whirligig-style roof vents with flat roof vents, saying they'll handle the venting just as well and look better. Am I getting taken? (I know the flat ones are cheaper.) If they're just as good, I'm happy since I'm sick of hearing the old ones squeak all the time.

A All things being equal, wind-driven turbine vents do move more air than flat vents (but only when the wind blows). The question: How much air must be moved? A largely arbitrary rule of thumb that's been adopted into most building codes calls for 1 sq. ft. of vented area for every 300 sq. ft. of attic space. So a 1,500-sq.-ft. attic must have 5 sq. ft. of vent space—half dedicated for air intake in the soffits and the other half for exhaust on the roof. (These can be ridge vents, wind turbines or the flat vents your roofer wants to install.)

In cold climates, good attic ventilation is important for preventing ice dams. It also keeps your home cooler in the summer, vents moisture that finds its way from the living spaces of your home into the attic and helps shingles last longer. The fact is, it's hard to overventilate an attic—generally, more is better.

If you don't like the looks of wind turbines, don't be afraid to use the flat vents; just be sure to follow the 300-sq.-ft. rule. But if you want to use wind turbines, buy high-quality ones that have permanently lubricated ball bearings or plastic bushings in the spinning mechanisms. Usually, it's the cheaper units with metal bushings that will squeak and eventually drive you (and your neighbors) out of your mind on windy nights.

PLASTIC BEARINGS

Wind-driven turbine vent

AIRFLOW

Flat roof vent

Rectangular Roof Vents

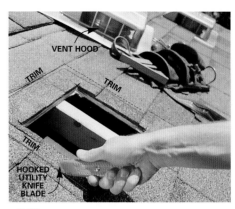

10 MEASURE the vent hood size and trim the topmost shingles with a hooked knife blade so they will butt against the vent hood on the top and the sides. You'll have to trim two or three rows of shingles (see Photo 12).

9 CUT a square hole in the roof the same size as the hole in the base of the vent you're installing. Locate the top of the hole about 15 in. below the peak of the roof. Mark the hole with chalk and set your saw depth to cut through the shingles and the roof sheathing only. Don't cut into any rafters. For a roof with a single layer of shingles, start with a depth of 3/4 in. Use an old carbide blade for cutting, and wear safety goggles and hearing protection because you will hit nails.

11 PULL nails as necessary so the vent's flange can slide into place. The best time to do this is when the shingles are cool (early morning). Use your flat pry bar to carefully separate the shingles from one another. Apply roofing cement around the perimeter of the hole.

12 HOLD the vent up at an angle and slide it into place. Then set it down into the roofing cement.

13 NAIL the flange to the roof on the front edge. Finish sealing the vent by applying cement to the areas where the shingles overlap one another and where they overlap the flange.

How to choose roof vents

We recommend two types of roof vents: heavy-gauge rectangular metal vents (Photo 13) and plastic shingle-over ridge vents with baffles (Photo 16).

tip Work in cool weather so you don't mar the shingles.

Ridge vents with baffles have several advantages: Their low profile and shingle cover make them blend into the roof, and they distribute ventilation evenly along the ridge. You're also less likely to damage the shingles when you install them.

Ridge vents cost about $10 per 4-ft. section and are available from roofing dealers and many home centers. Follow Photos 14 – 17 for installation tips.

Rectangular metal roof vents work best on hip or pyramid roofs that have a short ridge line. Look for galvanized steel vents. (They cost $6 to $10 and are available at roofing supply stores and some home centers.) Follow Photos 9 – 13 for installation tips. Consult a roofing supply store for special installation instructions if you have a metal, slate, cedar or tile roof.

Ridge Vents

14 REMOVE the old ridge cap with a flat pry bar or square-nose shovel. Pull out any nails left behind. Use a chalk line to mark your cutting line. First, pop a line along the very top of the ridge. Then pop a line 1-1/2 in. down from your ridge line on both sides of it. These will be your cutting lines.

15 CUT OUT a slot in the shingles and the sheathing with a circular saw equipped with an old carbide blade. For a single shingle layer, start with a blade depth of 3/4 in. and make sure it doesn't cut into the rafters. If you have an overhang, stop the slot short so the opening is only over the attic space, not the overhang. If you have a hip roof (no gabled ends), stop the slot 6 in. short of the beginning of the hip. Wear your goggles and hearing protection because you WILL hit nails. Sweep off the sawdust and open the slot with a flat pry bar.

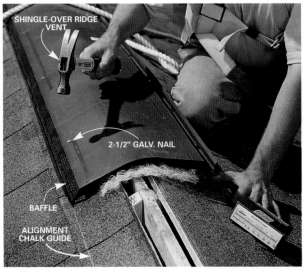

16 TO INSTALL a ridge vent, first pop a chalk line down from your ridge line equal to half the width of the ridge vent. Align ridge vent pieces. Nail one side of vent in place with 2-1/2-in. galvanized nails. To keep the line straight, finish nailing the side you aligned with your chalk line before nailing the other side.

17 COVER the vent with ridge cap shingles using 1-in. galvanized roofing nails. The vent will have a nail line marked on it. You can buy special ridge cap shingles for laminated shingles (shown here), or cut your own ridge cap from three-tab shingles (the shingle packaging will have directions). If you have to stop the ridge vent short of the end of the ridge, install the remaining ridge cap so that it slopes away from the vent.

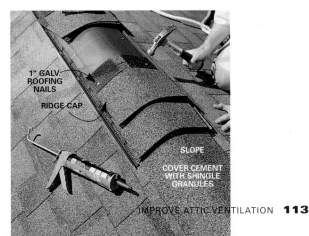

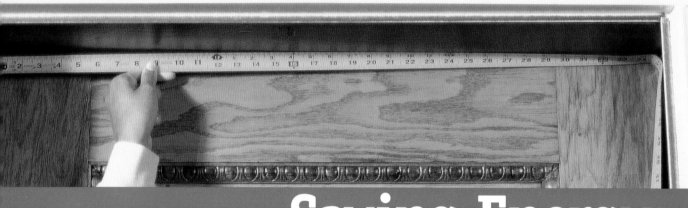

Saving Energy:

indows and doors are the weakest link of all of the other components—ceilings, walls and floors—that work together to create your home's "energy envelope." The insulating qualities of even the best-built high-tech windows and doors pale in comparison to that of the walls and ceilings that surround them. In short, these "holes in the wall" need all the help they can get. That "help" can range from installing new weatherstripping to installing caulk and replacement windows and doors.

Like so many other energy-saving projects, improving windows and doors offers collateral benefits. New windows usually mean lower maintenance and a quieter house. New storm doors usually mean not only fewer drafts in winter but fewer bugs in summer. Caulking windows, doors and siding can help your house look better and last longer. When you ponder the costs of improving your windows and doors, consider these added benefits as well.

Windows & Doors

Window tint films

Instant, affordable energy efficiency—winter and summer

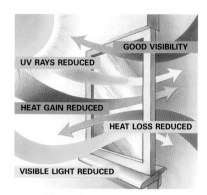

Low-E films reflect both outside summer heat and inside winter heat and offer fade protection.

If your windows let in too much heat in the summer and too much cold in the winter, a simple, affordable option to improve their efficiency is to apply low-E or tinting film. Low-E films offer these major benefits:

- Like reflective and nonreflective films, low-E films virtually eliminate the ultraviolet ray penetration, helping to reduce fading problems while doing little to affect window visibility.
- They reduce heat gain from the outside in the summer.
- During the winter, they reduce heat loss by 60 percent.
- Glare is reduced by filtering 50 to 60 percent of the incoming light.
- In the case of a broken window, the film helps hold the pieces of glass together.
- Most tint films come with complete directions. Follow them for best results.

1 CLEAN windows thoroughly. Spray window with wetting solution following manufacturer's directions.

2 POSITION film on dampened window, making sure it overlaps sash on all sides.

Quick tip*

PLASTIC-FILM STORM WINDOWS MAKE SENSE. You can reduce heat loss through older and single pane windows by 25 to 50 percent by installing special clear plastic film on the interior. Most install with tape and a hair dryer and cost as little as $4 per window.

3 SPRAY film surface with wetting solution. Make a single squeegee pass across the top, then use vertical passes down.

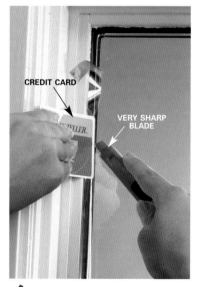

CREDIT CARD

VERY SHARP BLADE

4 TRIM excess film using a credit card shield and very sharp utility knife. After trimming, wet and squeegee a second time.

Installing combination storm windows

Add warmth, quiet and an extra layer of protection

Combination storm windows offer many benefits. They improve a window's thermal efficiency, improve security by adding a layer of protection, help protect primary windows against rain and hail, and act as a screen to allow ventilation. Some standard-size units are available at home centers; others must be special-ordered.

1 MEASURE existing window at inside edges of brick molding and order windows. Predrill holes along outer edges of storm window frame 2 in. from each corner and every 12 in. between.

BRICK MOLDING

EXTERIOR STOP

2 TEST-FIT the storm window. Use a belt sander to trim its lip, if necessary. Don't twist the window out of square to make it fit or it won't operate properly. Now apply a bead of silicone along the openings' top and sides but not the bottom.

EXPANSION SEAL

3 POSITION storm windows in openings. Lift window as high as possible, then lower expansion seal at bottom. Attach window with screws. Make sure moisture can pass freely through weep holes at the bottom.

Energy-Saving Goof

Thar she blows!

One fine fall day I was caulking around my garage doors. I went through one cartridge, loaded another, clipped off the tip, then went back to work again. But I noticed that the caulk wasn't flowing and the trigger was getting harder and harder to pull. Suddenly the caulk tube burst open like a can of refrigerator biscuits, covering the garage door, my arms and my face with blobs of gooey caulk. It was then I realized I had forgotten to puncture the inner seal of the cartridge before squeezing the trigger of the gun.

Replacing double-pane windows

Fix 'em for maximum energy efficiency

Insulated glass can get broken or lose the seal between the panes and permanently fog. Start by taking the entire sash to a shop that repairs windows. They'll measure the size and thickness of the insulating unit, help you identify the manufacturer, determine whether a window is still under warranty and discuss energy-efficient replacement options. Manufacturers recommend one of three methods for installing the sealed units. Savvy do-it-yourselfers can repair the units themselves. Sometimes it's easier and cheaper to replace the entire sash.

GASKET METHOD. With sash removed, take out screws that hold horizontal rails and vertical stiles together. Tap frame loose from gasket and glass with wooden block and hammer. Remove old gasket from faulty pane and install it on a new glass double-pane unit. Push two frame pieces together around the gasket and fasten the frame back together. Seal any gaps in corners using clear silicone.

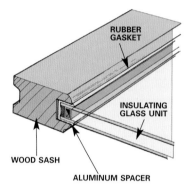

RUBBER GASKET

INSULATING GLASS UNIT

WOOD SASH

ALUMINUM SPACER

RUBBER GASKET

ADHESIVE TAPE METHOD. Pry out stops using a putty knife. Flip window over and slice through tape bond with a utility knife blade. Scrape old tape and clean lip with adhesive solvent. Lay new setting tape in place. Position spacing blocks against one side of frame, position glass against blocks and carefully drop it in place. Replace stops and seal gaps with clear silicone.

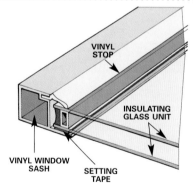

VINYL STOP

INSULATING GLASS UNIT

VINYL WINDOW SASH

SETTING TAPE

SETTING TAPE

CAULK METHOD. Carefully pry off wood stops. Flip window over and cut caulk with a utility knife. If necessary, break window after covering it with carpet. Soften adhesive using a heat gun, and then scrape and clean edges. Position spacing blocks, apply bead of neutral-cure silicone to frame and drop in new glass unit. Apply silicone to glass's stop side and reinstall stops.

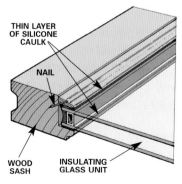

THIN LAYER OF SILICONE CAULK

NAIL

WOOD SASH

INSULATING GLASS UNIT

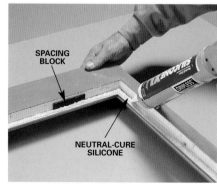

SPACING BLOCK

NEUTRAL-CURE SILICONE

Weatherstrip
a wooden entry door

Simple-to-install kits make it easy to stop annoying, energy-wasting drafts

Feeling a winter chill? If you run your hand around the perimeter of your closed door and feel a cool draft, your weatherstripping is probably worn, cracked or deformed.

Maintaining an airtight seal on your doors and windows usually won't save a lot of energy and money, but it's essential for stopping cold drafts and keeping your home comfortable. And in older, leaky homes, it actually can be a good money-saving strategy.

Replacing weatherstripping on newer windows and doors (less than about 35 years old) is fairly easy. You can usually slide out the old weatherstripping and push or slide new vinyl or foam into the grooves in the door or the surrounding frame. The biggest hassle is finding replacement

Project facts

COST
$10 to $20 per three-piece weather-stripping kit; $3 to $6 per door sweep (see p. 121 for details)
TIME
1 – 2 hours per door
SKILLS
Novice carpentry
SPECIAL TOOLS
Coping saw or hacksaw, depending on weatherstripping type

1 LIFT the door by the doorknob to check for loose hinges. If the door moves upward, tighten the top hinge screws. That might solve the draft problem!

CHECK FOR LOOSE HINGE

2 CLOSE the door and measure the top of the frame from side to side. Mark the length on the short section of your purchased weatherstripping with a clear, sharp line.

TOP JAMB

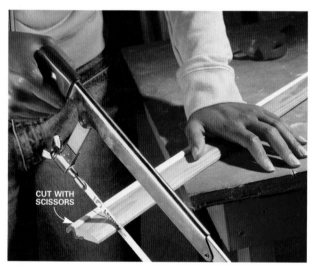

3 CUT the foam part of the weatherstripping with sharp scissors. Then cut the wood flange with a hacksaw or other fine-tooth saw.

CUT WITH SCISSORS

4 TAP 1-1/2-in. nails into the wood flange and position the weatherstripping so the entire length of the foam seals against the door. Tack the weatherstripping in place but don't drive the nails home yet. Then measure the length of the sides of the frame.

FLANGE

WEATHERSTRIPPING CONTACTS DOOR

DOOR SHUT

weatherstripping that exactly matches the old. See "How to buy weatherstripping," opposite, for advice.

Older windows, especially double-hung windows, are difficult to weatherstrip. If they're in bad shape, consider replacement windows.

Installing new weatherstripping on older doors (and doors

for which you can't find replacement weatherstripping) is fairly easy, and we'll show you how to do it here. Weatherstripping kits are available at most full-service hardware stores and home centers ($10 to $20; see photos, opposite). They include two side strips, a top strip and fasteners.

We'll also show you how to install a door sweep ($6) to stop drafts from coming under the door. A wide variety of these are usually available on the hardware store or home center shelf alongside weatherstripping.

Size up your leaky door

On the door shown here, the old, worn bronze weatherstripping was not replaced with new bronze because the project is difficult, especially around the latch plates. (You can still find several types of replacement bronze

Quick tip*

THE TWO-INCH HOLE IN YOUR WALL A 1/16-in. gap between the bottom of an exterior door and the threshold is equivalent to cutting a 2-in. square hole in your wall. When you apply weatherstripping, be meticulous.

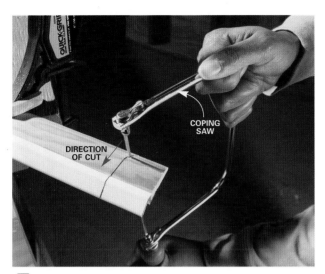

5 CUT one end of each side weatherstripping to fit the profile of the top piece. Mark the profile using a scrap for a guide, cut the foam with scissors and cut the profile with a coping saw.

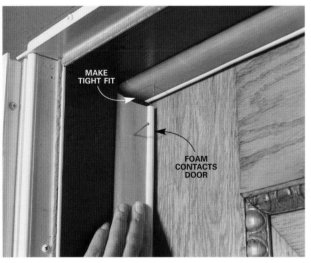

6 FILE or sand your cut for a tight fit. Then measure and cut the bottom to length (Photo 3). Position the weatherstripping so that the entire length seals to the door and tack it in place.

at full-service hardware stores.) The wrapped foam type shown is easier to install and more effective. Later you can paint the wood flange to blend with the frame.

Before you go out to buy your materials, check the door to make sure the draft isn't caused by loose hinge screws (Photo 1). If the screws no longer bite, you may have to glue wood plugs in the holes and redrive the screws.

Cut and nail— this stuff goes up fast

The weatherstripping kit will come with two long pieces for the side jambs and a short piece for the top jamb. Begin with the top and follow Photos 2 – 7 for the basics. Make precise measurements and cuts so you get a nice,

How to buy weatherstripping

You can usually find the types of weatherstripping shown below at well-stocked hardware stores and home centers. Many other types are available, but you'll probably have to order them from a catalog. Ask to see a catalog at your local hardware store and order through the store if possible. (An online catalog is available at www.mdteam.com.)

We like the wrapped foam type (A and B below and shown in our story). It's durable, retains its shape, withstands abrasions and conforms to a wide range of gaps. The metal flange with slots for screws (B) is a bit more adjustable than the nail-on wood flange type (A).

The vinyl or silicone bulb type (C) won't cover wide gaps as well as wrapped foam, but it has a smaller profile with a cleaner look.

Finding new weatherstripping to match the exact profile of the old can be difficult. If you know the door manufacturer or where the door was purchased, try there first. (Check the door and frame for a label.) Otherwise, call a local door or window repair service. (Look under "Doors, Repair" or "Windows, Repair" in your yellow pages.) They may stock the materials or tell you where to call. Replacement kits for the wrapped foam and magnetic (for steel doors) types are sometimes available at hardware stores and home centers.

A good Internet source for weatherstripping is the Energy Federation Inc. at www.efi.org.

Common weatherstripping types

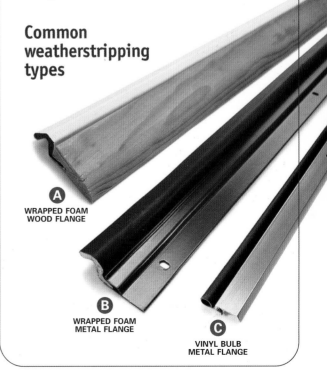

A WRAPPED FOAM WOOD FLANGE

B WRAPPED FOAM METAL FLANGE

C VINYL BULB METAL FLANGE

WEATHERSTRIPPING

7 OPEN and close the door several times to make sure the weatherstripping seals against the door and the door latches and locks. Adjust the weatherstripping as needed. Drive the finish nails home.

tip Follow the old carpenter's rule: Measure twice, cut once.

THRESHOLD

8 MEASURE the width of the door from inside and mark the length on your new sweep.

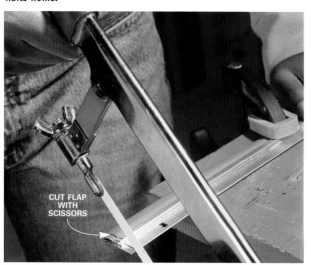

CUT FLAP WITH SCISSORS

9 CUT the flexible flap with sharp scissors or sharp utility knife. Then cut the flange with a hacksaw.

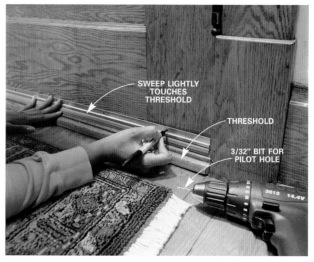

SWEEP LIGHTLY TOUCHES THRESHOLD

THRESHOLD

3/32" BIT FOR PILOT HOLE

10 POSITION the door sweep with the flexible portion lightly touching the top of the threshold. Then mark the screw positions and drill the pilot holes.

tip When you paint the wood flange, keep the paint off the foam.

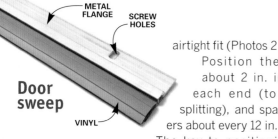

METAL FLANGE
SCREW HOLES

Door sweep

VINYL

airtight fit (Photos 2 and 3). Position the nails about 2 in. in from each end (to avoid splitting), and space others about every 12 in.

The key to positioning the new weatherstripping is to shove it against the door so it compresses slightly along its entire length (Photo 4). If you compress it too much, the door won't latch when you close it, a common rookie mistake.

The "coped" cuts on the side jambs make a clean, tight joint (Photo 6). Make this cut first, leaving plenty of length for the bottom cut.

It's critical to make sure that the door shuts and latches easily before you drive the nails home (Photo 7). However, the weatherstripping also needs to fit snug to the door over its full length. For small adjustments, pull the nails and start them in a new spot.

Install a door sweep

Shut the door, then look for daylight and feel for a draft coming under the door. If you see a lot of light or feel a draft, install a new door sweep.

The door shown here had old bulb-type weatherstripping attached to the threshold. While these types can be effective, you have to replace them every few years because foot traffic wears and crushes them.

Door sweeps last longer but won't always work if they brush or rub against the floor or carpet when you

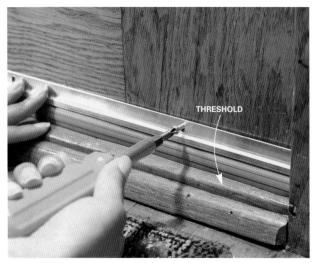

11 PUSH the sweep down against the threshold and drive the screws. Open and close the door to test the seal.

THRESHOLD

FELT PAD

NEW WEATHERSTRIPPING

12 CUT two 2 x 1-3/4-in. pads from 1/8-in.-thick felt. Nail the pads at the bottom of each side frame as shown. Open and shut the door and adjust the pads if necessary.

open the door. If the floor, carpet or rug is even with or higher than your threshold (the bottom of the door frame; Photos 8 and 11), you can't use a sweep.

For a replacement, choose a simple face-mount door sweep with a flexible vinyl flap because it's easy to mount and adjust. Photos 8 – 11 show you how to measure, cut and screw it to the door.

You'll be left with a pair of small gaps between the weatherstripping on the frame and the sweep, at the bottom corners of the door. Unless you want a perfectly airtight, draft-free door, don't worry about these gaps. However, Photo 12 shows one way to close them. It's not precise; use whatever thickness of felt (or combination of layers) fits between the door and frame without hindering the door operation.

Good work! You can look forward to a more comfortable winter.

Replacing a U-shaped astragal on a steel garage door

The hollow rubber weather seal on the bottom of steel doors is called a U-shaped astragal, and its job is to keep both cold winds and mice out of your garage. U-shaped astragals are sized according to their width as they lie flat. Choose the width that best fits your situation. Use a larger seal if you need to fill a wider gap between the door and the garage floor. The best source for U-shaped astragals is a garage door dealer.

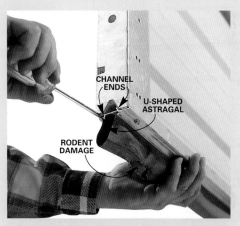

CHANNEL ENDS

U-SHAPED ASTRAGAL

RODENT DAMAGE

USE a flat-blade screwdriver to open the ends of the channels that hold the old seal on both ends of the door. Then pull out the old seal.

NEW U-SHAPED ASTRAGAL

LUBRICANT

SLIDE the new seal into the channels. To make the job easier, lubricate the channels with silicone spray or rubbing alcohol. After the seal is in place, crimp the channel ends on both ends of the door with pliers.

Hang a new storm door

Add an extra layer of protection from the cold with a storm door.

You no longer have to put up with a rusty old storm door that bangs shut every time the kids go out. Modern storm doors are stronger, smoother and a heck of a lot more handsome than older doors. In fact, installing a new one is one of the least expensive ways to dress up an entry and improve energy efficiency.

Replacing an old storm door is easier than you might think. Manufacturers have made installation more DIY friendly by providing standard sizes that'll fit almost any door opening and simpler installation kits. Still, you'll find some sticking points. The following step-by-step directions walk you through some tricks and techniques you won't find in any instruction manual.

If you have a hacksaw, screw gun, a short level and a pair of side cutters and two to three hours, you're on your way to saving the $100-plus cost of a professional installation. Replacing an old storm door or installing a new one is a perfect Saturday morning project, even if you have limited carpentry skills. Choose a storm door that fits the style of your home. Prices range from $100 to $500.

Selecting the door

To find the size of the storm door you need, simply measure the height and width of the main door. Most front entry doors are 36 in. wide and require a 36-in. storm door.

Shown here is a "full-view" storm door (opening photo). This door has removable screen and glass panels that you interchange each season. The other common type, a "ventilating" storm door, has glass panels that slide open or closed over the screen, much like a double-hung window.

Nearly every storm door sold is reversible. That is, you can install it with the hinge on either side. The manufacturer's directions tell you how to do it. When you buy it, you don't have to specify which way the door must swing.

You typically mount storm doors to the exterior door trim using "Z-bars." The hinge-side Z-bar may already be screwed to the door (ours was), or you may have to mount it once you determine the door swing direction. On some doors, you'll also have to drill holes for the latch.

Getting started

Begin the project by folding open the box and removing the glass storm panel. Set it and the screen panel in a safe place out of the wind. Then check for damaged or missing parts by comparing the contents with the parts list in the instruction manual. (The one shown had been returned, repackaged and sold as new. One of the parts had already been cut to length and the mounting screws were missing.) Use the cardboard as a work surface to prevent scratching the parts while you work on the door.

Then determine the door swing. In general, hinge the storm door on the same side as the main door. However, consider these exceptions:

- **Adjoining walls.** If there's an adjoining wall or rail, it's best to have the door swing against it; otherwise entry can be awkward, especially if you're carrying groceries.
- **Electrical.** Will the door open against any light fixtures? Will the doorbell or light switch wind up on the latch side where they belong?
- **Wind.** If there's a strong prevailing wind, it's best to have the door hinge side face the wind direction. That way, sudden gusts can't fling it open and break it.

Out with the old storm door

Taking off an old aluminum door is usually just a case of unscrewing the mounting screws on the door, closer and safety chain. But sometimes there's caulk around the frame. You can usually cut through the caulk with a utility knife. But worse yet, you could find old caulk between the frame and the door casing. If so, you'll have to pry the frame away with an old chisel and scrape the trim surfaces clean. A heat gun may help soften the caulk. Get rid of an old door by throwing the glass panel in the trash, and then cut up the aluminum frame and door with a circular saw and a carbide-tipped blade. Toss the pieces into the recycling bin.

Wooden storm doors generally have hinges that are mortised (notched into the wood) and screwed to the door casing. Don't worry about the hinge or latch recesses. When you install your new storm door, they'll be hidden behind the new door frame.

Why a storm door?

A traditional storm door was a real workhorse. It protected the handsome but vulnerable wooden main door from harsh weather and helped to insulate it.

Today's better insulated and protected main doors have little need for a storm door and are often eliminated from new homes, showing off fancy front doors. However, the "full-view" storm door (like the one shown here) still showcases the main door and, when screened, allows you to take advantage of those cooling summer breezes too.

1 FIND a flat area near the entry door, lay the box flat on the ground, fold it open and check to make sure you have all the parts.

2 ADD a trim extension if needed to doors with sidelights. Prime and paint the new trim, position it with a reveal equal to the other trim and then nail it into place.

> ✳ **tip** If your entry door trim needs paint, do it now. It's a pain in the neck painting around a new door, and you'll have a neater-looking job.

3 CONFIRM the door swing direction and fasten the hinge-side Z-bar to the correct side (if necessary). Mark a cutting line on the Z-bar 3/16 in. above the top of the door with a square. Slide the weatherstripping aside and cut the Z-bar with a hacksaw.

> ✳ **tip** Use an 18- to 22-tooth-per-in. hacksaw blade for smoother, easier cuts.

4 MEASURE from the outside lip of the threshold to the top door casing. Transfer the measurement to the bottom of the hinge-side Z-bar and cut it to length, matching the angle on the threshold.

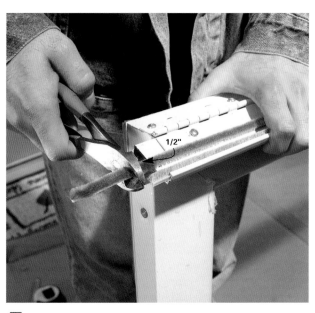

5 CENTER the weatherstripping in the Z-bar, then snip off the ends, leaving it 1/2 in. extra long at each end.

Prep the opening

Storm doors hang from the door trim, technically called "exterior casing." If the door has never had a storm door (as in our situation), you may have to extend the trim between the door and a sidelight (Photo 2). This is the most difficult situation you're likely to encounter. You have to rip a new trim piece to match the thickness of the other trim (usually 1-1/8 in. thick).

Manufacturers make storm doors a bit narrower than standard openings to make sure they'll fit. If your opening is typical, you'll have to "fur out" the sides to center

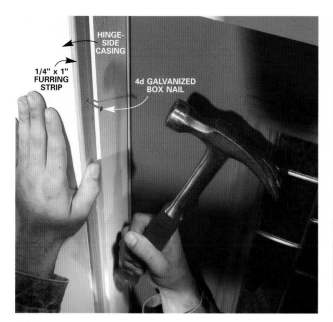

6 MEASURE the opening width and determine the furring strip thickness (see text). Cut a furring strip to length, then nail it to the inside edge of the hinge-side casing with four evenly spaced 4d galvanized box nails.

7 LIFT the door into the opening and pry it against the hinge-side casing with a twist from rubber-handled pliers on the latch side. Screw the hinge Z-bar into the door casing side.

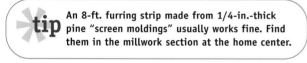

tip An 8-ft. furring strip made from 1/4-in.-thick pine "screen moldings" usually works fine. Find them in the millwork section at the home center.

8 SWING the door open, slip the top-side Z-bar into place and close the door to hold it. Adjust the gap between the Z-bar and the top of the door until it's even and screw it into the top casing.

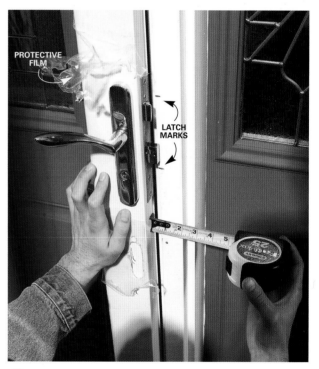

9 MOUNT the latch mechanism, then mark the position of the top and bottom of the latch on the door casing. If the space between the door and the casing is over 5/8 in., nail two 1/4-in.-thick furring strips to the inside of the casing, one above and one below the marks (see Photo 11).

the storm door in the opening. You'll nearly always need to install at least one 1/4-in. furring strip on the hinge side (Photo 6) and possibly even have to add another one to the latch side (Photo 11). To figure this out, measure the exact width of the opening, that is, the distance between the inside edges of the trim. (Measure at the

tip Your door may come with a protective plastic film. Only peel off those areas needed for installing hardware during installation (Photos 9 and 13). That way the door will be protected from scratches. After installation is complete, peel away the plastic.

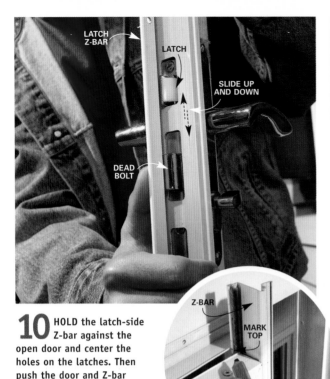

10 HOLD the latch-side Z-bar against the open door and center the holes on the latches. Then push the door and Z-bar against the doorframe and mark and cut the bottom at the angle of the threshold. Then mark the top (inset) and cut it.

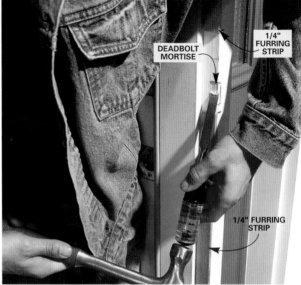

11 CLOSE the door against the casing with the deadbolt extended and chisel out the wood where the deadbolt hits. Slip the latch-side Z-bar into place, close the door against it and screw it to the casing, keeping a consistent 1/8-in. gap with the door.

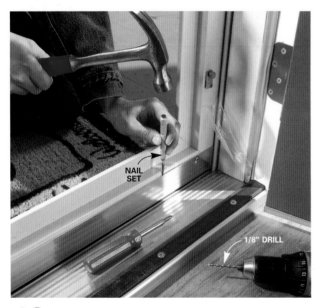

12 SLIDE the rubber weatherstripping into the door sweep and crimp the ends. Slide the sweep over the door bottom and tap it down to snug it to the threshold. Drill 1/8-in. holes through the adjustment slots and add the screws.

13 POSITION the closer bracket and screw it to the jamb. Attach the closer, level it and mark the screw positions on the door. Drill 1/8-in. pilot holes and screw the closer to the door. Repeat for the top closer.

middle, top and bottom.) The manufacturer's instructions will usually list the minimum width required. Subtract that width from your measurement and make the furring strip thickness along the hinge side about half the difference.

It's important to mount the door tightly to the hinge-side

trim. Pry against the latch side to make sure it snugs up tight (Photo 7).

Follow the photos with your instructions for the rest of the installation steps. Door latch and Z-bar systems vary. Cutting the latch-side Z-bar is a bit fussy. The idea is to

Adjust a storm door for a perfect close

IF YOUR STORM DOOR SLAMS SHUT or won't close hard enough to latch, try a few simple adjustments to make it close just right.

First, change the mounting position of the closer's connecting pin (Photo 1). To remove the pin, you have to first lock the door open with the hold-open washer to release the tension on the pin. But there's a good chance that your hold-open washer won't work. In that case, open the door and snap locking pliers (such as Vise-Grip pliers) onto the closer shaft to hold the door open. To repair the washer, slip it off the shaft, put it in a vise and make a sharper bend in it using a hammer. Or you can take the entire closer to a home center or hardware store and find a similar replacement for about $10. Some closers mount a little differently from the one shown here. For example, you may find that the door bracket, rather than the closer, has two pin holes.

If moving the pin makes matters worse, return it to its original position and try the adjustment screw (Photo 2). Turn it clockwise for a softer close, counterclockwise for harder. If your door has two closers, treat them exactly alike. Adjust both screws equally and make sure their pins are in the same position.

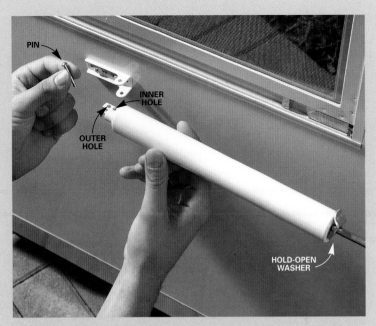

1 LOCK the door open and remove the pin. Connect the closer at the inner hole to make the door close harder. For a softer close, use the outer hole.

2 TURN the adjustment screw to make the door close harder or softer. Make a quarter turn, test the door and continue making quarter turns until the door closes just right.

center it on the latch and lock (Photo 10). Observe where it strikes the sill and cut the bottom at an angle that matches the sill. Then cut the top so it fits against the top Z-bar. Don't worry if the latch and lock bolt end up a bit off-center, as long as they work smoothly.

You may need to chisel out the latch or deadbolt pocket as shown (Photo 11). It all depends on the door latch style.

After installing the door sweep and closers, adjust the closer tension. Begin with the window panel rather than the screen in place. The closers should be set with the door at its heaviest. You may want to reset a gentler setting for the screen panel.

Finally, it's a good idea to save the boxes for the window and screen panel for off-season storage. Under a bed is a great safe storage location.

Install a new
Front door

We'll show you the techniques that will result in a perfect weathertight installation

It's not often that you can complete a project in a weekend that will save you money and dramatically improve the looks of your house. But that's what will happen when you replace a worn, drafty front door with a stylish, energy-efficient new one. And since modern doors come prehung in a weatherstripped frame, you don't have to be a master carpenter to do a first-class job.

Here you'll learn how to order a door that'll fit like a glove. Then you'll see, step by step, how to get your old door out and the new one in.

If you can handle basic carpentry tasks, you'll have no trouble installing a new prehung door in a day. Figure on another day to finish the details and start painting the door. You can complete most of the job with basic hand tools. You'll need a hammer, pry bar, tape measure, level, utility knife, nail set and saw. If you decide to install new interior trim, you'll also need a miter saw.

Shown here is a top-quality prehung wood door (Simpson Bungalow No. 7228) from a lumberyard. Including the special 2-1/2-in. wide exterior trim (casing), the total cost was $1,100. You could purchase a steel or fiberglass door for much less, but the style and crisp detailing of the wood door matched this house perfectly. The door arrived about two weeks after the order was placed.

1 TAP the hinge pins loose with a hammer and nail set. Then swing the door open and lift it off. Protect the floor with a dropcloth. The old door will be heavy.

2 PRY the interior trim loose from the doorframe. Protect the wall with a wide putty knife. If you plan to reuse the trim, first score the intersection between the molding and jamb with a utility knife.

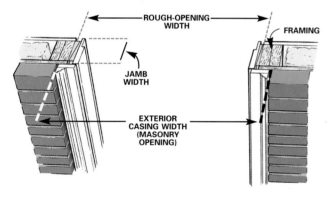

Figure A Measuring

Measure your old door

In most cases, simply order a new door the same size as the old one. If you alter the size or add sidelights, you'll have to reframe the opening and alter many details. This usually doubles or triples the size of the job. Here are the four sets of measurements you'll need to order a door (refer to Figure A, above, for extra details):

■ **Door size.** Measure the width and height of your old door. Round these up to full inches to find the size of the replacement door you'll need. If, for example, your

door measures 35-3/4 in. wide and 79-1/2 in. tall, you'll order a 36 x 80-in. door.

■ **Jamb width.** Measure from the back side of the interior trim to the back side of the exterior trim (Figure A). Specify this jamb width when you order your new pre-hung door. This guarantees that the interior trim will fit flush to the wall without adding "jamb extensions."

■ **Rough opening.** You'll have to remove the interior trim to get accurate measurements of the rough opening. Measure the opening width between framing members and from the bottom of the sill to the top of the opening. Compare these measurements to the rough opening requirements of your new door to make sure it will fit.

■ **Exterior opening** (or "masonry opening" if you have a brick or stone door surround). Measure to the outsides of the exterior casing and then from the bottom of the sill to the top of the trim.

Compare these measurements with those of a prehung door that has standard 2-in.-wide "brick molding" trim. If the framed door with standard trim is too small to completely fill the space or if you want a different trim style, you have three options. The best solution is to order a door with wider, flat casing to fit the opening. You can always add a piece of decorative molding to approximate the style of your existing exterior trim. (For this project, 2-1/2-in. flat

PRY BAR

CASING

3 SLICE the caulk joint between the siding (brick) and exterior trim and pry the trim from the doorjamb with a pry bar.

DOORJAMB

OLD DOORSILL

DOORJAMB

4 CUT completely through the side jamb with a handsaw. Pry the jambs loose and pull them out of the opening.

casing was ordered and the existing decorative molding was reinstalled.) Second, you can order your door with standard molding and fill the gap with additional strips of wood. The last option is to order the door without exterior molding and make your own to fit.

Start by tearing out your old door and preparing the opening

Photos 1 – 4 show how to take out the old door and frame. If you plan to reuse the interior moldings, pull the nails through the back side with pliers or a nipper to avoid damaging the face. Cutting through one side jamb makes it easy to tear out the entire frame (Photo 4).

After the doorframe is out, check the condition of the framing and subflooring in the sill area. Cut out and replace any rotted wood. If the sill on your new door is thinner than the one you removed, you may have to build up the sill area as shown in Photo 5. Set the sill height so the door just clears carpeting or rugs when it swings inward.

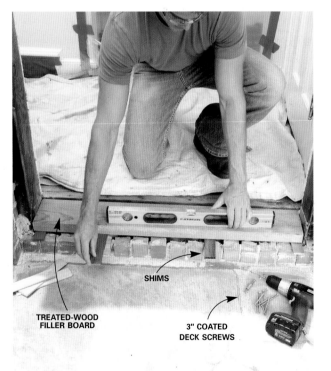

SHIMS

TREATED-WOOD FILLER BOARD

3" COATED DECK SCREWS

5 BUILD up the sill area to the proper height with treated lumber. Add shims to level it. Fasten it with coated deck screws.

6 COVER the rough sill area with self-sticking flashing tape. Wrap it up the sides of the opening and over the front edge. Set the door in the opening, plumb it and check the fit.

7 APPLY a bead of caulk along the sides and top of the door opening and at the sill according to the manufacturer's instructions.

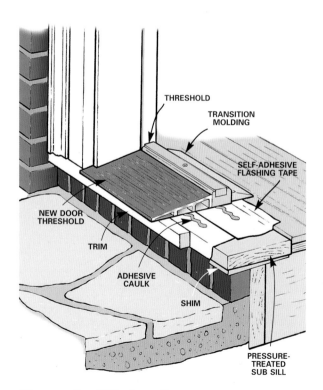

THRESHOLD

TRANSITION MOLDING

SELF-ADHESIVE FLASHING TAPE

NEW DOOR THRESHOLD

TRIM

ADHESIVE CAULK

SHIM

PRESSURE-TREATED SUB SILL

Figure B Sill detail

CHECK HERE FOR LEVEL

16d GALVANIZED CASING NAILS

PLUMB THE JAMB

TACK CASING HERE

8 MAKE SURE the doorsill is level. Then center the top of the door in the opening and tack it into place with galvanized casing nails. Plumb the hinge-side jamb and tack the bottom corners.

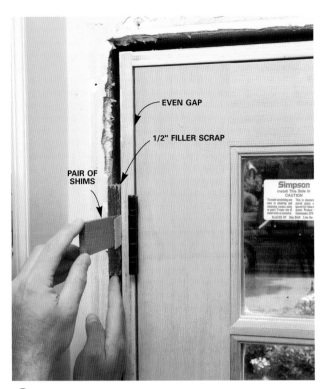

EVEN GAP

1/2" FILLER SCRAP

PAIR OF SHIMS

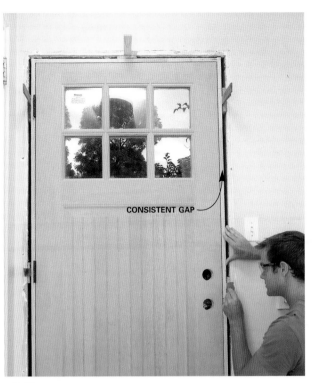

CONSISTENT GAP

9 SHIM behind each hinge. For large spaces, start with small squares of plywood. Then finish with pairs of shims. Make sure the hinge-side jamb remains plumb.

10 SHIM at the top, middle and bottom of the latch-side jamb and at the top until the gap between the door and the doorjamb is consistent. Score the shims with a utility knife and break them off.

Photo 6 shows how to protect the sill from water intrusion. Buy the flashing tape at a lumberyard. If you're installing a door in a newly constructed wall, you can buy a special plastic sill flashing kit instead. One brand is Jamsill (www.jamsill.com; call 800-526-7455 for ordering information). Details will vary depending on the doorway situation. The idea is to channel water away from the wood. If your home is built on a concrete slab, the doorframe will probably rest directly on the slab.

If your door is exposed to the weather, direct water away from the door with a metal drip cap (Figure C). Brick openings like this, and doors protected by porches with roofs, don't require a drip cap. You'll find drip caps at home centers and lumberyards. If the drip cap is damaged or missing, install a new one before you set the door frame in the opening. Cut the metal drip cap to fit and slide it under the siding and building paper (Figure C). If nails are in the way, slip a hacksaw blade under the siding and cut them.

3" SCREW INTO FRAMING

11 REPLACE a screw in each hinge with a 3-in. screw driven into the framing. Drive additional casing nails every 16 in. along the sides and top of the exterior trim.

Quick tip*

SEAL A DRAFTY DOOR Big screws heads in the threshold of newer entry doors can raise or lower the built-in narrow strip. If you can see light between the threshold and the door, raise the threshold where the light enters by turning the nearest screw counterclockwise.

12 FILL the space between the doorjamb and the framing with minimal expanding foam insulation. After the foam has expanded and skinned over, loosely stuff any remaining space with strips of fiberglass insulation.

MINIMAL EXPANDING FOAM

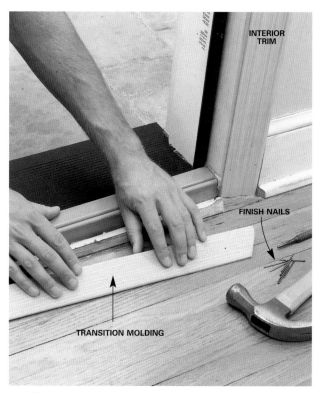

INTERIOR TRIM

FINISH NAILS

TRANSITION MOLDING

13 CUT and install new interior trim or reinstall the old trim. If there's a gap between the new sill and the existing flooring, cover it with a beveled transition molding.

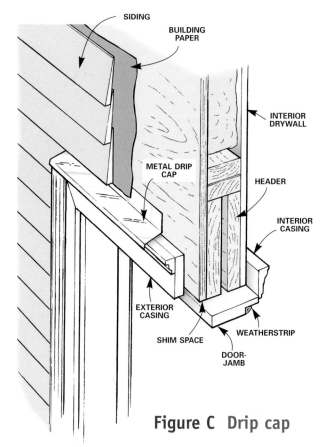

SIDING

BUILDING PAPER

INTERIOR DRYWALL

METAL DRIP CAP

HEADER

INTERIOR CASING

EXTERIOR CASING

WEATHERSTRIP

SHIM SPACE

DOOR-JAMB

Figure C Drip cap

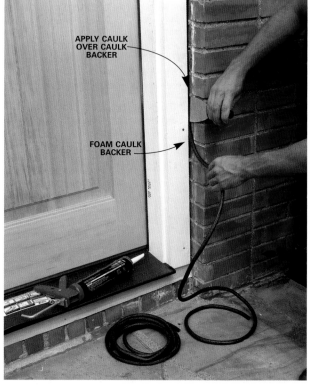

APPLY CAULK OVER CAULK BACKER

FOAM CAULK BACKER

14 PRESS foam caulk backer into the siding/trim gap. Apply a neat bead of caulk between the siding and the door trim. Cut a trim board to fit under the sill and screw it to the framing.

Solid shimming is the key to long-lasting, trouble-free operation

The brick opening shown here was level and plumb, but this isn't always the case. Start by checking the sill area with a 2-ft. level. If you're building it up as shown in Photo 5, it's easy to level it with shims at the same time. Otherwise, level the sill area with pairs of shims spaced about 4 in. apart.

Then set the door in the opening for a test fit. Hold a level against the hinge jamb and adjust the door and frame until the jamb is plumb. Check to see how the casing fits against the siding. If the siding is so far out of plumb that the door-frame and casing don't fit in, you either cut back the siding or trim the casing. It looks better if you can cut the siding, but it's usually more practical and easier to trim the casing. Mark the casing in areas that need trimming. Then take the door out and trim the casing with a belt sander or circular saw.

Make sure the building paper is intact around the frame edges. If not, slide strips of No. 15 felt behind the siding and tack it to the framing with staples. When you're sure the door will fit, caulk along the sill and behind the casing and tip the door into the opening. Photos 8 – 10 show how to shim and nail the door. The goal is to center the door in the opening and shim the sides until they're plumb and straight. Adjust the pairs of shims until the gap between the door and the jamb is consistent on the sides and top of the door. When you're happy with the fit, nail through the jamb into the framing at each shim location. Then replace one screw closest to the inside in each hinge with one long enough to reach the framing. This will keep the door from sagging over time (Photo 11).

After insulating the space around the door (Photo 12), install the interior trim. Photo 13 shows how to cover a gap between the doorsill and flooring. Complete the job by caulking the exterior (Photo 14). For gaps wider than 3/16 in., insert a foam backer (available at home centers, hardware stores and lumberyards) and apply caulk over it. Most doors require an additional trim board under the sill to support its outer edge. Finally, remove the door and paint or stain and varnish the door, jamb and trim.

Materials List

- Treated lumber to build up the sill (optional)
- Roll of flexible self-sticking flashing membrane
- Two tubes of polyurethane caulk
- Three packages of shims
- Two cans of minimal expanding foam
- Roll of foam caulk backing (optional)
- Transition molding (optional; Photo 13)
- One pound each of 12d and 16d galvanized casing nails
- One pound of 3-in. coated deck screws
- 4d, 6d and 10d finish nails

Buying a new door

Most home centers stock prehung exterior doors in a limited number of styles. Common jamb widths for stock doors are 4-9/16 in. and 6-9/16 in., and they usually include 2-in.-wide brick molding for exterior trim. These doors work great for newly constructed walls and for replacing doors in newer homes. But if, after measuring the jamb width and opening sizes for your existing door, you discover that you need a different size jamb or that your exterior trim is wider, then you'll save a lot of headaches by ordering a door to your exact specifications.

There are three types of doors to choose from. Steel doors ($150 to $300) are popular because they're inexpensive and require little maintenance. Fiberglass doors ($250 to $1,200) won't warp or rot, and the more expensive models are hard to tell apart from real wood. You'll find the widest selection of styles in wood doors ($300 to $1,500), but be prepared to spend extra time maintaining the finish.

Prehung exterior doors are available at home centers and lumberyards. If you can't find what you're looking for in stock, you can order it. Take along your measurements and a sketch showing which way the door swings.

If you plan to install a new entry knob and deadbolt, pick them out before you order the door. Then ask the salesperson to have the door drilled to accept your hardware. It'll cost a little extra, but it's well worth it to avoid the nerve-racking job of drilling into a new door. Don't forget to order hinges that will match the finish of your hardware.

Stop window and door drafts

Make your home more comfortable, and cut energy bills

1 SLICE through paint where the trim meets the wall and jamb. Put a new blade in your utility knife and make several passes over heavy paint buildup.

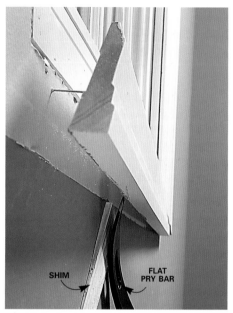

SHIM   FLAT PRY BAR

2 PRY away the trim gently with a flat pry bar. Protect walls with a shim or a scrap of wood as you gradually work the trim away from the wall.

If your windows or doors are a source of chilly drafts all winter long, the problem could be worn-out seals, weatherstripping or thresholds. Then again, sloppy installation might be to blame. When cold weather arrives, hold the back of your hand near the edges of windows or doors to track down the source of leaks. If you feel cold air flowing out from behind the trim, chances are the spaces around the window and doorjambs weren't properly sealed.

Plugging these leaks is a time-consuming job: You have to pull off the interior trim, seal around the jambs and then reinstall the trim. But if your doors and windows are otherwise fairly airtight, the payoff can be big too. Stopping drafts not only makes your home more comfortable but also cuts energy bills (air leaks are a major source of heat loss in most homes).

First investigate further: Remove one piece of trim from a window or a door. To prevent chipping or tearing paint, cut through the paint first (Photo 1). Slip a stiff putty knife under the trim and lift it enough to insert a flat pry bar. Don't simply force up one end of the piece. Instead, work along the length of the piece, moving your pry bar and lifting the trim off gradually (Photo 2). At mitered corners, watch for nails driven through the joint. To prevent these nails from splitting mitered ends, pry up both mitered

> **Caution:**
> Lead paint chips are hazardous. If your home was built before 1978, call your local health department for information on testing and handling lead paint safely.

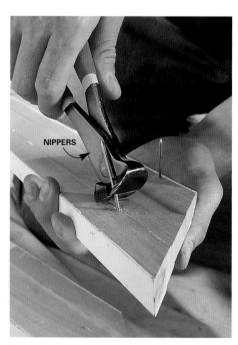

NIPPERS

3 PULL nails out through the back side of trim with nippers or pliers. Also write the location of each piece of trim on the back side.

FOAM SEALANT

WALL FRAMING

JAMB

4 PULL insulation from between the jamb and the wall framing. Seal the gap around the jamb with foam sealant. Be careful not to overfill and bow the jamb.

5 TACK each section of trim exactly in its original position with a couple of nails. Ridges in the wall paint can help you align each piece perfectly. Make sure the parts fit together tightly at the corners before you add more nails.

pieces together. Then pull them apart. When you're removing nails from the trim, pull them through the back side to avoid damaging the face of the trim (Photo 3).

With one piece removed, examine the space between the jamb and the wall framing. If the drywall covers the space, trim it back with a utility knife. If you see only a few loose wads of fiberglass insulation or no insulation at all between the jamb and framing, it's likely that all your windows and doors are poorly sealed.

To seal the gap, remove the remaining trim and inject foam sealant (Photo 4). Some sealants will push jambs inward as they expand, so be sure to use one that's intended for windows and doors (check the label). DAP Tex Plus was used here

because it's easy to clean up with a damp rag. Most expanding foams are nearly impossible to clean up before they harden.

Let the foam harden and trim off any excess foam with a knife before you reinstall the trim. Position each piece exactly as it was originally and tack each one up with only two nails (Photo 5). When all the pieces are in place, check their fit. With only a couple of nails in each piece, you can make small adjustments by holding a block against the trim and tapping it with a hammer. Then add more nails.

If your trim has a clear finish, fill the nail holes with a matching colored filler such as Color Putty or DAP Finishing Putty. With painted trim, it's best to fill the holes with spackle and repaint.

✳ Energy-Saving Q&A

Icy windows

Q Our winter temps reach minus 30 degrees F. We have low-E double-pane windows and maintain a low humidity level in our house (35 to 40 percent), but we still get ice on all of our windows. The only way I've found to defrost my windows is to aim fans at them. What can we do to remedy this situation?

A Double-pane windows with a low-E coating have an insulation R-value of about 3. Theoretically, they can sustain an indoor relative humidity of about 70 percent at 30 degrees F and 60 percent at 0 degrees F. With any higher relative humidity, condensation will form on the glass.

The glass edges of double-pane windows, the area you see wet and frosted, get considerably colder than the center of the glass. Depending on the sealing method, the edges can only sustain 45 to 55 percent relative humidity at 30 degrees F, and 25 to 35 percent at 0 degrees F before condensation begins. If you sustain a relative humidity at 40

percent or higher, your windows will be continually wet.

In your case, the simplest solution for controlling condensation is to reduce moisture sources. That means covering crawlspaces, sealing basement walls and floors, covering aquariums, reducing the number of houseplants, running ventilating fans during showers and while cooking, and making sure combustion devices are venting properly. Allowing more heat to get to the windows by keeping drapes open and circulating air with room fans will also help. Installing an air exchanger (an expensive option) will also lower indoor humidity.

When you shop for new windows, buy a type with higher-performance edge seals or consider triple-pane glass. Either will allow you to sustain a higher, more comfortable relative humidity in zero and subzero temperatures.

Exterior caulking
that lasts

Here's how to make caulk do its job and look good at the same time

With prepackaged tubes and slick caulk guns, caulking has become so quick and easy that it's almost fun. A squirt here, a squirt there. But don't rush through this step. A good caulking job ensures that you've sealed up all those energy-wasting gaps and cracks on the exterior of your home. It plugs the cracks where water can seep in and lift the paint. And it smooths over ugly gaps that make your home look shabby.

Here you'll find out what types of caulks and guns to buy to deliver fast and smooth results, yet still provide lasting protection. You'll also learn caulking techniques that'll result in an effective, long-term moisture barrier. Finally, you'll learn what caulk can't do and where you can go wrong when you apply it.

Buy a good caulking gun

Professional caulking guns begin at about $25, but even as little as six or seven bucks buys you a decent one (photo at left). The quality is all in the action. Better guns (even priced as low as $6) have smoother-operating, no-slip ratcheting mechanisms, easier-to-squeeze handles, and better pressure control, so you can deliver just the right amount of caulk where you need it. Look for one that's also "dripless," which means that it releases pressure when you relax your grip so you don't have that 2-in. bead of slop-over dribbling onto your shirt and shoes. A stiff wire attached to some guns comes in handy for puncturing the foil seal inside the nozzle.

If you have small hands, buy the longer-handled variety of gun, which is easier to squeeze. The trick is to compress the handle to a comfortable position with the mechanism released, then apply the caulk with a shorter handle movement.

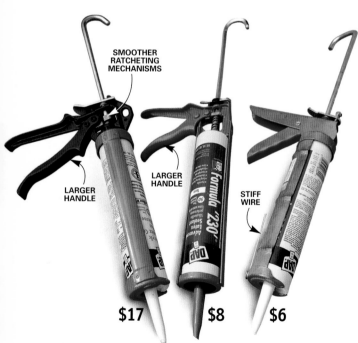

SMOOTHER RATCHETING MECHANISMS

LARGER HANDLE

LARGER HANDLE

STIFF WIRE

$17 $8 $6

Better caulking guns are sturdy and have smooth ratcheting actions and releases. Larger handles are easier to squeeze. The bent end of the rod hooks over ladder rungs. An attached wire conveniently pokes a hole in the tube seal.

Quick tip *

AVOID $2 CHEAPIES
A good gun is twice as fast and half as tiring.

Caulk to stop water and improve appearance

CAULK ALL EXTERIOR JOINTS that are vulnerable to water. Moisture is your home's worst enemy, so caulk around doors, windows, decks and other penetrations where water or wind-driven rain could get into the walls and rot the framing (Photo 2).

Caulk also protects wood siding and trim (Photo 4). Water soaking in through joints can cause paint to peel and siding to rot.

And finally, caulk gaps and cracks to improve your home's appearance (Photo 3). Stand back and look at each wall of your home. Then simply caulk distracting dark lines that you think will mar a neat paint job.

Four reasons to caulk:

1. To improve energy efficiency
2. To prevent rain and moisture from entering walls
3. To protect siding and trim
4. To improve appearance

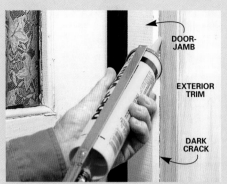

Seal the joints between trim pieces to block water and erase distracting dark lines. Otherwise, the paint will crack at these joints. Acrylic caulk works well for most joints.

Caulk decorative trim to improve its appearance. Apply and smooth a thin bead here to keep the corners crisp. A good caulking gun pays off to speed up this slow, painstaking job.

Follow the three-step caulking rule

Step 1: Prepare a solid base

Dig out old, loose caulk with a putty knife or sharp-pointed tool (Photo 1). Caulk hardens and cracks as it ages, usually breaking away from the wood, leaving it exposed to moisture. Clean loose caulk from cracks and gaps, but leave the caulk that still adheres well. (Poke at it with your putty knife. If it readily breaks away, dig it out.)

Then work primer back into the gaps. (Normally you'd do this during the paint scraping and priming stages, but if you missed spots, get them now.) Because primer adheres better to bare wood, it's the best base for caulk. This isn't the case with concrete, brick and other masonry surfaces. With these materials, use polyurethane caulk, which is sometimes called "self-priming" because it adheres so well.

1 CLEAN the joints by digging out old, loose caulk with a 5-in-1 tool or a stiff putty knife. Prime all bare wood, working the primer as far back into the joints as possible.

Step 2: Lay a ribbon of caulk

Rest the tip of the tube on the joint and squeeze on a ribbon that just covers the gap (Photo 2). Technique pays off here. Pull the tip of the tube along the joint, concentrating on covering the gap with a layer rather than completely filling it with a thick bead. The idea is to bridge the gap with caulk, not to fill it. A thick bead will crack and pull away from the wood when it hardens. A ribbon will stretch with the normal expansion and contraction of the wood (Figure A, below right).

For smoother caulking, cut the tip of the tube at a 45- to 60-degree angle so the hole is slightly smaller than the size of the gap you want to caulk (photo, bottom). It's much easier to squeeze out additional caulk than to clean up the mess caused by too much.

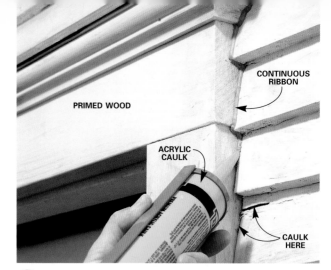

2 SQUEEZE a smooth, even ribbon of caulk over the joint, completely covering it. Squeeze steadily, resting the tip of the tube on the wood and dragging it along at an even pace to get an even flow.

3 MOISTEN a finger and press the caulk against both sides of the joint to ensure good adhesion, smoothing it as you go. Wipe away excess along the sides with a damp cloth. Don't caulk the horizontal joints between wood siding; your wall needs enough cracks to be able to "breathe."

Step 3: 'Tool' the caulk to ensure good adhesion and to smooth it

Dampen your finger (with water for acrylic, paint thinner for polyurethane) and run it along the joint, pressing the caulk against the sides and flattening and smoothing the surface (Photo 3), a process called tooling. The key to a durable caulk joint is to get good adhesion on each side of the joint (Figure A). Your finger will leave the joint slightly concave, but don't press the caulk tightly into corners trying to make them sharp. Acrylics and polyurethanes shrink 20 to 30 percent when they dry, so you can expect the concavity to increase.

Quick tip ✳

THE IDEA IS TO BRIDGE the gap with caulk, not to completely fill it.

Keep a wet cloth on hand to clean acrylic caulk from your hands and to wipe away excess. Work about 2 ft. of joint at a time, stopping to smooth each section. Otherwise, acrylic caulk will begin to skin over and won't smooth easily.

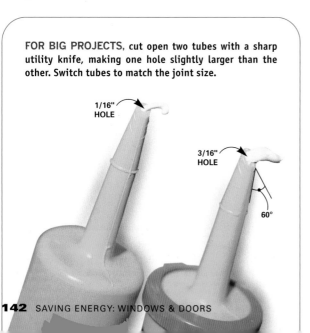

FOR BIG PROJECTS, cut open two tubes with a sharp utility knife, making one hole slightly larger than the other. Switch tubes to match the joint size.

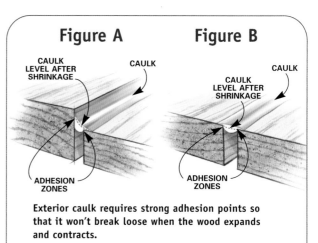

Exterior caulk requires strong adhesion points so that it won't break loose when the wood expands and contracts.

You need only two types of caulk

DESPITE THE VAST, CONFUSING ARRAY OF CAULKS on the home center shelf, you need only two types for your home's exterior—acrylic and polyurethane. Both types stick solidly to wood and most other building materials, accept paint well and retain their flexibility for years.

Acrylic

Use acrylic (sometimes called acrylic latex) as an all-purpose caulk (Photos 2 and 5). It's water-based, so you can smooth it and clean it off your hands and tools easily. Once spread, it skins over within minutes, so you can paint it almost immediately with an acrylic latex paint. Buy the highest-quality premium acrylic caulk available. Price is a good indicator—the more expensive, the better. Better acrylics typically cost $2 to $4 per standard 10-oz. tube.

> Acrylic is an all-purpose, water-based caulk.

Silicone acrylic is more flexible, a good feature, but if you buy it, make sure the label states that it's paintable.

Polyurethane

Polyurethane performs better than acrylic in all ways, but it's stickier and much harder to apply. You'll see how to use it in Photos 1 – 4 on pp. 144 and 145. You have to use mineral spirits or paint thinner for cleanup. Use it when you caulk concrete, stucco or other masonry and when you want extra-strong adhesion, for example, in areas especially vulnerable to water (Photo 2, p. 144). It costs $4 to $5 per tube.

> Polyurethane caulk has extra-strong adhesion.

Use backer rods to caulk wide joints

For a durable caulk joint wider than about 1/4 in., insert a special foam backer rod to fill the bulk of the gap. If you fill the entire gap with caulk, it'll soon harden and crack. To retain flexibility, your ribbon of caulk shouldn't be more than 1/8 in. to 3/16 in. thick (Figure C). Many home centers and full-service hardware stores carry foam backer rods in several sizes (photo at right). Otherwise, call a concrete products dealer.

Photos 1 – 4 on pp. 144 and 145 show the basic caulking steps for a wide gap. Shown is polyurethane caulk because it adheres better to stone than acrylic does. But it's tough to handle because it's super sticky. Keep a rag and paint thinner nearby for cleaning it off your hands and tools. If you're doing extensive caulking, wear plastic gloves to limit your skin exposure to paint thinner. Apply polyurethane sparingly; excess is difficult to clean off.

You can file an old putty knife to a round profile to use as a shaping tool (Photo 3, p. 145). Smoothing a wide joint so it looks nice takes practice, so begin with less-prominent joints.

1/2" FOAM BACKER ROD

5/8"

3/8"

Backer rods in a variety of sizes help seal large cracks.

Quick tip *

CHOOSE A CAULK COLOR that'll blend with concrete or other masonry. Then leave the caulk unpainted.

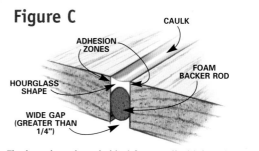

Figure C

CAULK

ADHESION ZONES

FOAM BACKER ROD

HOURGLASS SHAPE

WIDE GAP (GREATER THAN 1/4")

The hourglass shape is ideal for a caulked joint. The caulk flexes in the middle yet remains solidly anchored to the sides.

1 PRESS foam backer rod into gaps larger than about 1/4 in. using a putty knife or other blunt tool. Buy various sizes so you won't have to compress large rods into small gaps.

FOAM BACKER

2 LAY masking tape along the stone to ensure a crisp, even edge on the rough surface. Then spread caulk over the remaining gap.

MASKING TAPE

POLYURETHANE CAULK

Mini caulk gun for tight areas

An ordinary caulk gun is just too big and bulky for working in tight spots, such as behind a sink or at the back of a tub faucet. For these places, a 20-cc plastic syringe (without a needle) makes an ideal mini caulk gun. Just cut the syringe tip at a slight angle, pull out the plunger and load it with caulk. Syringes are available at pharmacies and farm supply stores.

A final step: Test for backdrafting

Exterior caulking on a large painting project has the side effect of making your house more airtight. Although increasing airtightness saves energy, it can have negative consequences too. (See "Where *not* to caulk," below.)

Where *not* to caulk

DON'T CAULK JOINTS THAT AREN'T AFFECTED BY WATER and won't mar the appearance of the final paint job. Two examples are horizontal joints under lap siding (Photo 3, p. 142) and the tops of drip caps over windows and doors where flashing carries water to the exterior. Joints protected by roof overhangs don't need caulk either.

Moisture generated inside must have ways to get out. If you seal your home in an airtight skin, you'll trap that moisture in the walls, especially in cold weather, and it'll soak the wood, cause rot and lift the exterior paint.

Still, a good caulking job will make your home more airtight. So afterward, check your gas- or oil-burning appliances to make sure they continue to vent waste gases properly.

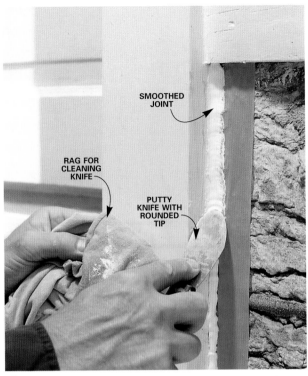

SMOOTHED JOINT

RAG FOR CLEANING KNIFE

PUTTY KNIFE WITH ROUNDED TIP

FINISHED JOINT

3 SMOOTH the caulk with a round-end tool to shape the joint and ensure good adhesion on the edges. Using a finger won't work on wider joints like this, especially with this sticky type of caulk. Keep a cloth dampened with thinner handy to clean off excess polyurethane caulk.

4 PULL OFF the tape before the caulk begins to harden. Otherwise, the caulk will stick to it and you'll have to cut it off.

A tighter house can cause potentially hazardous exhaust fumes from gas-, oil- or wood-burning devices to spill into the house rather than flow out a chimney or vent. This phenomenon is called backdrafting. Test your water heater for backdrafting (it's the most likely candidate) by closing all your doors and windows and running hot water until the water heater comes on. After about a minute, check the vent hood with a smoking match to make sure the exhaust pulls the smoke up the vent. If the vent isn't drawing properly, call in a heating contractor to find and correct the problem.

Quick tip*

A FEW TRICKS TO REMEMBER WHEN CAULKING:

- Use expanding foam to seal large gaps, especially around dryer vents, electrical service entry points and other places where utilities enter your home.
- Caulking inside is often more effective than caulking outside. Before repainting a room, caulk around "leaky" moldings.
- As a rule of thumb, you'll use 1/2 tube of caulk per door, 1/4 tube of caulk per window.

*Energy-Saving Hint

Caulking extender

If you have to get caulk into a tight spot, just tape a flexible drinking straw to the tip of your caulking gun and you'll be ready to caulk into any nook the straw will reach.

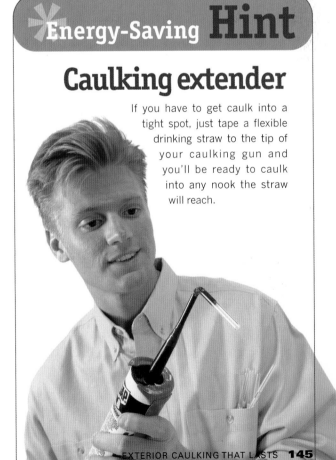

Energy-saving replacement windows

Out with the old and cold. In with the new and warm.

Are you ready to replace your drafty old windows with new energy-efficient units? You'll be glad to know that you don't have to tear off interior moldings or disturb exterior trim and siding.

Here you'll learn, step by step, how to remove the old sash from double-hung windows and mount either a new sash kit or a wood or vinyl replacement insert inside your existing window jamb. Even a beginner can do it.

Both the sash replacement kit and the wood or vinyl replacement insert fit in the space between the outside stop, called the blind stop, and the removable interior stop (see Figure A, opposite). The sash replacement kit is designed to replace the sash in double-hung windows only. Wood or vinyl replacement inserts, on the other hand, are self-contained units with their own jamb and sash and can therefore be slid into almost any type of window jamb. They are available as double-hung, sliding or casement-style windows.

> **CAUTION:**
> Houses built before 1978 may contain lead paint. Before disturbing any surface, get a lab analysis of paint chips from it (about $10 - 15 per sample). Contact your public health department for information on how to collect samples and where to send them.

Option 1

Wood or vinyl replacement inserts

For a maintenance-free window that doesn't require any painting or staining, consider vinyl replacement windows. Some companies even make a simulated wood grain interior. Since wood or vinyl replacement inserts have their own jamb, they can be installed in window jambs that are slightly out of square. Ask your window dealer for help measuring, though, since you'll have to downsize the window slightly to fit.

Shopping for replacement windows is a little trickier than buying sash kits because the quality of the windows varies dramatically and many are available only to contractors. The window we ordered cost $275 and arrived in about three weeks. Make sure to inspect and operate an actual working model of the window before you order. Look closely at details like the locking system, weatherstripping, and sash and frame joints. Then consider the overall appearance. Some windows, like ours, have narrow vinyl sash parts that allow more light and a better view than windows with wide sash frames.

Buyer's Guide
The following companies manufacture vinyl replacement windows. Call for the retailer nearest you.

CRESTLINE WINDOWS AND DOORS: (800) 552-4111. www.crestlinewindows.com

KVW division of Kolbe & Kolbe Millwork Inc.: (800) 955-8177. www.kkvw.com

VETTER WINDOWS & DOORS: (800) VETTER2. www.vetterwindows.com

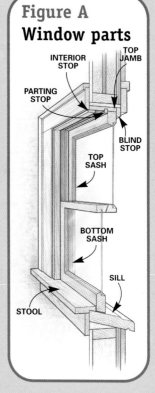

Figure A
Window parts

INTERIOR STOP
TOP JAMB
PARTING STOP
BLIND STOP
TOP SASH
BOTTOM SASH
SILL
STOOL

Option 2

Double-hung sash replacement kits

If you want to retain the authentic wood look of your old double-hung windows, sash replacement kits are the best option. You can order the sashes with grilles to match the rest of the windows in your house and paint or stain the wood. (You can choose grilles that either snap in or are glued to the glass.) But your old window jamb must be square and rot-free. Measure diagonally. If the diagonal measurements differ by more than 1/2 in., the new sash won't seal properly and you should replace the window or use a vinyl replacement window instead.

Double-hung sash replacement kits consist of two new wood window sashes, two vinyl jamb liners and installation hardware. They range in price from about $200 for a basic window with a snap-in grid to more than $400 for windows like ours with simulated divided panes. Features like energy-efficient low-E glass and maintenance-free exterior cladding are available for an extra cost. Contact one of the manufacturers listed at right for more information and to find out where to order windows in your area.

Buyer's Guide
Here are a few companies that sell double-hung sash replacement kits. Check your local lumberyard or home center for other sources.

JELD-WEN: (800) 535-3936. www.jeld-wen.com

KOLBE & KOLBE MILLWORK INC.: (800) 955-8177. www.kolbe-kolbe.com

MARVIN WINDOWS AND DOORS: (888) 537-8266. www.marvin.com

Option 1

Wood or vinyl replacement inserts

Start your replacement insert installation by removing the interior stop, sash and parting stop. The parting stop is usually caked with paint and difficult to remove. Use pliers to break out the lower section. If the upper sash is stuck, pry or break out the upper section of parting stop with a chisel. If your windows have spring balances or metal jamb liners rather than sash weights like ours, start by removing the interior stops (Photo 1). Then look for the screws or nails that secure the sash hardware and remove them. The goal is to remove all hardware back to the blind stops (Photo 2). You don't have to worry about dinging up the jamb and sill, because they'll be covered. If your window has a sash weight cavity, stuff it with insulation.

Make sure your window insert is square

Your wood or vinyl replacement insert will be slightly smaller than the window jamb opening to allow for shimming. The key to a window that operates smoothly and seals properly is getting the frame perfectly square and the sides straight. Photos 5 and 6 show how. Don't be afraid to remove the screws and readjust the window in the opening if necessary. In addition to checking the window by measuring the diagonals (Photo 5), open and close the sashes to make sure the tops and bottoms are parallel with the sill and top jamb and that the top and bottom sashes are parallel to each other where they meet in the middle. Keep tweaking the shims until everything is square and lined up. Then snug but don't overtighten the screws. Complete the installation by reinstalling the interior stops (Photo 7) and sealing up the exterior (Photos 8 and 9). You can also install wood or vinyl replacement inserts in casement and sliding window jambs. We won't talk about them in detail here. Be sure to read the installation instructions that come with each window.

STIFF PUTTY KNIFE

SMALL PRY BAR

INTERIOR STOPS

1 GENTLY PRY off the interior stops. Pry against a stiff putty knife to protect the wood. To minimize paint chipping on painted windows, score the joint between the window frame and stop with a utility knife before prying off the stop. Pull the nails through the back side of the stop with a nail nipper or pliers. Complete the window prep by following Photos 2 and 3.

CAULK BLIND STOP

2 SLIP the new window insert into place to make sure it fits. Then remove it and lay a bead of polyurethane caulk along the inside of the blind stop and the back side of the window stool.

HEAD EXPANDER

VINYL REPLACEMENT WINDOW

3 REST the bottom of the replacement window on the sill and tilt the window into place against the blind stop. If your window includes a head expander, position it over the top of the jamb first. Press the window tight against the caulked blind stop.

SCREW INTO JAMB

4 LOOSELY FASTEN the window into the frame with partially driven screws in the lower left and upper right corners. Close and lock the sash.

MEASURE BOTH DIAGONALS

5 MEASURE diagonally across the new window. Slide shims behind the screw holes in the four corners and adjust them until the diagonal measurements from opposite corners are equal. Drive screws through the upper left and lower right screw holes.

6 HOLD a level against the side jamb and slide wood shims behind each remaining screw hole until the side jamb is straight. Snug up all screws and check that the sashes slide easily and align perfectly where they meet in the middle. Be careful; overtightening screws could warp the vinyl jamb.

7 CUT OFF the shims with a sharp utility knife and then replace the interior stops and nail them in place with 4d finish nails.

8 STUFF fiberglass insulation in the gap under the sill of the new vinyl window. Measure the size of the gap and cut the vinyl filler strip to fit. Use a sharp utility knife and straight-edge or tin snips to cut the vinyl. Press the filler into place.

9 CAULK the joint between the new window and the blind stop and between the windowsill and the filler strip.

Double-hung sash kits

The toughest part of sash replacement is tearing out the old window. You have to pry off the stop (carefully for reuse) and the parting stop (which you can discard; see Photo 3, p. 152). You can either nail or screw the new liner clips in place (Photo 4). We chose screws because driving nails can be difficult in old window jambs. Be sure to leave a 1/16-in. space between the clip and the blind stop or the jamb liner won't snap in (Photo 4). Then replace the interior stops and top parting stop (Photo 5). Read the instructions included with your window for the exact procedure to use for lowering the sash lifts (Photo 6) and tilting the sash into place. If you have trouble pushing in the sash after you tilt it up, try working with one side at a time. Compress the jamb liner with one hand while you ease one top corner of the sash in with the other. Then repeat the process on the other side. Also position the top of the sash toward the center of the opening.

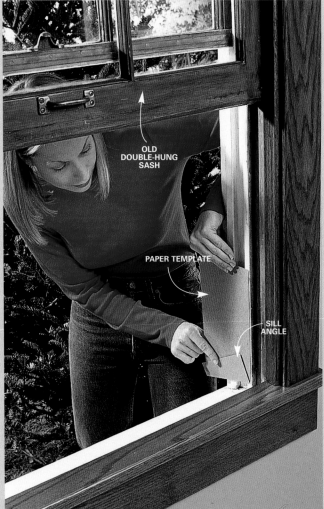

OLD DOUBLE-HUNG SASH

PAPER TEMPLATE

SILL ANGLE

Figure B
Find the sill angle

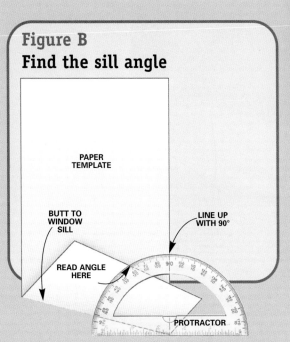

PAPER TEMPLATE

BUTT TO WINDOW SILL

READ ANGLE HERE

LINE UP WITH 90°

PROTRACTOR

1 ALIGN the edge of a heavy piece of paper with the window stop and fold the bottom to match the angle of the sill. Lay a protractor (Figure B) on the folded paper to determine the angle. Then measure the interior height and width of the window frame. Use these measurements to order your sash replacement kit.

Your old jamb must be solid

The window replacements we show must be installed in a solid, rot-free jamb. Inspect your old window frame carefully for signs of water damage. Pay particular attention to the sill. Probe with a screwdriver to uncover hidden soft spots. Normal exposure to rain and snow often causes the exposed parts of poorly maintained windowsills or the lower sections of the exterior trim to rot. An experienced carpenter can usually repair these areas with sections of new wood or you can use an epoxy repair system. Rot along the top or interior parts of windows, including the window jamb, is more difficult to repair and often signals a bigger problem. Don't mess with repairs. Plan on tearing out the entire window and installing a new one.

Measure carefully

There's nothing worse than discovering that your nonreturnable custom-sized window doesn't fit. Measure the width between the side jambs at the top, middle and bottom and record the smallest measurement. Measure all the way to the jamb, not the blind stop or parting stop (see Figure A). Now measure the height from the top jamb to the sill (see Figure A). Measure both sides and the middle and record the smallest measurement. Finally, determine the sill angle (Photo 1, p. 151) and specify this when you order a sash replacement kit to make sure the jamb liners fit tight to the sill. This step isn't necessary for ordering wood or vinyl replacement inserts. Keep a record of all correspondence with your window supplier and ask for written confirmation before the windows are ordered so you can double-check the sizes.

If your house was built before about 1940, you'll likely have double-hung windows with sash weights and cords like the ones shown here. Newer double-hungs may have springs or jamb liners instead, but once these are removed, the installation process is the same.

2 REMOVE the lower sash and cut the sash cords. If your window has weatherstripping or hardware other than sash cords, pry out or unscrew these to remove the sash.

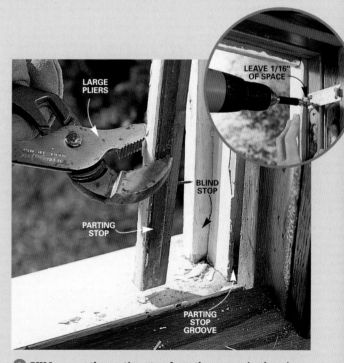

3 PULL or pry the parting stop from the groove in the window frame and discard it. Remove the top sash, cut the sash cords and take out the sash weight pulleys, sash weight cover and weights. Stuff the cavity with fiberglass insulation. Screw the jamb liner clips to the jamb with No. 6 x 3/4-in. pan head screws (inset). Position clips 4 in. from the top and bottom and space the remaining clips evenly between them. Leave a 1/16-in. space between the clips and the blind stop to allow space for the jamb liner to slide in.

VINYL JAMB LINER

JAMB LINER CLIPS

4 SNAP jamb liners over the metal clips after installing the sash stops and gaskets according to the instructions included with your window. Align the jamb liner so its outside edge fits between the blind stop and the metal clips. If your jamb liner has a vinyl flap facing the outside, make sure it lies over the blind stop. Press firmly over each clip location until you hear or feel the liner snap onto the clips.

4D FINISH NAILS

NEW PARTING STOP

5 SLIP the new parting stop into the groove in the top jamb with the weatherstripped edge facing the outside. Drill 1/16-in. pilot holes and nail the stop in place with three 4d finish nails. Replace the wood interior stops on the sides and top of the window and nail them in place with 4d finish nails.

SLIDE DOWN

SASH LIFT

FLAT-BLADE SCREWDRIVER

6 SLIDE the sash lifts down to within about 10 in. of the windowsill. Press down firmly with a flat-blade screwdriver. Twist the screwdriver slightly from horizontal to slide the lifts. Then twist back to horizontal to engage the lifts in their new locations.
CAUTION: Release pressure very slowly to make sure the clips are engaged before you remove the screwdriver completely.

NEW TILT-IN SASH

7 HOLD the top sash with the exterior facing up and the metal cams away from you. Tilt the sash and align metal pivots with the slots in the jamb liner closest to the exterior. Make sure the pivots are above the sash lifts. Tilt up the sash and press outward on the jamb liner while you snap the top of the sash into place between the jamb liners. Slide the sash down until the metal cams contact the sash lifts. Repeat the process on the lower sash.

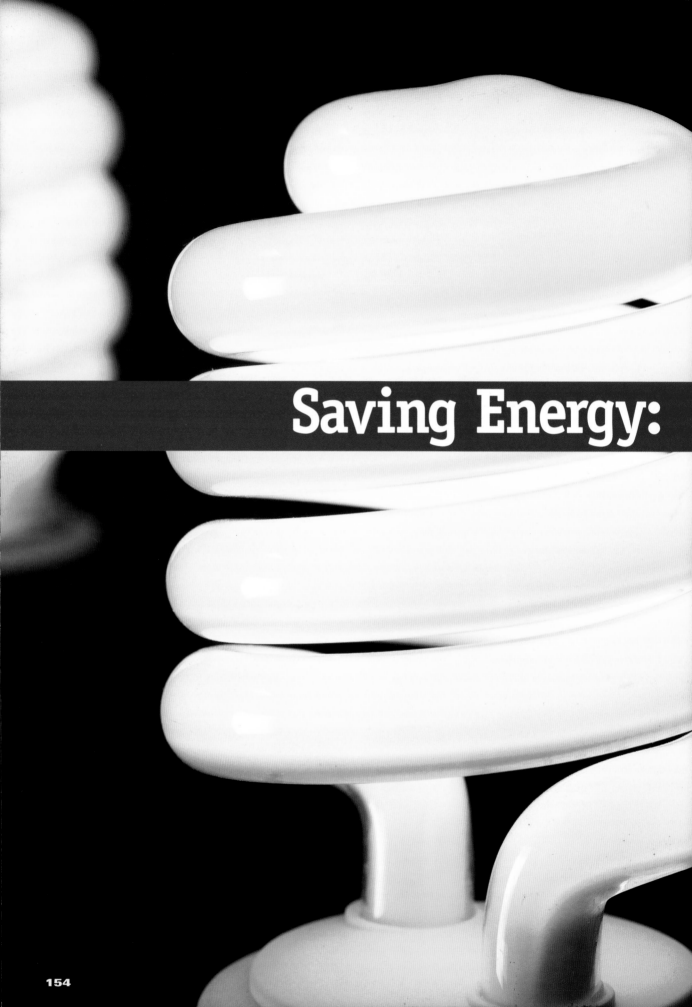

Saving Energy:

Installing energy-efficient light bulbs and using them, and other lights, wisely is perhaps the simplest and most easily accomplished form of energy conservation of all. It can be as simple as flicking a switch or screwing in a new bulb.

Compact fluorescent bulbs (CFLs) have come a long way since first being introduced two decades ago. Originally expensive, CFLs can now be purchased for as little as $3 apiece. That may be five times the cost of an incandescent bulb, but a single CFL can save $30 to $40 in electricity over the course of its lifetime, and last five to 10 times longer than its incandescent cousin.

Motion-activated lights, dimmers and homeowner habits can also greatly reduce lighting bills. Energy-efficient lighting is a good place to begin your energy saving plans.

Smarter Lighting

Compact
fluorescent bulbs
10 common questions; 10 commonsense answers.

1

CFLs vs. incandescent bulbs

Q How do compact fluorescent lights work and how do they differ from standard bulbs?

A Standard incandescent bulbs work by using electricity to heat up a thin filament inside the bulb. As the filament heats up, it glows, producing light. The drawback to standard bulbs is that most of the energy consumed—over 80%—goes into creating heat, not light.

CFLs work on a totally different principle. They consist of two basic parts: a gas-filled tube (what many of us would call the "bulb") and a ballast that contains the electronics. In simple terms, electricity from the ballast excites phosphors on the inside surface of the bulb; these phosphates in turn glow, producing light. Since CFLs don't waste as much energy creating heat, they're much more energy efficient. You see the savings when you compare the wattages; a 15-watt CFL provides about as much light as a 60-watt incandescent bulb.

Compact fluorescent bulbs—usually referred to by the initials, CFL—traveled the rocky path of most new products. Initially they were expensive (as much as $15 apiece) and fraught with problems (they appeared "dim," flickered, didn't come on instantly and burned out sooner than promised).

But that was then. New technology has solved most of the old problems. Today CFLs are one of the easiest and most effective ways of saving money on energy. It's as easy as screwing in a bulb and flipping a switch. Many CFLs can be purchased for around $3 and some utility companies offer discounts or rebates to customers who buy them.

That said, buying and using CFLs can still be confusing. The answers to these common questions will help you put these great energy-saving bulbs to best use.

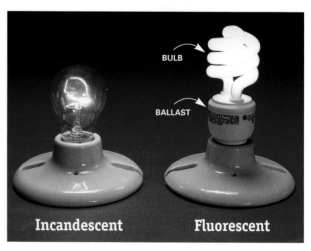

BULB

BALLAST

Incandescent   **Fluorescent**

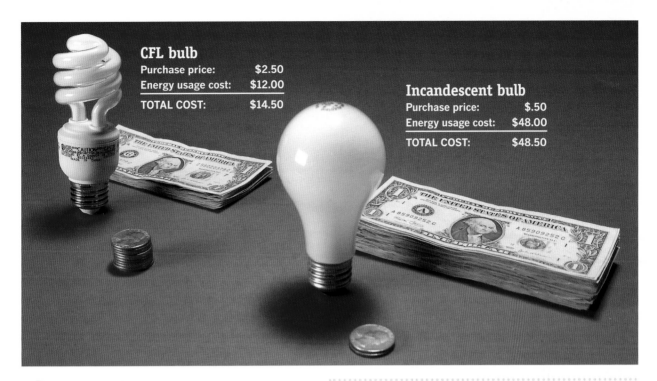

CFL bulb

Purchase price:	$2.50
Energy usage cost:	$12.00
TOTAL COST:	**$14.50**

Incandescent bulb

Purchase price:	$.50
Energy usage cost:	$48.00
TOTAL COST:	**$48.50**

2

Payback: How long? How come?

Q CFLs cost five or six times as much as regular bulbs. How long do I need to use them before I recoup my investment?

A Although CFL bulbs have come down dramatically in price, their electronic ballast and other features do make them more expensive to manufacture than incandescent bulbs. The payback period will vary based on how much electricity costs in your area. However, based on a cost of 10¢ per kWh, a 15-watt CFL will cost about $12 to operate over its 8,000-hour projected life span. Burning a 60-watt incandescent bulb with equivalent light output for the same length of time will cost about $48; a cost difference of $36 (and you'll need to buy four to eight bulbs since they have a much shorter lifespan). Based on those numbers, a CFL will pay for itself in about 500 hours (in about four months if the bulb is used four hours per day).

Quick tip

COOLER YET. Since CFLs generate less heat than standard incandescent bulbs, your air conditioner won't have to work quite as hard in the summer.

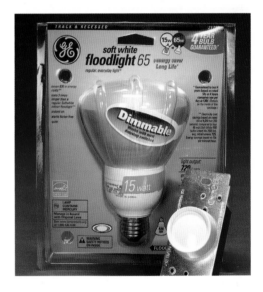

3

Dim the lights

Q Can I install CFL bulbs in fixtures that operate on a dimmer switch?

A Yes—but only if you buy the right ones. Look for CFLs that are labeled "dimmable" on the package; they have special ballasts that allow them to be operated using a standard incandescent dimmer switch. Expect to pay $3 to $4 more for a dimmable CFL than a regular CFL. Dimmable CFLs are available at most discount department stores, but they're relatively new, so you may have to search around town (or the Internet) to find them.

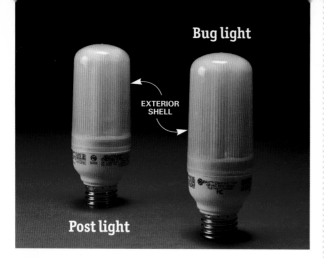

Bug light

EXTERIOR SHELL

Post light

4
Outside in the cold

Q Can I use CFLs outside and in my garage during the long, cold winter?

A Yes, they're great energy savers outdoors, but beware. Older fluorescent lights—both compact and tubular—are powered using magnetic ballasts. The lower the temperature, the more difficult it is for these bulbs to "get up to speed" and operate evenly. However, most CFLs made today have electronic ballasts that are much less sensitive to the cold.

If you're planning to use a CFL in an area exposed to the elements, purchase one designated for "exterior" or "outside" use. These usually have an extra translucent shell surrounding the fluorescent bulb to offer additional protection. Specialty bulbs like the "bug light" (above) and exterior floodlights are also available.

5
Best (and worst) places to use them

Q Are there some places where using a CFL makes more sense than others? Are there situations to avoid?

A Two scenarios make particular sense: 1. Since many CFLs have projected life spans of 8,000 hours or more, consider placing them in difficult-to-reach fixtures. It may mean climbing the ladder once every five years instead of once every year; 2. It also makes sense to use CFLs in light fixtures that are continuously "On" more than three to four hours per day.

Situations to avoid? Frequently switching a CFL "On" and "Off" and excess jostling can shorten its lifespan. Also, electronic ballasts are very sensitive to heat. Using CFLs that are not rated for use in enclosed fixtures can shorten the lifespan of a ballast (or bring about its demise altogether).

6
Lumens or watts?

Q Is there a formula or rule of thumb for determining fluorescent bulb wattage in order to get the same amount of light as that cast from an incandescent bulb?

A Generally speaking, if you divide the wattage of an incandescent bulb by 4 you'll come up with the equivalent wattage needed in a fluorescent. In other words, you'd replace a 60-watt incandescent bulb with a 15-watt fluorescent (60 divided by 4 equals 15), a 25- to 30-watt fluorescent to replace a 100-watt incandescent and a 35- to 40-watt CFL to replace a 150-watt incandescent.

But actual light output varies among brands. The most accurate way of comparing light output is to compare the lumens listed on the package of an incandescent bulb against that of a CFL. Be wary of CFLs that don't list the lumens on their packages, but only the "equivalent to" number. Sometimes the claims that their light output matches a certain incandescent wattage are misleading or wrong.

Modular CFL for dedicated fixture

BULB

BALLAST

SU13

Non-CFL pin-type

FC8T9/KB Kitchen & Bath 22W CHINA 6E CE

7
New CFLs on the block

Q I've seen smaller fluorescent bulbs that don't screw in. What's the story on pin-type fluorescent bulbs?

A The pin-type fluorescent bulb familiar to most of us is the classic circular kitchen bulb (above). These aren't considered true CFLs since the ballast is in the fixture itself, not built into the bulb.

But there is a new generation of pin-type bulbs, like the bulb shown at the top of the page. These are true CFLs, but they have a base designed to fit only into fixtures made specifically for these pin-type bulbs. Another unique feature of these bulbs is that the ballasts and tubes are separate. One of the reasons behind this modular design is that a typical ballast can last 30,000 hours, while a typical CFL bulb lasts 10,000. By making the parts independent, one only needs to change the bulb part that fails. These bulbs also meet the strict energy code in California.

8
Three-way bulbs

Q Are there three-way CFL bulbs, and if so, do they require a special lamp or light fixture?

A Yes, three-way CFLs are available, and no, you don't need a special lamp—usually. The three-way bulbs that ramp up to the equivalent of a 150-watt incandescent can be either circular or spiral in shape. Either way, they're quite large. For bulbs in that range, check to be sure they'll fit the harp and shade of your lamp.

Also make certain your three-way bulb is screwed in snugly. Unless the contacts on the bottom of the bulb make solid contact, your three-way bulb may work like a single-output bulb.

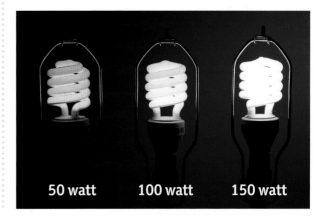

50 watt   100 watt   150 watt

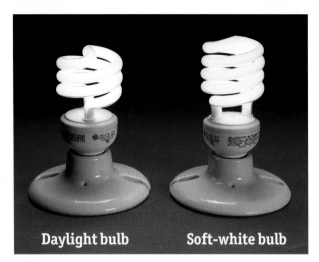

Daylight bulb   **Soft-white bulb**

9

The "quality of light" factor

Q I stopped buying CFLs because the first few I bought years ago seemed dim and the color of the light was weird. Are CFLs more like "normal" incandescent bulbs these days?

A The longevity of CFLs has been a double-edged sword. Since they last so long, some of the first generation bulbs— that indeed had problems— are still burning and giving people the wrong impression of the newer CFLs.

The newer bulbs and electronic ballasts flicker less, make less noise, start up faster and emit light very similar to that of the standard "Type-A" incandescent bulbs we're used to seeing. The spiral shape, which is often used in CFLs, casts light more like a standard incandescent bulb. The color of the light has improved dramatically. If you couldn't see the bulb, you wouldn't know whether the light was incandescent or fluorescent. "Daylight" bulbs (left in photo above), which broadcast a whiter light, are available for those desiring a cooler light with less of a yellowish cast.

10

Disposing of CFLs

Q What's the best way to dispose of a spent or broken CFL bulb?

A Manufacturers have taken steps to reduce the amount of mercury in CFLs, but they still contain a small amount—on the average, about 5 milligrams (roughly equivalent to the tip of a ballpoint pen). Special steps should be taken when disposing of CFLs. Recycling options include:

- Many municipalities have hazardous waste facilities that accept broken or spent CFLs. You can find information on sites near you by visiting www.earth911.org. Type your zip code into the "location" box, then click on "Household Hazardous Waste" and "Fluorescent bulbs" to find facilities in your area. Note that most facilities accept hazardous waste only during certain business hours and/or on certain days.
- Some retail stores offer a fluorescent bulb collection service. You may find some in your area by visiting the Web site listed above, then scrolling down to find the "Local Commercial Locations" section. Some ACE and other hardware stores serve as collection sites. Many IKEA stores also take back spent CFLs.
- There are a number of national organizations that can help. The U.S. Environmental Recycling Hotline (877-327-8491) can help you find local collection centers. Additional information for businesses and homeowners can also be found at www.lamprecycle.org.

NEVER send a CFL or other mercury-containing product to an incinerator. If a CFL breaks, sweep up the glass fragments and place them in a sealed plastic bag, along with the wet paper towel you use to pick up stray shards. Don't use a vacuum. Open windows to air out the house.

Special CFLs for special uses

If every American household replaced just one standard incandescent bulb with one high-efficiency compact fluorescent light bulb, enough energy would be saved to light over 2-1/2 million homes for an entire year! There used to be a limited number of compact fluorescent options, but now there are dozens. Here are a few:

TUBE CFLs have one of the smallest overall sizes and are available in a wide range of wattages. Some have a rated life of up to 15,000 hours.

REFLECTOR CFLs are available in a variety of beam spreads for indoor and track lighting applications. Some are dimmable and/or rated for use in recessed light fixtures.

DECORATIVE CFLs are available for fixtures where bulbs are exposed, such as bathroom strip lights or chandeliers. They're available in "candle," "globe," "bullet" and other shapes.

LARGE LOOP CFLs are ideal for ceiling fixtures and torchiere lamps. Many are modular with independent ballasts and bulbs.

Energy-Saving Q&A

How to choose CFL bulbs

Q I've looked at compact fluorescent bulbs at the home center, but I'm not sure what to buy. How do I know which provides as much light as a regular 60- or 100-watt bulb?

A First, look at the lumen rating, not the bulb wattage, to compare real light output. Then buy a compact fluorescent bulb (CFL) with 20 percent more lumens than the incandescent bulb you want to replace. For example, if a 60-watt incandescent bulb has 870 lumens, buy a CFL with at least 1,050 lumens. If you follow wattage guidelines on the package (such as a 13- to 17-watt CFL equals a 60-watt incandescent; a 25- to 27-watt CFL equals a 100-watt incandescent), you may not be satisfied with the light output. This is especially true if you're over 50, because older eyes take in only half as much light as 20-year-old eyes.

Another reason you need more lumens is that the CFL will dim over time. It will lose 20 to 25 percent lumen power after 4,000 hours (40 percent of a CFL's 10,000-hour-rated life). Incandescent bulbs lose minimal lumens, but their life is extremely short compared with that of CFLs.

Finally, while CFLs can last up to 10 times longer than incandescent bulbs, certain circumstances can shorten their life:

- Frequent on-off switching (it's best to use CFLs only in lights that are on more than three hours per day).
- Excessive vibration or impact (you may not want to install CFLs near doors).
- High humidity levels.

SCREW-ON COVER (750 LUMENS WITH COVER)

15 WATTS (900 LUMENS WITHOUT COVER)

New styles in Fluorescent Lighting

Energy-efficient fluorescent lighting will look great in any room— and you'll save on your electric bills

Large pendant light

Wall sconce

What you get

STYLE: These fixtures feature handsome glass shades, not plastic. Many other styles are available through lighting stores and catalogs (see the Buyer's Guide, p. 164).

ENERGY SAVINGS: Fluorescent bulbs consume about one-third as much electricity as a standard incandescent bulb to produce the same amount of light. Choose a fluorescent bulb in the 13- to 17-watt range to replace a 60-watt incandescent, an 18- to 24-watt fluorescent to replace a 75-watt incandescent and a 25-to 28-watt fluorescent to replace a 100-watt incandescent.

NICE LIGHT: The light looks identical to the light from an incandescent bulb. You can't tell the difference if you can't see the bulb.

LONG-TERM SAVINGS: These fixtures use only fluorescent bulbs. The bulbs last 8,000 to 10,000 hours compared with about 1,000 hours for incandescent bulbs. You can expect to save $10 to $40 per bulb before they wear out. The list prices quoted here include the bulb. Retail prices are often lower—sometimes much lower.

Small pendant light

Chandelier

Shade-style wall sconce

Ceiling light fixture

Double wall sconce

Buying tips

For the **biggest savings**, buy fluorescent fixtures for lights that you use at least **two hours a day**. The electricity saved adds up quickly for lights you keep on that long. The electrical savings on heavily used lights will soon make up for the higher purchase price of a fluorescent bulb.

Estimate the amount of light you need, then **go for a brighter fixture.** Fluorescent bulbs dim somewhat over their long (10,000 hours) life span.

You can't put a dimmer switch on most fluorescent fixtures . . . yet. The manufacturers are working on this, but for now, if you want to dim your lights, stick to special screw-in compact fluorescents or incandescent bulbs.

When you're buying an **outdoor fixture**, make sure the fluorescent bulb will **start in cold weather**. Most of these start at temperatures as low as 0 degrees F or lower. However, in cold weather, the bulb will require a few minutes to reach full brightness.

Unless you're highlighting a workbench, countertop or other work space, **buy "warm white"** bulbs (labeled as either 2,700 or 3,000 degrees K) for interior use. "Cool white" light (labeled as 4,000 degrees K) creates a more commercial atmosphere.

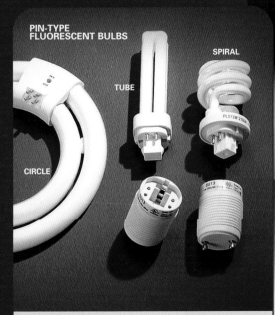

PIN-TYPE FLUORESCENT BULBS

SPIRAL

TUBE

CIRCLE

Globe-style outdoor light

Sconce-style outdoor light

Enclosed-style outdoor light

Fixtures, bulbs and ballasts

The fixtures shown here have a ballast and a pin-type fluorescent bulb that plugs into it (photo above). You can't screw in a standard incandescent bulb or even a screw-base compact fluorescent. The small ballast shown here is used in many of these fixtures. It accepts either spiral- or tube-shape bulbs. However, a ballast accepts bulbs of only one wattage level. You can't switch from a 13-watt bulb to an 18-watt bulb without switching ballasts.

Fixtures with higher light output utilize several small bulbs or one of several circle-type bulbs. These circle bulbs also have pin mounts.

Typically, the bulbs last 10,000 hours and the ballasts about 30,000 hours. At three hours per day, that's almost 10 years for the bulb and 30 years for the ballast! Sometimes you can find replacement bulbs ($5 to $10) at home centers and lighting stores. Pin configurations vary. Take the old bulb with you when you go to buy a replacement to make sure you get the exact same base. You can also order them through a lighting store or from an Internet source. (See the Buyer's Guide.) New ballasts cost $15 to $40. The ones shown above cost about $16. Order them through lighting stores.

Buyer's Guide

FIXTURE MANUFACTURERS
American Fluorescent: (847) 249-5970. www.americanfluorescent.com
Kichler Lighting: (866) 558-5706. www.kichler.com
Sea Gull Lighting: (800) 347-5483. www.SeaGullLighting.com

FLUORESCENT BULBS ONLINE
One online retailer of fluorescent bulbs is www.efi.org, which sells replacement pin-type bulbs as well as screw-base compact fluorescents, including dimmable bulbs. For other sources, type "compact fluorescent bulbs" into a search engine.

Bonus: lighting
handy hints

Fluorescent bulb storage

Safely store extra fluorescent bulbs in jumbo-sized vinyl-clad storage hooks in a handy location near your fixture in the shop, garage or basement. Cut the hooks off one end of a couple of mini bungee cords and use zip ties to attach the severed ends to the top of two vinyl-clad steel storage hooks. Store several fresh bulbs and mark your bad bulbs with a marker and store them until it's time to recycle.

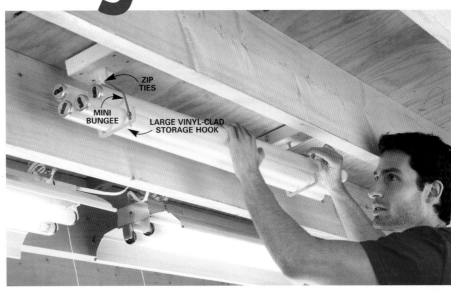

ZIP TIES

MINI BUNGEE

LARGE VINYL-CLAD STORAGE HOOK

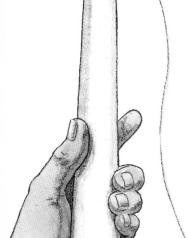

Longer-lasting light for garage door openers

Standard light bulbs can't take much vibration, so they may not survive long in garage door openers. For light that lasts, use a bulb designed to withstand hard knocks. "Rough-use" bulbs cost about $4 at home centers.

Bulb changer

Use this handy gizmo to get light bulbs out of high ceiling fixtures. It's a length of PVC pipe with a hardware store suction cup taped to the end. Just wet the rim of the suction cup, stick it to the bulb, and turn. The trick: make a small hole near the rim with a string attached. This makes it easier to get the suction cup off the bulb once it's in place.

Mark fluorescent bulbs for easy install

Fluorescent light bulbs can be a real hassle to install. You can't see where the prongs are, so you twist this way and that until it feels right. But if the prongs aren't locked in, the bulb can fall out, even though it lights up as usual. The solution is simple: Mark the orientation of the prongs on the bulb with a felt-tip pen.

Install a dimmer switch

ELECTRONIC DIMMER

Dimming a light decreases energy consumption and increases bulb longevity.

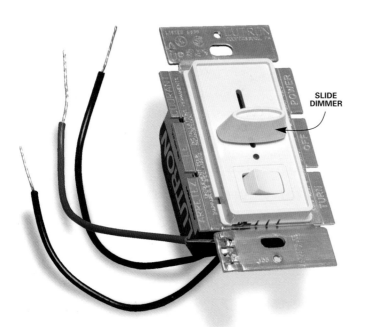

SLIDE DIMMER

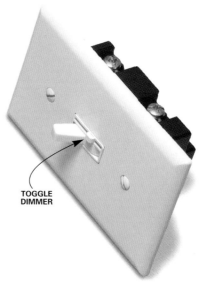

TOGGLE DIMMER

It doesn't take long to replace an ordinary light switch with a full-feature dimmer. But while you're at it, to make your home safer, you should upgrade the wiring to meet the latest requirements of the National Electrical Code. The step-by-step instructions here will show you how to install the dimmer, concentrating on details that will guarantee a safe installation.

The tools you'll need are inexpensive and will come in handy for all your electrical projects. You'll need a screwdriver, wire stripper, inexpensive voltage tester and needle-nose pliers to install a dimmer.

Double-check for hot wires in the box

Turn on the light and have a helper watch as you switch off the circuit breakers, or unscrew the fuses one at a time until the light goes out. Leave this circuit turned off while you work.

In Photo 1, we're using a non-contact voltage detector to double-check for voltage before removing the switch. These detectors are available at hardware stores and home centers for about $12. This type of tester is recommended because it'll detect voltage without direct contact with the metal conductor. That's huge—it means you can check potentially hot wires before you handle them. After you unscrew the switch and pull it away from the box, probe around inside the

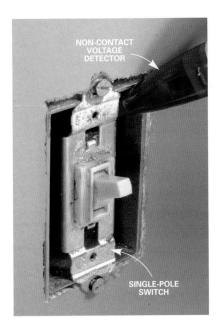

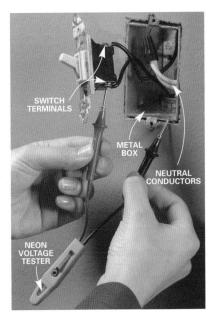

1 TURN off the power at the main circuit panel. Hold the tip of a non-contact voltage tester near each screw terminal to be sure the power is off. Then unscrew the switch and pull it from the box.

2 MEASURE the height, width and depth of metal boxes and refer to Figure A below to determine the box volume. Plastic boxes have their volume stamped inside.

3 TEST for a ground. Turn the power back on. Then place the leads of a voltage tester between each screw terminal and the metal box. If the tester lights, the box is grounded. Caution: Turn off the power again before proceeding.

box with the detector to make sure there are no other hot wires from another circuit.

Make sure the box is large enough

Too many wires and devices stuffed into a box can cause dangerous overheating, short-circuiting and fires. The National Electrical Code specifies minimum box sizes to reduce this risk.

To figure the minimum box size required by the electrical code, add: 1 for each hot and neutral wire entering the box, 1 for all the ground wires combined, 1 for all the clamps combined, and 2 for each device (switch or receptacle) installed in the box. Multiply this figure by 2 for 14-gauge wire and 2.25 for 12-gauge wire to get the minimum box volume in cubic inches.

To help determine the gauge of the wire in your switch box, look at the amperage of the circuit breaker or fuse in the main electrical panel. Fifteen-amp circuits are usually wired with 14-gauge wire and 20-amp circuits require 12-gauge or heavier wire.

Compare the figure you get with the volume of your existing box. Plastic boxes have the volume stamped inside, usually on the back. Steel box capacities are listed in the electrical code. Listed in Figure A is the volume of the most common steel boxes. If you have a steel box, measure it (Photo 2) and consult the chart to see if it's large enough. If your box is too small, replace it with a larger one. It's possible to replace a box without cutting away the wall, but it's a tricky job. It's better to just remove about a 16-in. square of drywall or plaster and patch it after the new, larger box is installed.

Test your ground before you connect it

New dimmers have either a green grounding wire or a green ground screw that you'll have to connect to a grounding source if one is available. Houses wired with plastic-sheathed cable almost always have bare copper ground wires that you'll connect to the dimmer. But test first using the procedure shown in Photo 3 to verify that the wire is connected to a ground.

Some wiring systems, like the one shown, rely on metal conduit for the ground. If you have one of these systems, Photo 3 shows how to test the metal box to verify that it's grounded. If it is, attach a short ground wire to the metal box with either a metal grounding clip

> **Caution:**
> If you have aluminum wiring, don't mess with it! Call in a licensed pro who's certified to work with it. This wiring is dull gray, not the dull orange that's characteristic of copper.

Figure A Common metal box sizes

Height/width/depth (inches)	Volume (cubic inches)
3 x 2 x 2-1/4	10.5
3 x 2 x 2-1/2	12.5
3 x 2 x 2-3/4	14.0

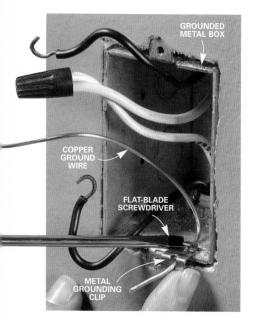

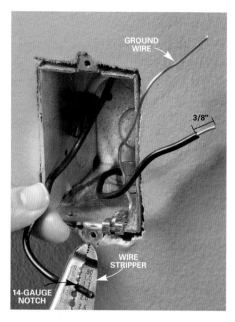

4 PRESS a grounding clip and 6-in. length of bare copper wire onto the metal box with a screwdriver. Cut away a little bit of drywall under the box to provide clearance for the clip.

5 BEND the ground wire back onto the clip and squeeze it down tight so it won't interfere with the dimmer switch.

6 CLIP off the bent end of each wire with the wire cutter. Strip 3/8 in. of insulation from the end of the wires.

as shown in Photos 4 and 5 or a green grounding screw screwed into the threaded hole in the back of the box. Then connect it to the dimmer.

If testing reveals your box isn't grounded, you can still install the dimmer, but you must use a plastic cover plate and make sure no bare metal parts are exposed.

The easy part is installing the dimmer

Some dimmers, like the one shown, have stranded wires attached. Photos 7 and 8 show how to install this type of dimmer. Others have screw terminals instead. For these, strip 3/4 in. of the insulated covering from the wires in the box and bend a loop in each with a needle-nose pliers. Place the loop clockwise around the screw terminals and close the loop around the screws with the needle-nose pliers. Then tighten the screws.

> **Caution:**
> Call an electrician if the original switch is connected to two white wires. This may indicate a dangerous switched neutral.

It doesn't matter if you reverse the two switch wires to a single-pole dimmer. But if you're replacing a three-way switch with a three-way dimmer, label the "common" wire (it'll be labeled on the old switch) when you remove the old switch so you can connect it to the "common" terminal on the dimmer.

In most cases, the two switch wires will be some color other than green or white, usually black. But one of the wires may be white if your house is wired with plastic-sheathed cable (like Romex). Put a wrap of black tape around the white conductor to label it as a hot wire.

Buying dimmers

IF THE SWITCH YOU'RE REPLACING is the only switch controlling the light, buy a standard single-pole dimmer ($5 to $30). If the light can be switched on and off from two or more switches, buy a three-way dimmer switch. But you won't be able to dim the lights from every switch location unless you buy a set of special dimmers (about $70 per pair) with advanced electronics and install one at each switch location.

MOST DIMMERS ARE DESIGNED to handle 600 watts. Add up the wattage of all the light bulbs you'll be dimming. Then read the dimmer package to make sure it can handle the load. Heavy-duty 1,000- and 1,500-watt dimmers are also readily available. Read the package if you'll be installing dimmers side by side in the same electrical box because the wattage rating is reduced to compensate for extra heat buildup.

FINALLY, you have to use a special device, not a dimmer, to control the speed of ceiling fans and motors. Some fluorescent lights can't be dimmed without altering the fixture.

PLASTIC WIRE CONNECTORS

STRANDED SWITCH WIRES

GROUND WIRE

NEW DIMMER

7 HOLD the wires together with the stranded wire protruding about 1/8 in. beyond the solid wire. Match the size of the wire connector you're using to the size and number of wires being connected. Check the manufacturer's specifications on the package to be sure. Twist a plastic wire connector clockwise onto the wires to connect them. Stop twisting when the connector is snug.

NEW DIMMER SWITCH

SCREW TO BOX

8 FOLD the wires neatly into the box. Screw the dimmer to the box with the screws provided. Finish the job by installing the cover plate and turning on the power to test the new dimmer.

MOTION-ACTIVATED LIGHT SWITCH

Instant garage light

Q We would like more light in the garage when we arrive home after dark. The bulb in the garage door opener isn't enough. What's a good solution?

A For more light, simply replace your existing light switch near the door leading to the house (in an attached garage) with a motion-activated switch that works by detecting a moving object that emits heat (such as a person or a car). Not only will this provide automatic instant light when the car arrives home, it also will light up the garage when entering from the house, and then shut off automatically.

The motion-activated switch shown (about $16) allows you to adjust the length of time the lights stay on from 5 seconds to 20 minutes. It also features an adjustable photo cell that can switch the lights on only when it's dark or when it's daylight, too. It also allows for manual on/off switching. Coverage area of the sensor is a 150-degree-wide pattern that senses 15 ft. on the edges of the pattern and 30 ft. dead ahead of the sensor.

When buying the switch, make sure you don't exceed the switch's maximum wattage rating or volt amperage (VA) rating. To calculate it, simply add up the total wattage of all bulbs, and multiply that total by 1.25.

Halogen bulbs —

They burn brighter and are up to 20% more energy efficient. Here's where to use them.

Incandescent

If you're an average homeowner living in the average house, 32 light bulbs will blaze away in your hallway, refrigerator and workshop tonight. The lion's share of those bulbs will be the standard 50¢ incandescent, screw-base type—a bulb based on simple yet ingenious technology that has remained the same throughout its 100-plus year history. But two upstarts are challenging this old standby: compact fluorescent lights (CFLs), because of their tremendous efficiency, and halogen bulbs, because of their longevity and brighter, whiter quality of light. For the lowdown on halogen bulbs, read on.

How halogens are different

Standard incandescent bulbs (Figure A) work on a very simple principle: Electric current passes through a thin tungsten filament inside a gas-filled bulb. The resistance that the filament puts up causes it to heat up and glow. The gas inside the bulb— traditionally, argon—prevents the filament from combining with oxygen and burning out. As the filament glows, microscopic amounts of tungsten burn or evaporate from the filament and are deposited as "soot" on the bulb wall. When enough tungsten has evaporated, the weakened filament finally breaks (usually from the shock of being clicked on) and POOF, you've got a burned-out light bulb.

Halogen bulbs (like the one shown in Figure B) function similarly, but with a few key differences: They're composed of a small, pressurized, peanut-size bulb inside a larger outer shell.

Figure A

When **STANDARD ARGON-FILLED** bulbs glow, minute amounts of tungsten evaporate from the filament and are deposited as "soot" on the inner shell of the bulb. This burned-off tungsten has two drawbacks: The "soot" gradually reduces light output, and it slowly weakens the filament until it becomes thin and breaks and the bulb "burns out."

COST: About 50¢ for a 75-watt bulb
LIFE SPAN: 750 to 1,250 hours
LIGHT OUTPUT: 1,180 lumens for a 75-watt bulb
BEST USES: The best and most affordable all-purpose bulb around. Good for general lighting in bedrooms and other living spaces where you want "soft" light and for fixtures with bulbs that are in the line of sight.

– a brilliant idea

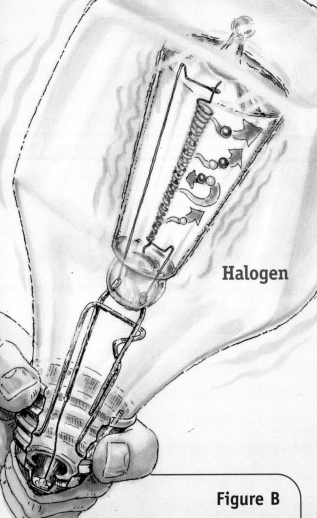

Halogen

The gas inside this inner bulb is halogen. When tungsten evaporates from the filaments of these bulbs, the halogen combines with it, escorts it back to the filament where it's redeposited, then heads out to round up more escaped tungsten particles. Since there's less soot on the bulb's shell, light output remains strong, and since filaments are constantly being rebuilt, the bulbs last longer. But the key difference—and the quality that makes them useful and unique—is they emit a whiter, brighter and more easily focused beam of light, almost like real sunshine.

Bright benefits of halogen lights

The pure white light halogens emit makes them ideal for certain fixtures and situations.

■ For reading and other exacting tasks, the bright light reduces eyestrain.

■ For display lighting, where you want to highlight artwork, photos, crystal or architectural features, the white focused light makes colors appear more vibrant. Halogen spotlights allow pinpoint focus. Using standard bulbs for general lighting in the same room heightens the effect of halogens even more.

■ For outdoor use, halogen floodlights cast a brighter, easier-to-see-by light. And since they last twice as long as standard bulbs, you won't need to struggle to reach hard-to-access outdoor fixtures as often. They have other benefits too. They're 10 to 20 percent more energy efficient and cheaper to operate. They burn brighter longer (a halogen bulb will still be cranking out 94 percent of its original light output near the end of its life, while a standard bulb diminishes to a measly 82 percent).

Of course, not everyone or every place loves halogen. They cost at least four times as much and don't give off that warm glow of a standard bulb we're accustomed to. And they have an intense glare; they need to be shaded, shielded or directed so the filament isn't in your line of sight.

Halogen bulbs burn hotter

Halogen bulbs burn hotter than standard incandescents, so care must be taken in their use. It's possible for the protective outer shell to break and for the inner bulb to continue working (though the outer shells are incredibly durable). This can pose a hazard, as the hot inner bulb can explode if moisture hits it. Dispose of any damaged bulbs just like you would an incandescent bulb. And, as you should do before replacing any bulb, check the light fixture label to make sure a halogen bulb is compatible and within the fixture's listed limits.

Figure B

When high-tech **HALOGEN-FILLED** bulbs glow, small amounts of tungsten burn off the filament, but instead of being deposited on the bulb shell, they combine with argon, which redeposits the tungsten back onto the filament. This has two advantages: The globe isn't darkened by soot, and the filament lasts longer, since it's continuously being "rebuilt."

COST: About $4 for a 75-watt bulb

LIFE SPAN: 2,000 to 2,500 hours (some manufacturers guarantee lights for two years or more)

LIGHT OUTPUT: 1,300 lumens for a 75-watt bulb

BEST USES: In track and recessed fixtures that you want to focus light on a particular area or object; in desktop, reading or other work-area lights where you want bright, focused light; in fixtures that are tough to reach; in banks of light where you want all the bulbs (new or old) to glow at the same intensity.

Tame a hyperactive motion detector

Save you—and your neighbors—from unwanted "trips"

An outdoor motion detector light can save electricity and scare off intruders. But if passing cars or the neighbor's dog constantly triggers the light, you don't get either benefit. To stop unwanted "trips," you have to limit the "detection zone," the area where the sensor can see moving objects.

First, aim the detector. Turn the sensor head right or left and up or down so that its field of vision is roughly centered on the area you want to cover. To make the head stay put, you may have to tighten screws or ring nuts (Photo 2) on the arm that supports the head. Next, set the "on-time" switch to "test" (Photo 1). This will let you determine the detection zone by walking across the detector's field of vision. When it sees you, the light will go on for a couple of seconds. (Your detector may need a one- or two-minute warm-up period before it starts to work.)

If the detection zone in front of the detector is too long, aim the head down slightly. If the zone is too short, raise the head, but keep it at least 1 in. from lightbulbs and lamp covers. When the range is about right, make finer adjustments using the range dial (Photo 1). It may be labeled "range" or "sensitivity." Start with the dial set at the maximum range and turn it down to shorten the zone.

If the zone is still too wide, narrow the lens opening with electrical tape (Photo 2). This is a trial-and-error process that can take a few minutes. Normally, you need to apply narrow blinders only to the right or left ends of the lens, but you can cover as much of the lens as you like. When the length and width of the zone are just right, reset the on-time switch.

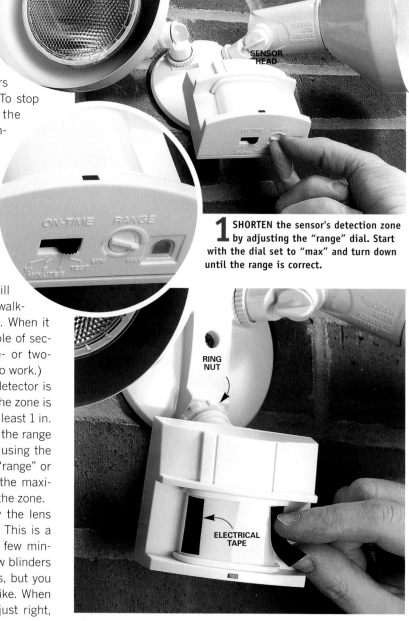

1 SHORTEN the sensor's detection zone by adjusting the "range" dial. Start with the dial set to "max" and turn down until the range is correct.

2 NARROW the detection zone by sticking electrical tape blinders on one or both sides of the sensor's lens.

Three cool, energy-saving light devices

1. Program a light to turn on and off automatically

Replace a light switch with the Programmable Wall Switch Timer and forget it. This device turns all of the lights controlled by a particular switch on and off automatically.

Light stairwells during the night for bathroom runs, turn the lamp on and off to fool cat burglars while you're on vacation, or maybe control the front porch light during prime visiting times. Very cool lighting controller for around $30 plus shipping.

Sporty's Tool Shop, (800) 776-7897, www.sportys.com/shoptool

2. Switching switched lights to motion activated

Wanna have the lights turn on automatically when you walk into a room? It's easy. Just replace the light switch with a motion detector light switch. They're especially useful for rooms where you have to grope in the dark for the switch (think garage) or dangerous areas where good light is imperative (think stairwells). They also have conventional on/off switch positions. You'll find a version in any well-stocked electrical department at home centers or hardware stores. Expect to pay $20 to $50 depending on amperage and quality. If you're just controlling a light, buy a cheap one. If you're switching several lights or lights and an exhaust fan, choose one with higher amperage.

3. Motion-activated porcelain lights

If one of your hobbies is shutting off the storage closet light, take heart. You can install the Automatic Light Socket. It's as easy as unscrewing the light bulb, screwing in the Light Socket and then screwing the bulb back into the unit. It contains a motion detector that detects movement up to 12 ft. away and turns on the light, which stays on for four minutes and then shuts itself off. Around $40 plus shipping.

Sporty's Tool Shop, (800) 776-7897. www.sportys. com/shoptool

FRONT WALK AND FRONT DOOR

DARK OR DEEPLY SHADED AREAS

DECK

DRIVEWAY AND GARAGE

PATIO

BACK WALK AND BACK DOOR

Motion detector lighting

Automatic night lighting when and where you need it.

Why come home at night to a dark door? Or try to walk an icy sidewalk you can't see? Or pay to leave a light on all night when you only need it for a minute or two?

Outdoor lights that are automatically activated by motion detectors can solve all these problems—and others. They'll automatically come on to light up the kids who cut through the yard or the intruder on the deck, and they'll even expose the furry critter that's been raiding your garbage can.

In most cases, motion detector lights are easy to install if you're simply replacing an existing outside light fixture. And they won't cost you a fortune: Prices range from about $25 for a basic two-bulb floodlight—like the one shown here—to about $60 for a decent-quality front door light.

Here you'll learn how motion detector lights work, the best places to put them, and the how tos for a safe and trouble-free installation.

Figure A Motion detector and light styles

1. Flood   2. Decorative   3. Remote

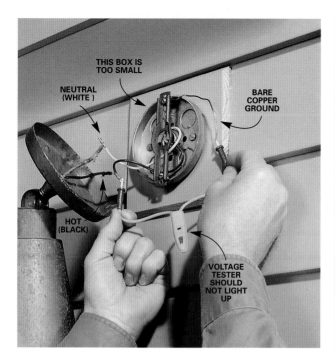

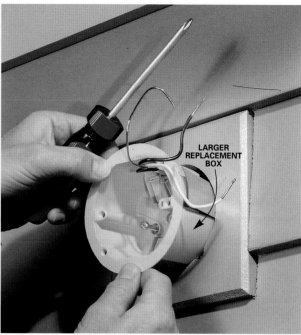

1 TURN OFF the power to the fixture at the main panel, then test the wires to make sure the current is off. Rub one lead of a voltage tester ($3 at hardware stores or home centers) against the ground wire and rub the other lead first against the hot wire (black), then the neutral wire (white). If the tester lights up in either case, the power is still on. Shut off the correct circuit at the main panel.

2 INSTALL a replacement electrical box if your existing box is too small (see "Size Requirements of Electrical Boxes," p. 176). Plastic boxes have the size in cubic inches stamped on them.

How motion detectors work

Motion detectors are small electronic eyes that detect infrared waves—heat waves that radiate from moving objects. When the detector senses an object moving across its field of view—especially warmer objects such as people, animals and cars—it electronically turns on the lights. The light stays on anywhere from 1 to 20 minutes, depending on how you preset the timer. Then the detector automatically shuts the light off unless it continues to sense movement. A photocell deactivates the light during daylight hours.

Most motion detectors have a semicircular field of view of up to 240 degrees and a distance range, adjustable on most detectors, that extends to 70 ft. or more. The detector will react to the movement of your dog, an approaching person, a passing car or sometimes even wind-blown leaves.

Nuisance "trips," such as blowing leaves or a passing car, can fool the detector and turn the lights on when you don't want them. These can be annoying to both you and your neighbors, and in fact, some homeowners won't install motion detector lights for this reason.

However, you can solve most unwanted switching-on by adjusting the distance-range setting and by carefully aiming the sensor to limit its field of view. You can also narrow the field of view even more by applying tape to the sensor, as shown in Photo 7. If nuisance trips concern

you, be sure to buy a light that has an adjustable distance-range setting, and an aimable detector unit as shown in Figure A, Nos. 1 and 3.

Motion detectors allow you to operate the light in the conventional, manual way, usually by flipping the switch off for a second, then back on. This allows you to keep the light on at night when you want to, even when there's no motion. By double-flipping a second time, you return to automatic.

Where to put them

For best effectiveness, position motion detector sensors to cover the walks leading to your front and back doors and the driveway (see large illustration, p. 174). That way the lights will come on when you come home at night. You can also use them to light up decks, patios and any potentially hazardous locations such as around stairways and swimming pools.

If improved security is a priority, position the lights to cover all the approaches to your house, including fence gates, the patio door, the darker areas of your yard, and around trees and bushes. Good lighting can't guarantee security, of course, but it's one of the best low-cost ways to get unwanted intruders to back away.

Ideally, it's best to mount motion detector lights 6 to 10

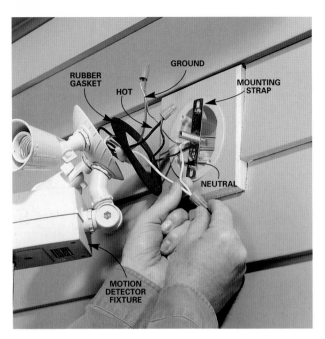

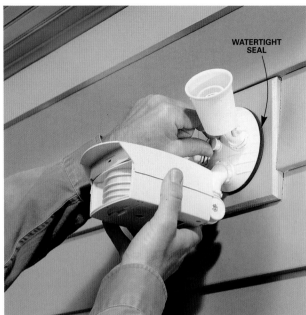

3 MOUNT the light fixture according to the manufacturer's instructions. Run the wires through the rubber gasket. Then connect the neutral wires (white), hot wires (black) and ground wires (green or bare copper) with wire connectors.

4 SCREW the fixture in place. Make sure the rubber gasket seals the edges of the box so moisture can't get in. Apply a bead of clear silicone caulk around the edges if necessary.

Computation table for electrical box size

Wires entering box (neutral and hot)	2
Ground wires (combined total count as 1)	1
Clamps	1
Fixture itself	2
Total	**6**

- 14-gauge wire requires 2 cu. in. space per wire.
- 2 cu. in. wire x 6 wires = 12 cu. in.
- New box = 16 cu. in., so it's large enough.

ft. above the ground and position them so that most movement will occur across the sensitivity zone rather than directly toward the detector.

Obviously you can't always do that if you use existing light locations. One solution is to buy a remote motion sensor unit that you can mount some distance away from the light itself. Remote sensors cost $15 to $25. The wires connecting them to the light are low-voltage and not dangerous, so you don't have to enclose them in metal or plastic conduit.

Installing motion detector lights

Motion detector lights are easy to install, but each brand has a few different details, so read the instructions. You'll find the basic information printed on the outside of the box. Read the box before you buy the unit so you know

what you're getting. You'll find more detailed instructions inside the box.

The step-by-step photos and tips here provide a general guide of how to do the job. In most cases, you'll simply replace an existing fixture with the new one, as shown. Make sure to turn off the power to the fixture at the main panel before removing it.

However, if you have to run a new electrical line and install a switch, the job can get much more complex. Outdoor electrical lines must be encased in approved conduit and weatherproof electrical boxes. If you're not familiar with conduit or the rules for running new electrical circuits, call in a licensed electrician.

Working with old electrical boxes can be tricky too. Sometimes they don't contain a ground wire (bare wire or one with green insulation) or other grounding means such as metal conduit. The National Electrical Code requires all electrical boxes and fixtures to be grounded. If you're not sure yours is, check with your electrical inspector to determine if you have to run a new ground wire.

Size requirements of electrical boxes

You also need to check out the size of your electrical box. A shallow box like the one shown in Photo 1 no longer meets code requirements, and must be replaced with a larger box, as shown in Photos 2 and 3.

The computation table, above left, gives the method for calculating minimum box-size requirements. To do the calculation, count the number of wires coming into the

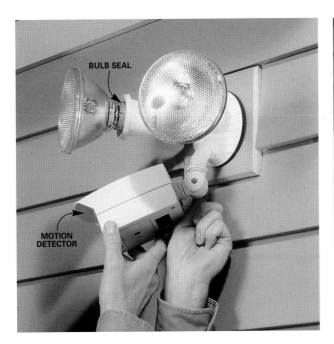

BULB SEAL

**MOTION
DETECTOR**

5 AIM the motion detector at the field of view you want covered. (Later, you can aim the detector lower to reduce the field of view if nuisance trips are a problem.) Point the light bulbs to the area you want lit. Keep the bulbs as far away from the detector as possible.

**RANGE AND TIMER
ADJUSTMENTS**

6 SET the detector's distance range as desired. You can also reduce this later, if necessary, to eliminate nuisance trips. Also set the timer shutoff control. On most units you can choose automatic shutoff after either 1, 5 or 20 minutes.

box. However, some other things besides wires are counted as "wires" for computation purposes. For example, all the cable clamps used count for one wire, and always count the fixture as two wires. Then multiply this total wire number by 2 cu. in. for 14-gauge wire (or 2.25 cu. in. for 12-gauge wire, even if there's just one of the heavier wires in the box).

The computation method given here sometimes overestimates the minimum box size required by code, but it simplifies the calculation.

Additional installation tips

- The cover of an outdoor electrical box must be waterproof. Seat the rubber gasket carefully (Photo 4). And if you are placing it against a rough surface, caulk it as well.
- Moisture can seep into the detector and light sockets and ruin them. To prevent this, either locate the fixture under an eave or other protected area or buy one that has bulb seals (Photo 5) and angle the bulbs downward so water can't run into the socket.
- Heat from the light bulb itself can confuse the detector. Keep the bulb and detector as far apart as possible (Photo 5).
- Adjust the field-of-view angle and set the distance range of your motion detector to avoid nuisance trips from normal passing traffic, animals, pools of water, air conditioners, heating vents and wind-blown trees and shrubs (Photos 5 – 7).
- Get an electrical permit from your local department of

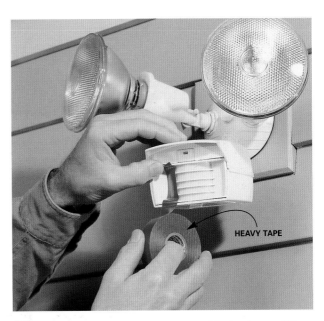

HEAVY TAPE

7 COVER a portion of the detector lens with plastic tape if it becomes necessary to narrow its side-to-side field of view more than the adjustments will allow.

inspections. Check for special local rules and have your work inspected when finished.

- CAUTION: Don't let your ladder or your body touch lethal overhead power lines while you're working.
- CAUTION: Aluminum wiring requires special handling. If you have aluminum wiring, call in a licensed pro who's certified to work with it. This wiring is dull gray, not the dull orange that's characteristic of copper.

Recessed lights
Insulating to prevent heat loss.

BLOW-IN CELLULOSE INSULATION

CEILING DRYWALL

Attic

Living room

HIGH-TEMPERATURE CUTOFF SWITCH

Label

BULB

Recessed-light detail

TRIM

Recessed light fixtures that are rated IC (insulation contact) are designed so that insulation can be installed in direct contact with them. These fixtures have a high-temperature cutoff switch that turns off the lamp if excessive heat builds up. If they cycle on and off, that's the reason.

To resolve the problem: First, check the information on the fixture label (p. 179) to make sure the bulb is an acceptable type and wattage. Second, check the fixture label to make sure the trim is compatible with the housing (p. 179) The wrong trim can trap too much heat inside the fixture housing. Look for a part number on both the housing and the trim and call a supplier to confirm their compatibility. Third, if the housing allows the bulb to be adjusted up and down, move the bulb down. Fourth, the thermal protector might be defective and require replacement. This is a tough one to diagnose. If you have several lights turning on and off, the protectors are probably OK. A single problem light might well have a faulty protector. Call in a licensed electrician to fix it.

If you've tried these fixes and the light is still cycling off and on, build an airtight box around the problem light, as shown. You have to do it from within the attic (not a pleasant working environment!). Cut the box from 2-in.-thick rigid extruded foam board, then glue and screw the joints. Caulk all seams and penetrations from either inside or outside the box. It's important to make the box airtight to keep warm air from escaping into the attic. It provides air space around the fixture to help prevent overheating, yet interior air cannot get into the attic, and your insulation is still intact.

Well-insulated recessed light

AIRTIGHT
CAULKED JOINTS

2" RIGID
INSULATION
BOARD

3" MINIMUM

IC-RATED
FIXTURE
HOUSING

EXISTING
CEILING
JOINT

2'-0"

Manufacturer's label

NOTE: THIS LABEL APPLIES ONLY TO THIS SPECIFIC FIXTURE.

HALO® H5ICAT

WARNING – RISK OF FIRE. USE WITH HALO TRIMS ONLY FOR
EACH LAMP TYPE & WATTAGE INDICATED. SEE TRIM FOR NO.   **IP**

TRIM NO. NO. DE GARNITURE NO. DE BORDILLO	LAMP SIZE AND TYPE PUISSANCE ET TYPE D' AMPOULE TAMANO DE LAMPARA Y TIPO	
5000, 5001	75 WATT, R30 MAX	
5010, 5020	50 WATT, R30 MAX	
5010, 5020	60 WATT, BR30 MAX	
5000, 5001, 5020	75 WATT, PAR30 MAX	
5010, 5060	50 WATT, PAR30 MAX	
5021	40 WATT, A19 MAX	
ERT513	50 WATT, PAR20 MAX	
5001	50 WATT, R20 MAX	
5001, ERT513	65 WATT, BR30 MAX	
5000, 5001, ERT513/WHT	75 WATT, PAR30L MAX	

Suitable for damp locations
convient aux endoits mouilles
Apropiado para zonas humedas

Also listed as suitable for use in wet locations - covered ceiling installation only - when used with HALO shower trim Cat N5 5050p:

Tambien idoneo para uso en zonas mojadas lechos cubierta solo cuando se usen con luz para ducha HALO bordillo Cat N5 5050p:

Maximum of (8) N0 12 AWG through branch circuit conductors Minimum 90 degrees C supply connection.

For trims (para bordillos) 5050p:s 5070 5071 see trim for Lamp type & wattage (vea bordillo para tipo de lampara y valvio)

ADVERTENCIA RIESGO DE INCENDIO

Use con bordillo de HALO solamente para cada tipo de lampara y valios indicados vea bordillo para no

WL – 464

TRIM
NUMBER

TYPE
OF BULB

MAXIMUM
BULB SIZE

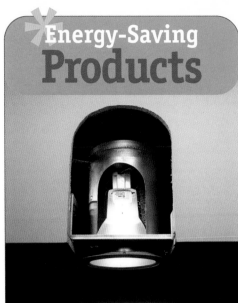
Recessed CFLs

The trend toward energy-efficient lighting has recently expanded to recessed lights. Rather than installing conventional recessed fixtures, you can now install fixtures for fluorescent lights only. Each fixture comes with a built-in ballast and accepts a pin-based compact fluorescent bulb. You'll get the same amount of light using only about one-third the electricity.

The housing, cone trim and light (each sold separately) cost a total of $110 and are available (usually by special order) at lighting stores.

Juno, (847) 827-9880. www.junolighting.com

Long-lasting bulbs for recessed lights

You can save energy by using standard compact fluorescent light bulbs (CFLs) specially designed for use in standard recessed light fixtures. Bulbs with different beam spreads are available to suit a variety of situations, and some are dimmable. And like most other CFLs, they'll last three times as long as their incandescent counterpart. Offered by GE and other bulb manufacturers.

Saving Energy:

*S*aving water may, at first glance, seem to be an oddball inclusion in a book on saving energy, but let's take a second glance. Even a slowly dripping faucet can waste 2,000 to 3,000 gallons of water per year. And if that faucet is dripping hot water, it's wasting the energy used to heat that water as well.

As you can conserve coal, oil and electricity through maintaining and upgrading your heating and cooling systems, you can conserve water—another precious commodity—by maintaining your plumbing systems.

Finally, you can put a stop to the "mental energy" that's wasted while you listen to the annoying drip, drip, drip of an ailing faucet or showerhead.

Conserving Water

Repair
drippy faucets

Leaky faucets waste water and the energy that heats it

Usually the hardest part of repairing a faucet is finding the right replacement parts. Hardware and plumbing supply stores normally carry parts for common models, but if you have a faucet from a small manufacturer, you may have to special-order replacement parts. (Sometimes it's easier to simply replace the whole darn faucet.) Most repair kits include thorough instructions and some of the specialized tools you'll need.

Examine the faucet closely to determine where the leak is coming from. Leaks around the base of a spout require a different repair than a drip from the end of a spout. After you turn off the water supply, open the valve in the center position to relieve water pressure.

Pay close attention to the order and orientation of the parts as you remove them. A digital camera is handy for recording each step in case you forget later. Set the parts aside in the order you removed them. When all the

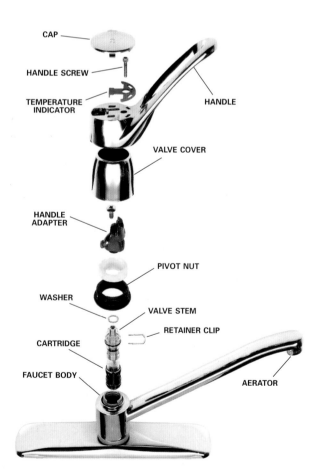

CAP

HANDLE SCREW

TEMPERATURE INDICATOR

HANDLE

VALVE COVER

HANDLE ADAPTER

PIVOT NUT

WASHER

VALVE STEM

RETAINER CLIP

CARTRIDGE

FAUCET BODY

AERATOR

1
Cartridge-type faucet

Cartridges are used in both single- and double-handled faucets. If the levers or knobs on your two-handled faucet turn only 90 to 180 degrees, you most likely have a cartridge-type faucet. On a cartridge faucet, the handle is secured to the faucet by a screw that's hidden under a cap.

To stop drips at the spout or correct problems with hot and cold mixing, remove the cartridge and replace either the O-rings on the cartridge if they're damaged or the entire cartridge.

Don't be surprised if the cartridge seems stuck. It may take considerable force to pull it out. Really stubborn cartridges require the use of a special cartridge-pulling tool.

Quick tip*

PLAN AHEAD
If you don't find shutoff valves under the sink, you may have to turn off the main valve to your entire home. Let your family know ahead of time when you're going to make your repair.

parts are out, inspect the interior of the valve for bits of deteriorated gaskets or mineral deposits. To clean these surfaces, use a cloth or fine-abrasive nylon pad.

Slow water flow can be caused by plugged holes in the faucet body. Use a small screwdriver to clean them out. Before you replace worn parts and reassemble the faucet, hold a rag over the faucet and open the water shutoff valve slightly to flush out loosened debris, catching it in the rag. Here are other tips to remember when you repair a faucet of any type:

- Always take old faucet parts with you to the store to get an exact match.
- Plug or cover drains and strainer baskets to avoid losing small parts.
- Line sink with a towel to prevent dropped tools from damaging it.
- Slow flow is frequently caused by a plugged aerator. Simply remove it, clean it and return it to its place. If it still works poorly, replace it.
- Always pay attention to alignment of parts as you reassemble the faucet.
- Many faucet manufacturers offer a lifetime guarantee. Take them up on it if yours drips or malfunctions.

A faucet dripping at the rate of one drop per second can waste nearly 2,000 gallons of water per year.

2
Ball-type faucet

Water flow and temperature in a rotary-ball faucet are controlled by a hollow plastic or steel ball that rotates in a socket.

If water is leaking around the base of the handle, you may be able to fix it by removing the handle and simply tightening the cap. If it still leaks, replace the O-rings around the faucet body. If the faucet drips from the end of the spout, replace the seats and springs.

Plastic or brass balls are softer than stainless steel balls and can become scratched by debris. Inspect the ball and, if you see damage, replace it with a stainless steel ball. Be sure to align all the parts properly as you reassemble the faucet.

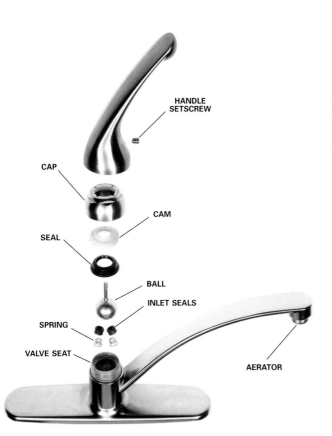

HANDLE SETSCREW

CAP

CAM

SEAL

BALL

INLET SEALS

SPRING

VALVE SEAT

AERATOR

Quick tip*

TOTAL RECALL
Pay close attention to the order and orientation of parts as you remove them. A digital camera comes in handy in case you forget.

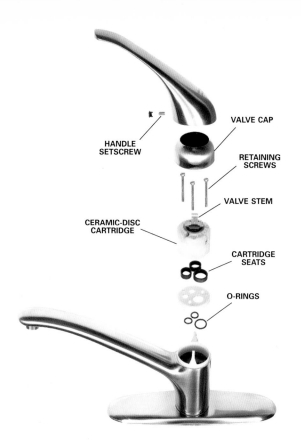

HANDLE SETSCREW

VALVE CAP

RETAINING SCREWS

VALVE STEM

CERAMIC-DISC CARTRIDGE

CARTRIDGE SEATS

O-RINGS

3
Ceramic disc-type faucet

Ceramic-disc faucets are like cartridge faucets, except discs inside the cartridge control the water flow. This type of valve is sturdy and reliable and rarely needs fixing. In fact, many manufacturers offer a lifetime warranty on the cartridge. Leaks can result from faulty rubber seals or a cracked disc inside the cartridge. Since replacement cartridges are expensive, start by replacing the seals and reassembling the faucet. If it still leaks, replace the cartridge.

Quick tip*

TRACKING DOWN PARTS. Look for the brand name stamped on the faucet. Knowing that will help if you need to order new parts.

4
Outdoor-type faucet

Most outdoor faucets, including the freeze-proof one shown, have a washer at the end of the valve stem. Freeze-proof faucets are particularly prone to worn washers because, when the faucet is turned off, it continues to drain for a few seconds; consequently, people tend to turn the faucet tighter, damaging the rubber washer. Before beginning your repair, turn off the faucet's water supply.

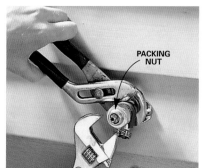

PACKING NUT

1 UNSCREW the handle and remove the packing nut. Hold the faucet steady while loosening the nut to avoid twisting the interior pipe. Even hard copper pipe can be twisted.

2 PULL stem out of faucet. For removal, some stems have to be turned so a key lines up with a slot; reattach handle to turn and pull stem.

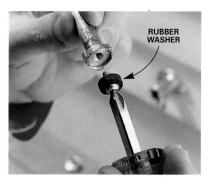

RUBBER WASHER

3 REMOVE and replace rubber washer on the stem end. If there are rubber O-rings on the stem, replace these as well.

5
Washer-type faucet

A leaky faucet has a torturous way of wearing on nerves and water resources. Even a slow drip can waste hundreds of gallons per month. Luckily, most dripping washer-type faucets can be cured in 30 minutes for less than a dollar.

To repair a washer-type faucet, you'll need to replace the washer on the bottom of the valve stem and sometimes the valve seat as well. Replace washers for both the hot and cold water while you're at it, not just the one that's leaking. Before you begin, turn off the water-supply valves and close the sink stopper so small parts won't disappear down the drain.

Most faucet handles are secured by a screw, which is sometimes covered by a snap-on cap or button. You may need to tap, wiggle or pry the handle a bit to remove it. The washer on the end of the valve stem may be flat or beveled. The new washer should be the same profile and fit snugly inside the circular lip without having to be forced.

With your finger, feel down inside the area where the stem assembly enters the faucet to determine whether the valve seat is rough or grooved. If it is, replace it with a new valve seat that exactly matches the old in diameter, height and threads.

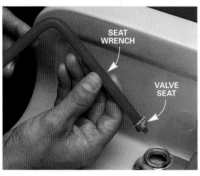

1 REMOVE the screw holding the handle, then loosen and remove the packing nut. Remove the stem assembly.

PACKING NUT

2 REMOVE the worn washer and replace it with the correct type: flat or beveled. The new washer should fit snugly without being forced.

3 USE a seat wrench to remove the worn valve seat. The new seat must match the old one exactly in diameter, height and number of threads.

SEAT WRENCH

VALVE SEAT

4 LUBRICATE the working parts of the stem assembly with heat-proof faucet grease. Reassemble faucet.

HEAT-PROOF GREASE

✻ Energy-Saving Goof

Strike one, you're out!

I needed to replace the ballcock assembly on our running toilet. Once all the nuts were loosened, I tried to remove the assembly, but it wouldn't budge. I decided to give it a little help by gently hitting it with a hammer. Unfortunately, one of my gentle swings missed and hit the side of the tank, splitting it. Now I know to keep my hammer away from the toilet. I also know how to install a new one!

Fix a running toilet

A toilet that runs is both annoying and wasteful

A toilet that won't stop running can drive you crazy, and can waste more than 20,000 gallons of water per year. But there is good news: You can put an end to this water wasting yourself, even if you have no plumbing know-how. You may be able to solve the problem in just a few minutes without spending a dime. At worst, this fix will cost a few hours and $20 in toilet parts.

Finding the problem is usually simple

A toilet runs constantly because the fill valve that lets water into the tank isn't closing completely. A toilet runs intermittently because the valve opens slightly for a few minutes. In either case, you have to figure out why that valve isn't stopping the incoming water flow.

First, look for leaks. A leak in the tank can make a toilet run constantly or intermittently. If your toilet is leaking, you've probably noticed it already. But take a look just to be sure. If you find leaks coming from the tank bolts or flush valve, you'll most likely have to remove the tank from the bowl so you can replace the tank bolts, the rubber washers and the gaskets on the flush valve. If there are leaks around the fill valve, tighten the locknut (see Photo 6, p. 189). Leaks can come from cracks in the tank, too. In that case, the only reliable solution is a new toilet.

If you don't find any leaks, lift off the tank cover. At first glance, the array of submerged thingamajigs inside may look intimidating. But don't let them scare you. There are really only two main parts: the flush valve, which lets water gush into the bowl during the flush; and the fill valve, which lets water refill the tank after the flush. When a toilet runs constantly or intermittently, one of these valves is usually at fault.

To determine which valve is causing the trouble, look at the overflow tube. If water is overflowing into the tube, there's a problem with the fill valve. Fill valve fixes are shown on the next page. If the water level is below the top of the tube, the flush valve is leaking, allowing water to trickle into the bowl. That slow, constant outflow of water prevents the fill valve from closing completely. To fix a flush valve, see pp. 190 and 191.

For these photos, the fronts and backs of new toilets were cut away to show you how to replace these parts. Your toilet won't look so pristine inside. You'll find scummy surfaces, water stains and corrosion. But don't be squeamish—the water is as clean as the stuff that comes out of your faucets.

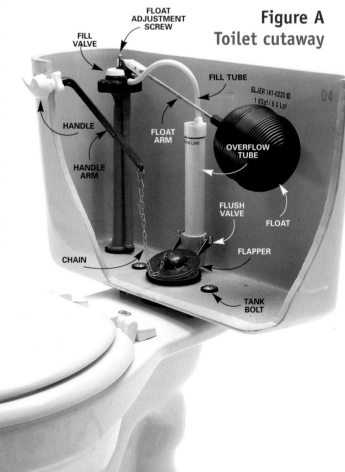

Figure A
Toilet cutaway

FLOAT ADJUSTMENT SCREW

FILL VALVE

FILL TUBE

ELJER 141-0220
1 6Gpf / 6 0 Lpf

HANDLE

FLOAT ARM

WATER LINE

OVERFLOW TUBE

HANDLE ARM

FLUSH VALVE

FLOAT

CHAIN

FLAPPER

TANK BOLT

1
Repair the fill valve

You may have to replace the fill valve, but these three fixes are worth a try first.

Fix 1: Adjust the float

If your valve has a ball that floats at the end of a rod, gently lift the rod and listen. If the water shuts off, you may be able to stop the running by adjusting the float. Some fill valves have a float adjustment screw on top (see Figure A). If there is no adjustment screw, bend the float arm (photo below). If you have a Fluidmaster-style fill valve, make sure it's adjusted properly (Photo 8, p. 189.) You don't have to empty the tank to make these adjustments.

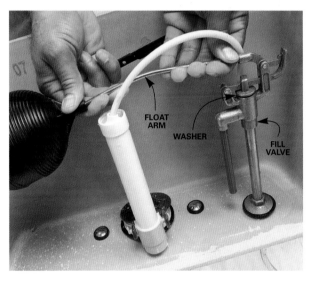

Gently bend the float arm down to put extra pressure on the valve. (To adjust a float that doesn't have an arm, see Photo 8.) Then flush the toilet to see if it works.

Fix 3: Replace the washer

When you remove the cap to flush out the valve, inspect the washer for wear or cracks. Replacing a bad washer is cheap ($1) and easy (photo below). But finding the right washer may not be. The most common washers are often available at home centers and hardware stores. Other styles can be hard to find. If you decide to hunt for a washer, remove it and take it to the store to find a match. Plumbers usually replace the whole fill valve rather than hunt for a replacement washer.

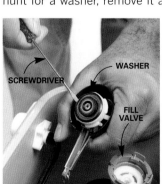

REPLACE a worn, cracked valve washer by prying the old washer out of the cap with a small screwdriver. Press the new one into place.

Fix 2: Flush the valve

Hard water, debris from old pipes or particles from a break in a city water line can prevent a flush valve from closing completely. Running water through it from the supply line will clear the debris. Photos 1 and 2 show you how to do this on one common type of valve. Even though other valves will look different, the clearing process is similar. However, you may have to remove a few screws on top of the fill valve to remove the cap.

1 REMOVE the fill valve cap. On this type of valve, press down and turn counterclockwise. Remove screws on other types of valves.

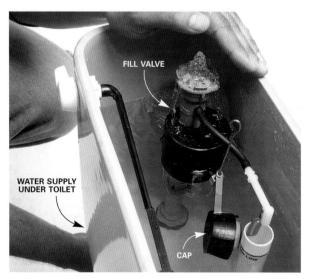

2 COVER the valve with your hand. Turn on the water (cautiously, so you don't get a cold shower!) and let it flush out the valve for a few seconds.

Fix 4: If you can't fix the fill valve, replace it

Replacing a fill valve requires only a few basic tools (adjustable pliers and a pair of scissors) and an hour of your time. A kit containing the type of valve shown here and everything else you need costs about $12 at home centers and hardware stores.

Your first step is to shut off the water. In most cases, you'll have a shutoff valve right next to the toilet coming either through the floor or out of the wall. If you don't have a shutoff, turn off the water supply at the main shutoff valve, where water enters your home. This is a good time to add a shutoff valve next to the toilet or replace one that leaks. This is also a good time to replace the supply line that feeds your toilet (Photo 6). A flexible supply line reinforced with a metal sleeve costs about $7 at home centers and hardware stores. Photos 1 – 8 show how to replace the valve. If the height of your valve is adjustable, set the height before you install the valve (Photo 5). If your valve is a different style from the

1 REPLACE the fill valve. Turn off the water at the shutoff valve. Flush the toilet and hold the flush valve open to drain the tank. Sponge out the remaining water or vacuum it up with a wet/dry vacuum.

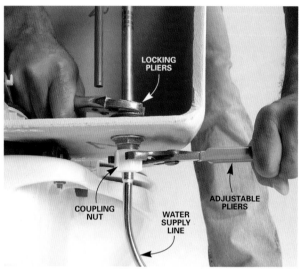

2 UNSCREW the coupling nut that connects the supply line. If the valve turns inside the tank, hold its base with locking pliers. Tip: Throw a towel on the floor underneath to catch water that will drain from the line.

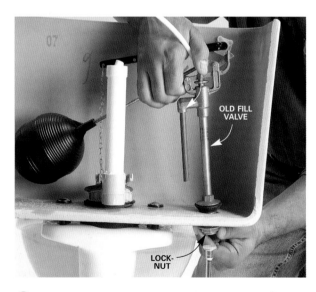

3 REMOVE the locknut that holds the valve to the tank. Push down gently on the valve as you unscrew the nut. Pull out the old valve.

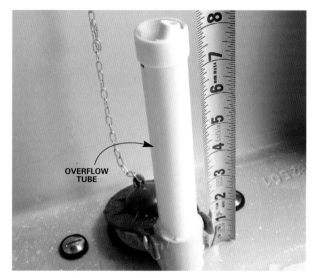

4 MEASURE the height of the overflow tube. Measure to the top of the tube, not to any water level label on the tube.

one shown, check the directions. After mounting the valve (Photo 6), connect the fill tube (Photo 7). The fill tube squirts water into the overflow tube to refill the toilet bowl. The water that refills the tank gushes from the bottom of the fill valve. When you install the valve and supply lines, turn the nuts finger-tight. Then give each another one-half turn with pliers. When you turn the water supply back on, immediately check for leaks and tighten the nuts a bit more if necessary.

Quick tip*

WASTE NOT, WANT NOT. A leaking toilet can waste 55 gallons of water per day or more. It pays to fix it fast! And don't worry about putting your hand in the tank. The water is the same as what comes out of the tap.

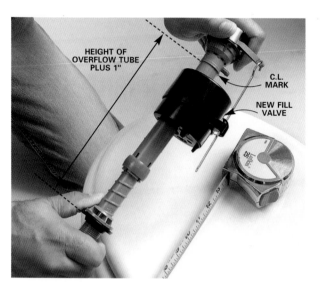

5 ADJUST the height of the new fill valve by holding the base and twisting the top. The height from the base to the CL (critical level) mark should be the height of the overflow tube plus 1 in.

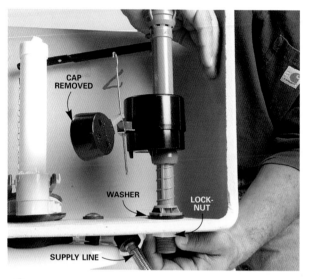

6 REMOVE the cap, press down to compress the washer and screw on the locknut. Connect the supply line and flush the valve as shown in Photo 2, p. 187. Reset the cap and check for leaks.

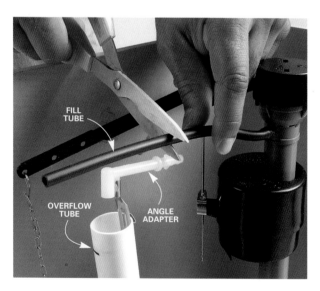

7 SLIP the fill tube onto the fill valve. Clip the angle adapter onto the overflow tube. Then cut the tube to fit and slip it onto the angle adapter.

8 TURN on the water to fill the tank. Pinch the spring clip and slide the float up or down to set the water level 1 in. below the top of the overflow tube or to the water line marked on the tank.

2
Fix the flush valve

When a flush valve causes a toilet to run, a worn flapper is usually the culprit. But not always. First, look at the chain that raises the flapper. If there's too much slack in the chain, it can tangle up and prevent the flapper from closing firmly. A chain with too little slack can cause trouble too. Photo 3 on p. 191 shows how to set the slack just right.

Next, test the flapper as shown in Photo 1. If extra pressure on the flapper doesn't stop the running-water noise, water is likely escaping through a cracked or corroded overflow tube. In that case, you have to detach the tank from the bowl and replace the whole flush valve. Since the overflow tube is rarely the cause of a running toilet, that repair is not shown here.

If pressing down on the flapper stops the noise, the flapper isn't sealing under normal pressure. Turn off the water, flush the toilet to empty the tank and then run your finger around the rim of the flush valve seat. If you feel mineral deposits, clean the flush valve seat with an abrasive sponge or ScotchBrite pad. Don't use anything that might roughen it. If cleaning the flush valve seat doesn't solve the problem, you need to replace the flapper.

Replacing your flapper may require slightly different steps than we show (Photos 2 and 3). Your flapper may screw onto a threaded rod or have a ring that slips over the overflow tube. If you have an unusual flush valve, finding a replacement flapper may be the hardest part of the job. To find a suitable replacement, turn off the

1 PUSH down on the flapper with a yardstick and listen. If the sound of running water stops, the flapper needs replacing.

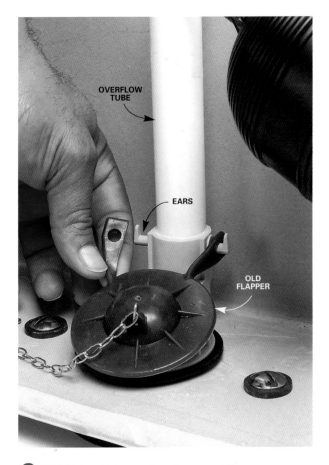

2 REMOVE the old flapper from the ears of the overflow tube and detach the chain from the handle arm.

water, take the old one with you to the home center or hardware store. (Turn off the water before removing the flapper.) You may not find an identical match, but chances are you'll locate one of the same shape and diameter. If not, try a plumbing supply store (in the yellow pages under "Plumbing Supplies") or search online (a good source is www.doplumb.com). It helps to know the brand and model of your toilet. The brand name is usually on the bowl behind the seat. In some cases, the model or number will be on the underside of the lid or inside the tank. Matching an unusual flapper can become a trial-and-error process. Even professional plumbers sometimes try two or three flappers before they find one that works well.

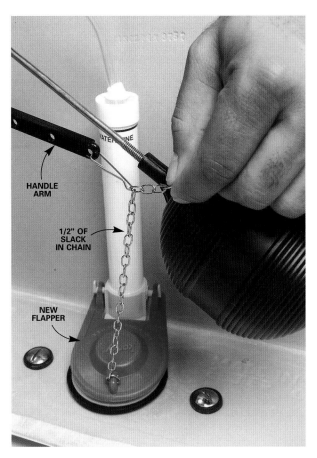

3 ATTACH the new flapper to the overflow tube and hook the chain to the handle arm. Leave 1/2 in. of slack in the chain. Turn the water back on and test-flush the toilet.

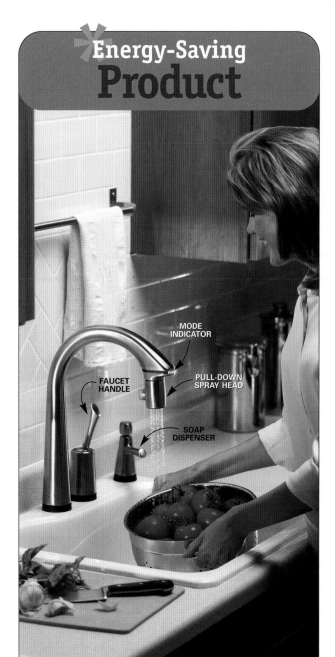

Hands-free kitchen faucet

When your hands are full, you don't want to set down your load to turn on the kitchen faucet. With a hands-free faucet like this one from Brizo (www.brizo.com), you don't have to. Water starts and stops when you lightly tap the faucet or use the hands-free feature. Pulling out the spray head also turns on the water.

The "Smart Technology" on/off switch distinguishes between the pan sitting in the sink and a pan placed under the faucet to be rinsed. You can also turn the faucet on conventionally with the handle.

In search of the perfect flush

Toilet technology puts an end to wasted water

In 1994 Congress decided to conserve water by requiring toilets to use no more than 1.6 gallons per flush. It was a good idea, but when manufacturers came out with their first water-saving models, they hadn't yet figured out how to make toilets perform as well as before (most toilets at that time used 3.5 gallons or more). So homeowners got stuck with toilets that required two or even three flushes to clear and clean the bowl. These wimpy toilets plug up more often too. Their design is poor, and there isn't much you can do to improve them. The only real solution is a new toilet.

Manufacturers have refined old designs and developed entirely new systems to make water-saving toilets work better. But there are still some weak flushers out there, so do some research before you buy (see below). When you're shopping, you'll find three types of flushing systems:

Quick tip*

TO SEE HOW WELL 80 TOILET MODELS CLEARED SOLID WASTE in a recent laboratory test, go to: www.cwwa.ca/home_E.ASP. Click on "CWWA Maximum Performance Testing of Popular Toilets Reports."

FOR REAL-WORLD EXPERIENCE AND OPINIONS on various models from plumbers and homeowners, click on "Terry Love's Report on low-flow toilets" at www.terrylove.com.

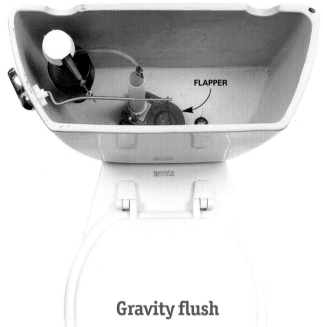

FLAPPER

Gravity flush

This is the system toilets have used for over a century: The flush valve (flapper) opens and water rushes down through the bowl. Manufacturers have steadily improved tank and bowl designs to create a more powerful flush with less water. One of the most effective improvements was to simply enlarge the flush valve from 2 in. to 3 in. or more.

Pros:
- **Cost.** Some of the models that perform well in lab tests cost as little as $150.
- **Easy to maintain.** Diagnosing problems and finding replacement parts is relatively easy.

Cons:
- **Tanks can sweat.** If condensation forms on the tank of your current toilet, the same problem will likely occur with any gravity toilet.
- **Big differences in performance.** There are still a lot of wimpy flushers out there. You have to do your homework to find a model that performs well (see "Quick Tip," at left).

Quick tip*

PUT IT TO THE TEST. Pressure-assist toilets are common in public restrooms, so you can take one for a test drive at an office or business. Just lift the tank lid and look for the pressure tank to see if it's a pressure-assist model.

Pressure-assist

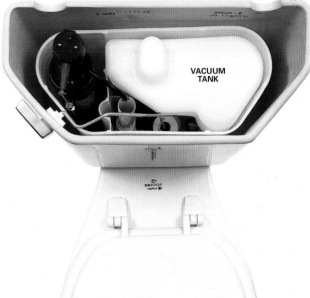

Vacuum-assist

These toilets have a pressure tank inside that works like a big water balloon. Water fills the tank and is held there under pressure. When the flush valve opens, pressure and gravity combine for an explosive flush.

Pros:

- **Powerful flush.** When it comes to clearing the bowl of solid waste, pressure-assist models generally outperform other types.
- **No sweat.** Because water is held inside a pressure tank rather than the porcelain tank, condensation won't occur on the outside of the toilet.

Cons:

- **Cost.** Starting at about $240, pressure-assist models cost more than some of their cousins.
- **Repairs.** Diagnosing problems, finding parts and making repairs can be a headache.
- **Noise.** Pressure-assist toilets create a loud flush.

This is the latest flush innovation. The porcelain tank contains a vacuum tank that's connected to the trapway (the large tube that carries water out of the bowl). When the toilet is flushed, water flowing out of the tank creates suction in the vacuum tank and trapway to help suck waste out of the bowl.

Pros:

- **Easy repairs.** Vacuum-assist toilets use the same type of fill and flush valves as gravity models, so they're simple to repair.
- **Strong flush.** Vacuum-assist toilets do well in lab tests. In clearing solid waste, they outperform most gravity types but don't do as well as many pressure-assist models.
- **No sweat.** Like pressure-assist models, vacuum-assist toilets store water in an inner tank, so condensation won't form outside the porcelain tank.

Cons:

- **Cost.** Starting around $180, vacuum-assist models cost slightly more than some gravity models.
- **Limited choices.** There are currently only two vacuum-assist toilets from major manufacturers: Briggs' Vacuity (www.briggsplumbing.com) and Crane's VIP Flush (www.craneplumbing.com).

Water-conserving sprinklers

Lower your water bill by watering smart

When it comes to saving water when watering a square garden, you have two great choices: a rotary sprinkler with a fairly square pattern that matches your garden size, and a rotary impact sprinkler with a circular pattern larger than your square garden (see photos below and p. 195).

Oscillating sprinklers (not shown) aren't water efficient. Any sprinkler that produces a fine mist or launches water skyward will cause water to evaporate as well as be blown off target. Oscillating sprinklers also lack uniform coverage because the water delivery rate tends to be much heavier at the sides than at the center of the pattern.

A good rotary sprinkler will deliver a fairly square pattern and water a square garden evenly. Check the box to determine its maximum coverage area. This sprinkler type will be suitable for more soil types as well. You can reduce the water volume for slower watering of poorly absorbing, heavy clay soils, or increase the volume for faster-absorbing sand or loam soils. The goal is to make sure all the water is absorbed, not running away from the garden. While reducing water volume does reduce coverage, it adds versatility beyond your garden. Your sprinkler will fit smaller flower beds or limited landscaped areas. Wheels on the sprinkler help when you're moving it.

Rotary Sprinklers
- Uniform water coverage
- Irrigation speed adapts to soil types

Pulsating sprinklers (rotary impact)

- Fairly uniform water coverage
- Highly adjustable pattern

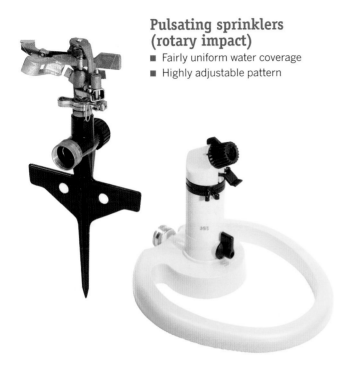

The second choice is a rotary impact (or pulsating) sprinkler (shown above). It uses a water-driven flapper that hits an anvil and drives the nozzles in a circular pattern. Most models are highly adjustable, from changing the circle diameter to watering a portion of a circle and to changing droplet size. You'll have some water waste covering a square garden with a larger circle, and coverage isn't as uniform as it is with the rotary sprinkler. However, they do a good job of keeping water close to the ground to minimize drift and reduce evaporation.

A 72-in.-tall pulsating sprinkler (not shown) is very useful for large gardens as plants grow and become tall enough to interfere with sprinkler patterns. An elevated sprinkler is more costly, but you can always build a platform or use a bucket to elevate your sprinkler above your tall tomatoes.

Finally, it's smart to measure the amount of water you apply. A good rule of thumb is to make sure your garden gets an inch of rainfall or irrigation per week, wetting the top 3 to 5 in. of soil. And it's always best to water in the morning, giving plants the rest of the day to dry so leaf diseases won't develop.

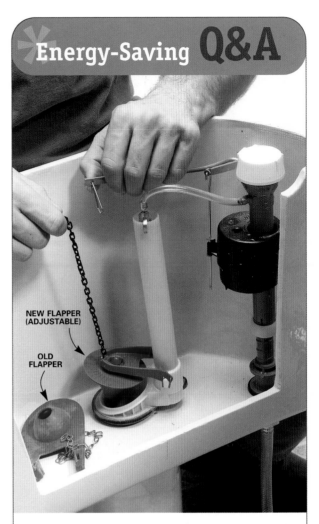

NEW FLAPPER (ADJUSTABLE)

OLD FLAPPER

Two flush fine; one doesn't

Q I recently installed three identical toilets in my home. Two flush fine, but the flapper on the third falls back and stops the flush too soon. I wind up flushing it two or three times, which wastes water. I've tried adjusting the chain length and water level, but nothing has helped. What else can I do?

A Most likely the problem toilet developed a manufacturing defect in the bowl or passages during the casting process. Defects can occur on any toilet but are more often found in lower-priced types. The easiest solution is to experiment with different flappers. You can usually find a variety of them at home centers and hardware stores. Start with one that's similar to the original. Then try one of the adjustable types, which you can set to stay open longer. Keep in mind that any flapper that solves the problem will probably increase the flush volume, from the standard 1.6 gallons to the 2- to 3-gallon range, but you'll still save water in the long run. As a last resort, take the toilet out and return it.

Micro Irrigation

Use less water and spend less time watering

Whether you're growing roses to win prizes or just trying to keep a few flower beds looking good, you know that keeping your plants well-watered is critical. Micro irrigation—a network of plastic tubing and low-volume drippers and sprinklers that reach every part of the garden you want to water—takes the hassle out of watering and keeps your water utility bill to a minimum by putting water only where it's needed.

The materials are inexpensive (you can get started for less than $100) and easy to install, using nothing more than a pruning shears and a special hole punch tool. Once you lay out the tubing and connect the drippers, sprinklers or sprayers, you'll be able to water your plants by simply turning on the water and letting it run for an hour or two. Add a battery-operated controller for about $40 more and you won't even have to remember to turn

on the water. It'll turn the water on and off automatically at the times you select.

Micro irrigation saves more than time and energy; it saves water by distributing it more efficiently. Because you use dozens of watering devices to replace one regular sprinkler, you have much greater control over where the water goes and how much is supplied to each plant. Instead of flooding the ground all at once, micro irrigation lets you apply a small amount over longer periods, allowing it to soak into the plants' root zone for maximum benefit. And since runoff and evaporation are kept to a minimum, micro irrigation uses less water.

Here you'll learn the basics of micro irrigation, including planning tips and step-by-step installation instructions. For more details, especially in the planning phase, read through one of the manufacturers' free planning guides or browse the Internet sites we've listed (see Buyer's Guide on p. 200).

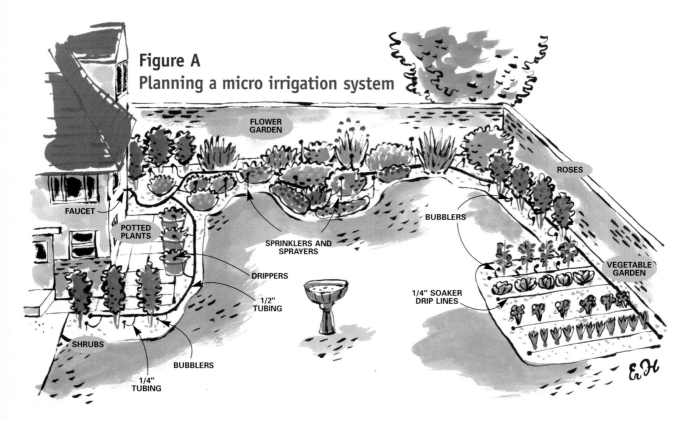

Figure A
Planning a micro irrigation system

FLOWER GARDEN

ROSES

FAUCET

BUBBLERS

POTTED PLANTS

SPRINKLERS AND SPRAYERS

VEGETABLE GARDEN

DRIPPERS

1/4" SOAKER DRIP LINES

1/2" TUBING

SHRUBS

BUBBLERS

1/4" TUBING

1 MOUNT a "Y" with shutoff valves to your faucet. Then attach the (optional) timer, backflow preventer, filter, pressure regulator and adapter.

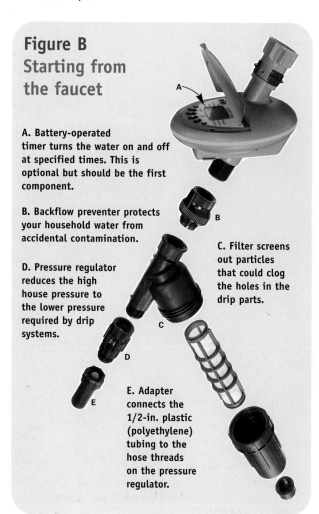

Figure B
Starting from
the faucet

A. Battery-operated timer turns the water on and off at specified times. This is optional but should be the first component.

B. Backflow preventer protects your household water from accidental contamination.

C. Filter screens out particles that could clog the holes in the drip parts.

D. Pressure regulator reduces the high house pressure to the lower pressure required by drip systems.

E. Adapter connects the 1/2-in. plastic (polyethylene) tubing to the hose threads on the pressure regulator.

Make a sketch and plan the system

If this is your first venture into micro irrigation, start small and experiment to get a feel for how the system works. Choose one or two flower beds or a garden and install a simple one-zone system.

The basic planning strategy is to pick the best watering device to serve each type of plant. Then determine a flow rate that supplies adequate water to every plant in the watering zone. Set up the system to run between one and two hours at a time, two or three times a week.

Start by measuring your garden and making a simple sketch. Choose the type and flow rate of the watering devices based on your soil and the plants' water needs. Mark these on the plan and draw in the tubing route to connect them. This will involve a little guesswork. See "Drippers, bubblers, sprinklers and sprayers" on p. 201 for information that will help you choose the right watering device. Try to cover all the root zones of your plants. Don't worry about getting everything perfect at first. Add a few extra of each type of watering device and buy the watering devices, tubing and the basic parts shown in Figure B for the faucet hookup. Once you see how the system works, you'll find it's easy to relocate or add emitters to get a more balanced water flow or better coverage.

Planning rules of thumb:
- Use 1/2 gallons per hour (gph) drippers in clay soil, 1-gph drippers in loam and 2-gph drippers in sandy soil.
- Add the gph rate of all drippers, bubblers, sprayers and sprinklers you plan to use. If you're using 1/2-in. tubing for the main line, limit the total to between 150 and 220 gallons per hour (check with the manufacturer).
- Limit the length of 1/2-in. tubing on one zone to a maximum of about 200 ft.
- Limit the total gph on a length of 1/4-in. tubing to 25 to 30.
- If you're burying lines, call (888) 258-0808 to have your underground utilities marked.

As you add to the system, it's best to divide your yard into groups of plants that have similar watering requirements. With this strategy, you add a separate system (zone), starting at the water source, for each group of plants or area of the yard.

For help with planning a large, more complicated system (and for the best prices), work with a retailer that specializes in micro irrigation (see Buyer's Guide on p. 200).

Begin at the outside faucet

Figure B and Photo 1 show the parts you'll need and the order in which to install them. The Y-splitter with shutoffs allows you to keep the drip system on all the time (and

1/2" POLY TUBING

2 CONNECT the 1/2-in. poly tubing to the faucet end. Then lay the tubing through the garden according to your plan. Stake it down about every 5 or 6 ft.

operated by a controller) and still use your regular garden hose (Photo 1). You don't have to use a controller, but you must use a backflow preventer. Some of these components are available with hose thread or pipe thread, so make sure to match the thread type when you buy parts. Joining hose thread to pipe thread will result in leaks.

Lay the 1/2-in. tubing

Next, run the 1/2-in. tubing to the garden bed (Photo 2) and position it according to your plan. The tubing will be more flexible and easier to work with if you let it sit in the sun for a while to warm up. Remember, you can cover the tubing with decorative mulch later to hide it. Cut the tubing with pruning shears. Use T-fittings to create branches and elbows to make 90-degree bends (Photo 3). Be aware that there are a few different sizes of what's called "1/2-in." tubing, depending on which brand you use. Buy fittings to match the brand of tubing you're using. If you need to join two different brands of tubing or you're not sure which you have, you can buy universal fittings that will work on all diameters of tubing. Use special plastic tubing clamps to nail the tubing to the house or deck.

You can bury 1/2-in. poly tubing in a shallow trench to conceal it as it crosses a path or small section of lawn, but for longer lengths, especially in high-traffic areas, we recommend substituting 1/2-in. PVC pipe instead. Buy adapters to connect the 1/2-in. poly tubing to the ends of the PVC pipe. Check with your local plumbing inspector before burying any pipe to see whether special backflow prevention is required.

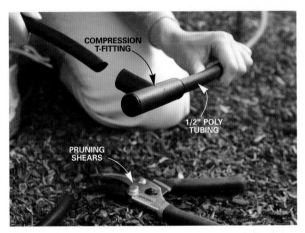

COMPRESSION T-FITTING

1/2" POLY TUBING

PRUNING SHEARS

3 CUT the tubing with a pruning shears and install T- and 90-degree fittings where they're needed. Twist and press the tubing firmly into the fitting.

HOLE PUNCH TOOL

1/2" POLY TUBING

4 PUNCH holes in the tubing wherever you want to install a watering device. Push and twist until the tip of the punch creates a clean hole.

Connect the emitters

Now add the various types of emitters for the particular plants—drippers, sprayers, sprinklers or drip line. The technique is simple. Use a hole punch tool to poke a hole in the tubing wherever you want to add a watering device (Photo 4). You can insert a dripper directly into the hole in the 1/2-in. tubing or use a barbed connector and connect a length of 1/4-in. vinyl tubing. Then connect a watering device to the end of the 1/4-in. tube (Photo 6).

You can buy sprinklers and sprayers as assemblies that include a barbed connector, a short length of 1/4-in. tubing and a plastic stake (Photo 5), or buy the parts separately and assemble them yourself. Remember to buy a selection of 1/4-in. barbed fittings, including T-fittings, elbows, connectors and hole plugs. You can press any of these fittings into a punched hole in the 1/2-in. line and connect 1/4-in. tubes to feed the emitters. T-fittings allow you to

BARBED CONNECTOR

run 1/4-in. tubing in opposite directions from the main line or to branch off a 1/4-in. tube. Use connectors to extend a 1/4-in. tube that's too short. If you punch a hole in the wrong spot or want to remove a fitting, push a hole plug into the hole to seal it.

When your installation is complete, run water through the tubing to flush out any dirt. Then cap the ends (Photo 7). Now you're ready to turn on the water and see how your new micro irrigation system works. Let the water run for an hour. Then check around your plants to make sure the root zone has been thoroughly wetted. Fine-tune the system by adjusting the length of time you water or by adding or relocating watering devices.

Maintain your system

- Clean the filter once a month (more often if you have well water with a lot of sediment).
- Inspect the drippers occasionally to make sure they're working.
- In cold climates, prepare for winter by removing the shutoff Y-splitter, backflow preventer, controller, filter and pressure regulator and bringing them inside. Remove end plugs and drain or blow the water out of the system. Replace the caps and plug the faucet end of the tubing as well.

Buyer's Guide

DIG Irrigation Products: (800) 322-9146. www.digcorp.com.

DripWorks: (800) 522-3747. www.dripworks.com.

The Drip Store: (866) 682-1580. www.dripirrigation.com.

Raindrip: (800) FOR-DRIP. www.raindrip.com.

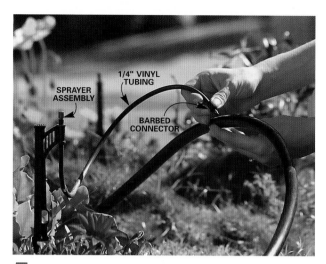

5 PRESS a barbed connector into the hole in the 1/2-in. tubing. If the 1/4-in. tubing isn't already attached, add a length of 1/4-in. tubing to reach your dripper, sprayer or sprinkler location.

6 PRESS pressure-compensating (PC) drippers, sprinklers or sprayers onto the end of the 1/4-in. tubing. Use a stake to support the dripper and anchor it in the root zone of the plant.

7 FLUSH the system by running water through it. Then use end cap fittings to close the open ends of the 1/2-in. tubing.

Drippers, bubblers, sprinklers and sprayers

One of the first things you'll notice when you're browsing the brochures or Web sites is a wide variety of watering devices. Here are the basic types and a few things you need to know about each one. While the ones shown here are the most common, there are many other, more specialized emitters. See the micro irrigation catalogs for the other types and their uses.

Drippers (20¢ to 70¢ each)

Use these to water individual plants, or buy "inline" drippers and use them in a series with a 1/4-in. tube. Drippers work great for container plants too. They're color-coded for different flow rates between 1/2 and 4 gph. In general, use lower flow rates for less porous soil, like clay, to allow more time for the water to soak in. Buy pressure-compensating (PC) drippers to maintain a steady flow despite the water pressure.

MIKE KRIVIT

Bubblers (45¢ to 70¢ each)

A cross between drippers and sprayers, many bubblers are adjustable for flows up to 35 gph and diameters to 18 in. Since they put out more water than drippers, they're good for larger plants like roses, tomatoes and shrubs.

Sprinklers (45¢ to $2 each)

These are miniature versions of sprinklers you might use in the yard. Most have flow rates between 14 and 40 gph and cover a radius of 3 to 30 ft. Since most sprinklers have a relatively high flow rate, you can't use more than about 15 or 20 in one zone of 1/2-in. tubing.

Sprayers (45¢ to $1.70 each)

These are like sprinklers without moving parts. You can choose a spray pattern from a quarter circle up to a full circle, or buy sprayers with adjustable spray patterns. They spray from 4 to 34 gph and up to a radius of about 12 ft. Use sprayers to water ground cover or densely planted flower beds.

Soaker drip line (20¢ to 35¢ per linear foot)

Also called emitter tubing, drip line consists of 1/2-in. or 1/4-in. tubing with built-in drippers. It's available with emitters spaced different distances apart for different flow rates. Drip line is great for vegetable gardens or rows of plants. You can use it to encircle shrubs and large plants, or lay it out in a grid pattern as a substitute for sprinklers in a densely planted flower bed. Use 1/4-in. drip line for maximum flexibility.

Repair drippy showers

OLD CARTRIDGE

NEW CARTRIDGE

Constant dripping wastes water and wears on nerves

When your single-handle shower faucet drips and drips, refusing to completely turn off, don't assume you have to replace the whole faucet. Most faucets can be repaired in an hour for less than $50.

Shown here are the fixes for a cartridge-style faucet. Cartridge valves have a single handle and operate when the cartridge slides in and out. Don't confuse them with single-handle ball-style faucets, which have a dome-shaped casing under the handle.

Turn off the water at the fixture shutoff valves or at your home's main valve. Turn on a faucet to make sure the water is off. Remove the handle as shown in Photos 1 and 2. If the handle sticks, try heating it with a hair dryer set on "hot." If you still can't get it off, use a special handle puller ($10 to $20 from a plumbing parts distributor or home center).

Virtually every faucet manufacturer has a different method of securing the cartridge to the faucet body. Look for a clip or spring and remove it (Photo 3). Cartridges are often difficult to pull out. Some manufacturers

HANDLE SCREW

HANDLE CAP

HANDLE KNOB

H

1 TURN OFF the water supply to the shower. Then pry off the handle cap with a small pocketknife to expose the internal handle screw.

2 LOOSEN and remove the handle screw. Pull off the handle and set it aside.

include a removal cap with new cartridges. Align the cap with the old cartridge ears and try to twist the cartridge loose. Then pull it out with pliers.

If you can't budge the old cartridge, you'll need a cartridge puller ($20 to $30 from a plumbing parts distributor). Make sure the one you buy works on your brand of faucet. Look on the handle or trim for the faucet brand or manufacturer. A knowledgeable person at a plumbing parts store may be able to identify the brand and model from a photo. Review Photos 4 and 5 for instructions on using a cartridge puller. Make sure

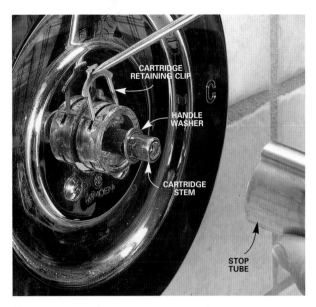

3 PULL OFF the stop tube. Pry up the cartridge retaining clip with a small screwdriver or awl. Remove the handle washer and then twist the cartridge stem loose and pull it out with pliers.

you twist the cartridge loose before pulling it out (Photo 4). Take the old cartridge with you to a plumbing parts store or a home center to find an exact replacement ($15 to $25).

Lubricate the cartridge sides, O-rings, retaining clip, cartridge stem and handle screw threads with plumber's grease. Slide the new cartridge into the faucet body. Some cartridges can only be installed one way (to avoid reversing the hot and cold), so follow the enclosed instructions. Reassemble the remaining faucet components.

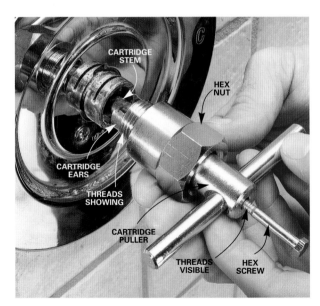

4 IF IT'S STUCK, use a special cartridge puller. Unscrew the hex screw and hex nut until threads are visible. Slide the puller over the cartridge stem, aligning the tool ears with the cartridge notches, and twist to loosen.

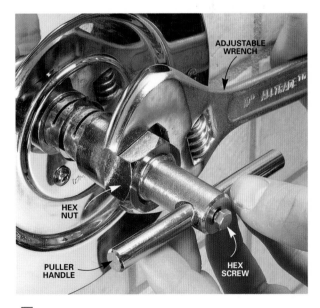

5 TURN the hex screw by hand until it bottoms out. Snug up the hex nut by hand and tug on the cartridge puller handle. If the cartridge won't pull out, hold the puller handle steady and tighten the hex nut two full turns. Pull the cartridge out of the faucet body. Buy an identical replacement cartridge, align it properly and reassemble the parts.

Inspect your tires!

And improve your gas mileage

Most drivers don't give their tires a second thought until they make strange noises or, worse yet, go flat and leave them stranded. Here you'll find out how to check your tires' air pressure, when to rotate tires, and the telltale signs of tire wear and what to do about it. You'll drive more safely, improve your gas mileage and extend the life of your tires.

Maintain tire pressure

Check your tire pressure regularly and give your tires a quick inspection every time you fill up with gas (photo above). Pressure is measured in pounds per square inch (psi) with a tire pressure gauge. You can buy one at any auto parts store. The $10-and-up dial and digital gauges perform better in the long run than the less-expensive pencil-style gauges. Tires typically lose pressure slowly (usually about 1 psi per month). If you neglect them, they can get dangerously low, build up excessive heat, wear unevenly and deteriorate faster—all of which spell bad handling and reduced mileage.

To get an accurate reading, check the tire pressure when the tires are "cold." Obviously

DIGITAL GAUGES

DIAL GAUGE

PENCIL GAUGE

Note: For the proper inflation pressure for your vehicle tires, look for an inflation chart on the driver's-side door post or in your manual. Front and rear pressures may differ.

"cold" can mean completely different things in a northern Minnesota winter and an Arizona summer. For tire pressure, however, it simply means the air temperature inside the tires is the same as the air temperature outside the tires. The temperature usually takes about three hours to equalize after your tires are hot from driving. For the proper inflation pressure, look in your owner's manual or look for a sticker on the driver's-side door post. Note: Extremely low temperatures (below 0 degrees F) may cause the inflation valve to stick, and all the air will leak from the tire. So if it's really cold, drive the car a few miles to warm the tires first. The reading may be a bit higher, but at least you won't be stranded.

Rotate regularly

Many auto owners know they should rotate their tires but they still don't do it. When you rotate tires from one wheel to the next, you distribute the wear more evenly over all four tires, giving them a longer life. This service is usually provided free by the tire dealer or you can get it as part of a maintenance contract for just a few dollars. Or take a half hour and do it yourself. Manufacturers differ on the rotation pattern, and the process can differ depending on whether you have a rear-wheel-, front-wheel- or four-wheel-drive auto, so check your owner's manual. Most vehicles should have their tires rotated every 4,000 to 8,000 miles, or about every other oil change.

Watch for uneven wear

Check the condition of your tire treads every month or so and watch for the telltale signs of uneven wear (see Figure B).

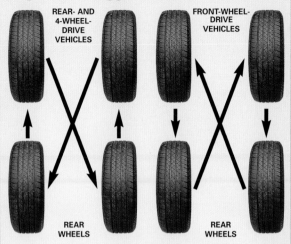

Figure A Suggested tire rotation

REAR- AND 4-WHEEL-DRIVE VEHICLES

FRONT-WHEEL-DRIVE VEHICLES

REAR WHEELS

REAR WHEELS

Note: If your vehicle has directional wheels or tires, rotate them front to back on the same side of the vehicle. Check with your dealer or tire manufacturer if you're unsure.

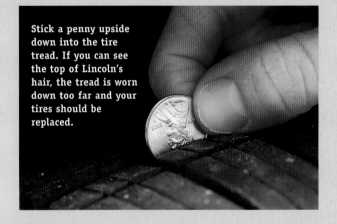

Stick a penny upside down into the tire tread. If you can see the top of Lincoln's hair, the tread is worn down too far and your tires should be replaced.

Figure B Reading tread wear patterns

If your tires show wear on the center of the tread only, you have over-inflated tires. Check the tread depth and replace the tires if necessary or fill them to the proper pressure.

If your tires show wear on the outer edges of the tread, you're probably driving on underinflated tires. Check the tread wear and replace the tires if necessary or fill them to the proper pressure.

If your tires are worn on either the inside or outside of the tread, you'll need to have your vehicle's alignment checked.

WEAR ON CENTER

WEAR ON OUTER EDGES

WORN ON ONE SIDE

Overinflated

Underinflated

Bad Alignment

Change your filter!

Clean air filters and PCV valves help your engine run more efficiently

You take your car in for an oil change. The work is almost done when the technician comes out to talk to you. He's holding your air filter and PCV valve and recommending that you replace both because they "look dirty." Without missing a beat, he explains how critical the air filter is to the efficient operation of your car. He tells you that a clogged air filter, or one that's nearly clogged, can easily cost you 10 percent in gas mileage. With gas prices going through the roof, he adds, replacement will probably save you more than the cost of the filter. Plus, a dirty PCV valve, well, that's never a good thing. Then he waits for your decision. It's tough to make up your mind about a $25 air filter and an $11.95 PC-whatchamacallit valve when you don't know what to look for.

It's not difficult to check the air filter and PCV valve yourself. Here's what you need to know:

Air filter check

First, ignore the dirt on the leading edge of the air filter pleats. All air filters accumulate dirt on the leading edge in as little as a few thousand miles. Yet most last for about 12,000 miles. You want to know how much dirt has penetrated deep into the pleats. To test the true condition of your filter, hold a shop light behind it. See how much light passes through the inner pleats and compare yours with the three sample photos (below, right). The filter shown on the left is totally clogged and cost the owner a fortune in wasted gas. The filter in the middle shows a clogged area, but the rest of the filter has decent light transmission. It's borderline, and the owner could probably squeeze 2,000 to 3,000 more miles out of it. It should be replaced at the next oil change interval. The filter on the right shows how much light passes through a new filter.

1 FOLLOW the black plastic duct to the air filter box. Unscrew or unsnap the latches. Remove the filter. Note that the screen always faces the engine. The pleats face the incoming air.

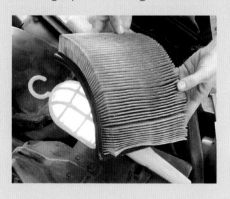

replace   borderline   new

2 HOLD the filter over a shoplight and compare it with the photos above. Reinstall or replace.

The PCV story

The PCV (positive crankcase ventilation) valve is a one-way valve that recycles crankcase gases back into the engine to burn. A plugged PCV valve can result in a rough idle and poor mileage. Worse, it can cause costly oil leaks. Always follow your manufacturer's replacement recommendations. And never replace a PCV valve simply because it "looks dirty." All used PCV valves look dirty. Photos 1 and 2 show two ways to check its real condition.

1 REMOVE the PCV valve from its grommet. With the engine off, shake the valve. If it's good, you'll hear a solid clicking sound.

2 OR, CHECK it in place with the engine running. Pull the PCV valve from its housing and place your thumb over the PCV valve opening. You should feel it click. If the click sounds or feels mushy, replace the valve.

SPARK
PLUG
BOOT

Worn plug wires and boots can start to leak voltage, resulting in poor combustion and lousy gas mileage.

Replace spark plug wires before they wear out

1 USE your digital camera to record the route of each wire. They have to go back the same way.

Do spark plug wires wear out? You bet. That's because spark plug wires aren't actually made of wire. They're made of delicate carbon fibers. Over time, the carbon breaks down and the fibers separate, causing high electrical resistance. High resistance degrades the spark, resulting in poor combustion, misfires, lousy gas mileage and ultimately a glowing "Check Engine" light. If you let that condition go on too long, the wires can start to leak voltage to nearby engine parts, causing arcing, severe performance problems, and even ignition component failures.

That's why it pays to replace your spark plug wires before they wear out. Change them during spark plug changes (whenever your owner's manual recommends, or between 60,000 and 100,000 miles). Here you'll learn which materials and tools you'll need and all the steps required to do a quality job of your own. You'll save about $80 on shop labor charges and ensure that you won't be

Wire Puller

Lisle 51750 Adjustable Spark Plug Wire Puller, $22.95.

3 USING a wire puller, twist the boot to break the seal from the plug and then pull off the old plug. Match the old wire length to the new wire.

Dielectric grease

Dielectric grease is available at any auto parts store.

COIL END

SPARK PLUG END

4 APPLY dielectric grease to both the plug and the coil/distributor end of each wire. Route the wire and press it onto the plug/coil tower until it clicks.

Wire options

The premium replacement exactly matches the factory connectors. The economy wire doesn't.

Economy brand, $22.99

Premium brand, $41.99

Factory

2 UNCOIL the new spark plug wires and sort them by length.

in for the costly diagnostic fees associated with worn spark plug wires. The whole job is pretty easy and will only take about an hour.

Before you start the job, use a digital camera to record how the wires attach to the coil/distributor/coil pack and the path they take to each plug. Notice how each wire wraps around the others and how they are arranged in the plastic retaining clips. They're arranged that way for a reason: to prevent cross-firing and interference with other engine sensors. So be sure to put them back in the same manner.

When you're at the auto parts store, buy a premium set of wires. The economy wire sets don't match the factory connectors, and the individual wires can be either too long or too short for some vehicles. The premium set, shown here, carried a lifetime warranty; the economy set, only two years. Next, invest in a spark plug wire puller tool (Photo 3). A wire puller tool makes removal much easier

and saves a lot of busted knuckles. To use it, simply grasp the boot with the rounded jaws, rotate left and right, then pull straight out. This is a tool that's worth the investment.

Some manufacturers precoat the insides of the plug and coil/distributor boots with dielectric silicone grease. The grease prevents the boots from sticking to the plug or coil/distributor. It also provides an additional layer of insulation to prevent voltage from traveling down the inside of the boot. If your set isn't precoated, purchase a small tube of silicone grease and run a bead around the inside of each boot.

Then remove one old wire at a time and match it to a replacement wire of the same length. Route the new wire and push the boot onto the plug or coil/distributor until you feel it click. Repeat the procedure for each wire.

Saving Energy:

AX4393-1
MADE IN MEXICO
: 01/2006
S. Gals. 40
DESIGN CERTIFIED
MAL
*CSA 4.1a–2002
by Rheem Mfg. Co., Montgomery, AL-36117

⚠ WARNING

⚠ DANGER

Nearly 25 cents of each energy dollar goes to heating the water used in washing machines, dishwashers, showers and sinks. For the most part, water heaters are kept "out of sight and out of mind," hidden away in the basement, garage or far corner of a utility closet. But paying even a little attention to them can yield big energy savings. Lowering the temperature setting to 120 degrees F will both save energy and help prevent scalding accidents. Wrapping your water heater in an insulated jacket can further reduce your water heating costs by up to 10 percent.

Appliances and water heaters that carry the ENERGY STAR label or a higher "energy factor" number may cost more in the short run, but will help conserve energy and money in the long run.

Appliances & Water Heaters

New-generation water heaters

Power-vented units cost more but save big in the long run

PVC PIPE

BLOWER

POWER-VENTED WATER HEATER

When it's time to replace your aging water heater, install a high-efficiency power-vented unit to save energy and dollars in the long run. This type of venting system is different from what you see on most gas water heaters. Most older water heaters have a "natural-draft" type of vent (photo below, right), where the hot waste gases rise through an open draft diverter and into metal pipes, which eventually lead to the outdoors. Running one of these vents is complicated and may be expensive. It's best left to a professional.

In contrast, a power-vented type (left) relies on a fan to blow the exhaust gases out. Since this method doesn't rely on the natural buoyancy of hot air, the vent pipes don't have to go upward. They can go out horizontally, which usually makes them much easier to install. Further, the fan dilutes the exhaust with cooler air so you can run the vents with easy-to-assemble PVC pipe. Power venting is an especially good solution for more energy-efficient, tightly built homes, where a good natural draft is difficult to establish.

However, you should be aware of several drawbacks: (1) You may notice the sound of the fan. Ideally the water heater will be in a room away from the main living area so it doesn't become bothersome. (2) You have to provide a standard electrical receptacle near the unit to supply power for the fan. (3) You have to make sure you have adequate "makeup" air to replace the air being blown out. (4) And finally, power-vented water heaters cost at least 50 percent more than a natural-draft water heater. Figure somewhere in the $450 to $650 range, plus installation. You can find power-vented water heaters wherever water heaters are sold; almost every major water heater manufacturer makes them.

If you decide to install one yourself, read the instructions carefully and make sure to follow all venting procedures. And call your local building department and ask if you need a plumbing permit to do the work.

NATURAL-DRAFT WATER HEATER

DRAFT DIVERTER

The hot exhaust gases from a natural-draft water heater rise through an open draft diverter and out through a metal duct.

A more
energy-efficient
water heater

> **tip** Set your water heater's dial to 120 degrees F. If the dial doesn't have numbers, check the water temperature with a cooking thermometer. Higher temperatures increase sediment buildup and the risk of scalding injuries.

Simple maintenance = increased efficiency and life span

Water heaters often work perfectly for a decade or more without any care, so they're easy to neglect. But a few minutes of TLC once a year pays off by extending the tank's life span and maintaining your water heater's efficiency and safety.

First, test the pressure-relief valve located on the top or side of the water heater (Photo 1). This valve opens automatically if the pressure inside the tank gets too high. (Excess pressure can actually cause the tank to explode.) If the valve doesn't release water when you lift the lever, replace the valve ($12 at home centers and hardware stores). Replacement is simple; turn off the water, drain the tank, unscrew the discharge pipe and then unscrew the old valve. Wrap the threads of the new valve with sealant tape and screw it in. If your valve is several years old and has never been tested, it might leak after you test it. In that case, replace the valve.

Next, close the shutoff valve on the cold water supply pipe that feeds the water heater. Then turn on the hot water at any faucet to release the pressure inside the heater's tank. Leave the faucet on until you finish your work. If you have an electric heater, turn off the power at the main panel. With a gas heater, turn the gas control dial to "Off."

Drain the tank to flush out sediments that have settled to the bottom of the tank. Sediment buildup shortens the life of your water heater and adds to your energy bill by reducing its efficiency. Draining 2 or 3 gallons of water is usually enough to flush out sediments, but always let the water flow until you no longer see particles in the bucket. **Caution: The water is scalding hot.**

Don't worry about any gurgling or groaning noises coming from the heater; it's just air entering the system as water drains out. If the drain valve won't close tightly when you're done, drain the tank completely, unscrew the old valve and screw in a new one ($8). To restart the water heater, open the shutoff valve and let the hot water run at any faucet to purge air from the system. Then turn on the power or relight the pilot.

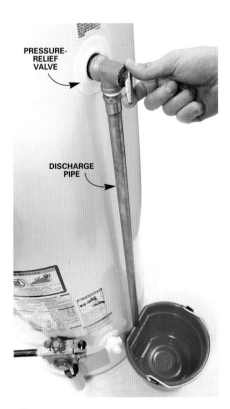

1 PLACE a bucket below the discharge pipe and gently lift the lever on the pressure-relief valve to test it.

2 OPEN the drain valve slowly and let the water run until it's clear and free of sediments. CAUTION: The water is hot!

Electric water heater tune-up

Bad elements and sediment buildup affect efficiency

If you're getting lukewarm water from your electric water heater, most likely one of your water heater's two heating elements—upper or lower—has gone bad. And since the lower element does up to 90 percent of the heating, that one usually wears out first. If you're comfortable with plumbing and electrical tools, you can do the repair yourself, but if you're at all hesitant, call a plumber.

First, shut off the power to the water heater at the fuse or breaker box. In almost every case, you'll remove two fuses or click two breaker handles (they may be pinned together). At the water heater, remove the two access panels and use a voltage meter, neon voltage indicator or voltage-sensing device to make sure there's no voltage running through any of the wires. This is no place to fool around; high-voltage wires, damp floors and water create a dangerous work setting. Make certain there's no power!

Disconnect the two wires attached to the element. Use a water heater continuity tester to test each element (Photo 1). Attach the alligator clip to one screw and touch the probe to the other screw; no light indicates a burned-out element. Perform a second test. Keep the alligator clip in place and touch the probe to the metal plate surrounding the element. If the element is shorted out, the tester bulb will light up.

To replace the element, keep the power off, open the nearest hot water faucet, then drain the unit through a hose connected to the drain valve. Remove the bad element (Photo 2), which may be held in place with four bolts or screwed directly into the tank. It may require a special element wrench for removal. Take the element to a home center or appliance parts store and exactly match the wattage, voltage, length and mounting style of the old element. The one shown cost $8. Install the new element and gasket (Photo 3), reconnect the wires, close the drain valve, refill the tank and check for leaks. If all systems are go, you can turn the power back on.

Unpolished stainless steel elements, specially designed to resist lime buildup and burnout, cost three times as much as the standard element shown, but come with a lifetime warranty. These dark gray, often wavy or U-shaped elements, are a wise investment for homeowners who get their water from a well or other water source high in lime.

There are other, less common causes of lukewarm water. The thermostat controlling each element can go bad, with the upper one being the most likely culprit.

1. Test the element

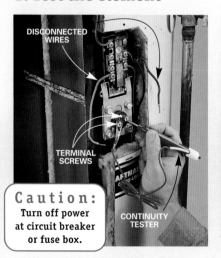

DISCONNECTED WIRES

TERMINAL SCREWS

CONTINUITY TESTER

Caution: Turn off power at circuit breaker or fuse box.

2. Remove bad element

BRACKET

BAD ELEMENT

BOLTS

3. Install new element

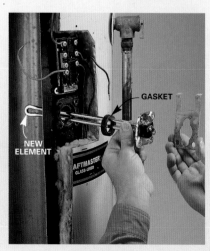

GASKET

NEW ELEMENT

Sediment can lower the efficiency of your water heater.
Drain tank and sediment every 6 to 12 months.

SEDIMENT

DRAIN VALVE

HOT WATER OUTLET PIPE
Distributes hot water throughout house.

COLD WATER INLET PIPE

COLD WATER SHUTOFF VALVE
Shut this off before draining the tank for
repairs. Power must be turned off first or
elements will burn out.

240-VOLT WIRING
Circuit will be protected by
two fuses or circuit breakers.

ELECTRICAL JUNCTION BOX

Some continuity testers come
with instructions on how to conduct a thermostat test. Replacing
the thermostat doesn't require
draining the tank.

The dip tube can also break
off, allowing the cold water to
feed into the top of the tank
rather than the bottom. This cold
water scoots right out the hot
water line, rather than starting at
the bottom where it gets warmed.

Occasionally, wires leading to
the heater get disconnected—but
tracking this down is absolutely a
pro-only task.

PRESSURE RELIEF VALVE
Provides safe outlet for overheated or overpressured water
to escape.

**UPPER THERMOSTAT AND
HIGH TEMPERATURE CUTOFF**
Thermostat senses water temperature and controls heating
element.

OVERFLOW PIPE
Must terminate within 18" of
floor for safety.

DIP TUBE
Directs cold water to bottom
of tank where it's heated, then
rises. In rare cases, tube can
break and must be replaced.

UPPER HEATING ELEMENT
In most units, only one element
is on at any given time. Lower
element clicks on during non- or
low-use periods. Upper element
clicks on during heavy use.

FOAM INSULATION

ANODE ROD
Sacrifices itself; it corrodes, rather
than the tank. Replacement rod
can be installed.

TANK
Most are porcelain or glass-lined
steel. If welded seams leak, the
entire unit must be replaced.

LOWER HEATING ELEMENT
Does up to 90 percent of all the
heating, thus most likely to wear
out first.

SEDIMENT AND SCALE
Depending on where your water
comes from and how it's treated,
your tank may have only a thin
layer or several inches of it.

LOWER THERMOSTAT
Water temperature (at both
thermostats) can be raised or
lowered with adjustment screw.
The recommended setting is
120 degrees F.

DRAIN VALVE
Remove sediment by attaching
hose and draining tank every
6 to 12 months.
Caution: Turn off power first!

ACCESS PANEL

Gas
water heater
tune-up

Flush the tank, fix broken dip tubes, save energy

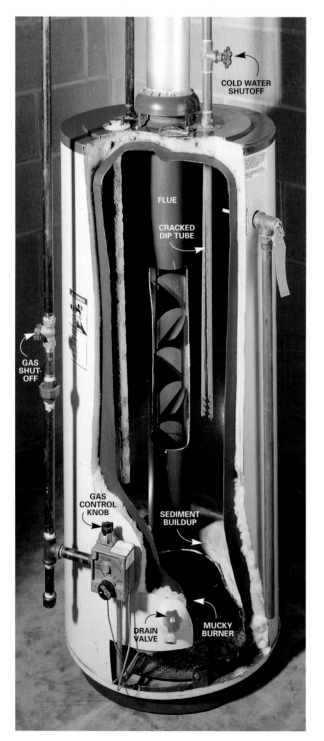

The most likely cause of a sudden hot water shortage from a gas water heater is a broken dip tube. But you should also clean the burner and give the tank a good flushing annually to get the most efficiency and life from your water heater.

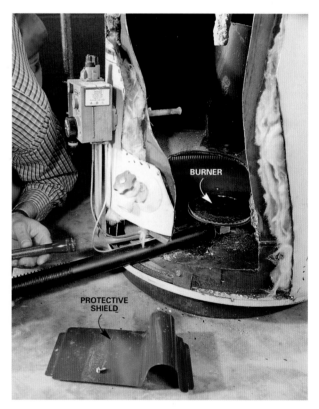

USE a vacuum to clean loose dust, soot and flakes of rust from the burner. These deposits can cause poor combustion, reducing the burner's efficiency.

Quick tip*

ELECTRIC VS. GAS WATER HEATERS
In some areas of the country, electric water heaters cost almost three times as much to operate as their natural-gas counterparts. When it's time to replace your electric water heater, consider converting to natural gas or propane.

1
Replace a broken dip tube

The dip tube, which is made of plastic and held in place by a built-in flange, carries the incoming cold water to the bottom of the water heater tank. When the dip tube breaks, cold water enters the tank at the top, mixes with the hot, and makes it seem as though you have very little hot water.

Consider replacing your straight dip tube with one that's curved. It will slow down the buildup of sediment by agitating the particles and keeping them suspended so they are flushed out.

Quick tip *

ENERGY STAR WATER HEATERS Currently there are no ENERGY STAR standards for water heaters. For information on selecting an energy-efficient unit, visit www.eere.energy.gov

2
Flush the tank

Most plumbers will tell you that sediment buildup reduces the capacity of your water heater and lowers its efficiency. Sediment buildup can also contribute to early corrosion and tank failure. That's why it's a good idea to flush the tank annually, especially if your water contains a lot of sediment.

Before you flush your water heater, turn the gas control knob to "Off" and let the water cool. Plan on replacing the drain valve with a 3/4-in. full-port ball valve with water hose adapter and a 3/4-in. x 3-in. galvanized nipple. This setup, coupled with a curved dip tube, will increase the water flow, provide a large opening for debris to escape, and generally help clean the tank better.

> **Caution:**
> Lever-type ball valves like the one shown can be easily opened by children.

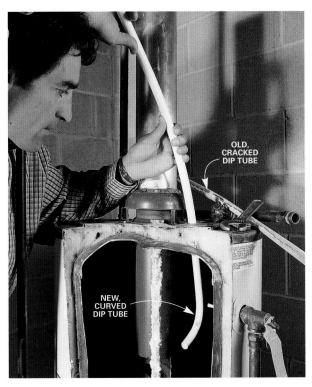

Replace the dip tube by first disconnecting the cold water supply. If you're lucky, there will be a union, which makes disconnecting it easy. You may have to cut the 3/4-in. copper pipe and sweat a joint later. Dig out the old dip tube with your finger. The tube may be cracked like the one in the photo above, or it may be broken or even missing.

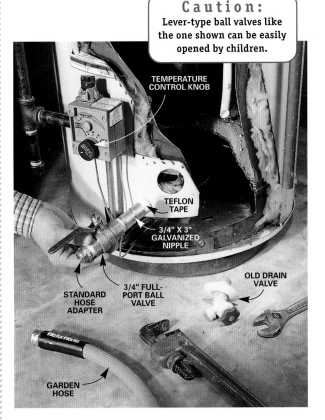

Drain as much water as possible with the factory valve. Then, remove it and install the new valve. Turn the water on and keep the drain valve open. The curved tube will agitate the particles and help with the flushing.

Save energy with a
tankless water heater

Tankless water heaters use 30 to 50 percent less energy than units with tanks, saving a typical family about $100 or more per year, depending on water usage. Tankless units (also called "on demand" units) heat water only when you turn on the faucet. They usually operate on natural gas or propane. The main advantage is that they eliminate the extra cost of keeping 40 to 50 gallons of water hot in a storage tank, so you waste less energy. They also offer a continuous supply of hot water, which is ideal for filling a big hot tub or a whirlpool. They're more compact than a standard water heater and mount on a wall.

The primary disadvantage is the upfront cost. The smaller units ($500) that you often see won't produce enough hot water to serve most households. They'll only serve one faucet at a time—a problem if you want to shower while the dishwasher is running. Larger units that can handle the demand of a whole family run $1,000 and up. (Regular tank water heaters cost $300 to $500, and they last 10 to 12 years, compared with 20 years for a tankless unit.)

But because tankless units have high-powered burners, they also have special venting requirements (a dedicated, sealed vent system, which requires professional installation). Natural gas burners often need a larger diameter gas pipe, which could easily add $500 to $1,000 to the initial installation cost.

The bottom line: When you're pricing a unit, be sure to get an estimate or firm bid on installation costs. This is not a do-it-yourself project unless you have pro-level skills. You can find tankless water heaters at many home centers and plumbing specialty stores. Ask if the unit qualifies for a federal tax credit.

Figure A
Tankless water heater details

When a hot-water tap is opened, the heating elements turn on. Water is heated as it flows through the heat exchanger.

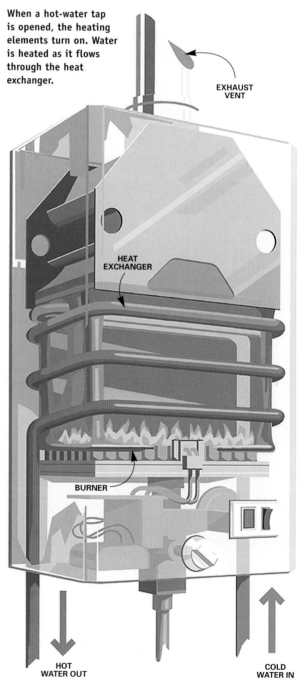

EXHAUST VENT

HEAT EXCHANGER

BURNER

HOT WATER OUT

COLD WATER IN

5 minutes to a more efficient refrigerator

You can eliminate more than 70 percent of service calls with this simple cleaning step. Skip this chore and you'll be contributing to your appliance repairman's retirement fund. Not to mention handing over $5 to $10 a month extra to your utility company because the fridge isn't running efficiently. Do it twice a year or more often if you have shedding pets. Their fur clogs up the coils fast.

Condenser coils are located on the back of the fridge or across the bottom. These coils cool and condense the refrigerant. When the coils are clogged with dirt and dust, they can't efficiently release heat. The result is your compressor works harder and longer than it was designed to, using more energy and shortening the life of your fridge. Clean the coils with a coil cleaning brush and vacuum. A coil cleaning brush ($6) does a thorough job and will easily pay for itself (look for one at appliance parts stores). The brush is bendable to fit in tight areas. It can be used for cleaning your dehumidifier and air conditioner coils too.

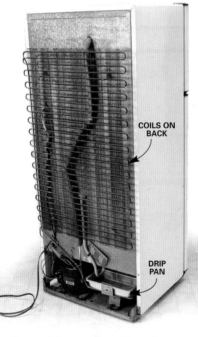

COILS ON BACK

DRIP PAN

Some refrigerators have the coils on the back of the unit. Brush and vacuum these coils in the same manner as coils found under a refrigerator.

Quick tip*

OLD REFRIGERATORS GIVE THE CHILLS
Refrigerators account for more than 15 percent of the electrical usage in most homes. The good news is, today's refrigerators use less than one-half the amount of electricity used by those made 20 years ago.

Caution: Always unplug your fridge before working on it!

GRILLE

VACUUM WITH NOZZLE ATTACHMENT

COIL CLEANING BRUSH

1 UNSNAP the grille at the bottom of the refrigerator to access the coils. If your coils are located on the back, you'll have to roll the fridge out to get at them.

COIL CLEANING BRUSH

CONDENSER COILS

2 CLEAN the coils with a special coil cleaning brush to loosen the dirt and dust. Vacuum the coils as you brush. Be careful not to bend the fan blades. A gentle brushing will do the job.

Maximize your
dryer's efficiency

The most likely cause of inefficient clothes drying is a buildup of lint that's constricting the flow of air that carries away moisture, and there are two reasons you should be worried about it. First, a dryer running at 50 percent efficiency means a lot of wasted energy dollars. Second, every year in the United States, 13,000 fires are reported that start at or in the dryer (both gas and electric), and lint buildup is one culprit. To remove that lint and get maximum efficiency from your dryer, first unplug it, then take the following steps.

Minimize obstructions in the duct system by:

1. Replacing any flexible ducting, especially the Slinky-type plastic stuff, with 4-in. rigid metal duct. The smooth sides of rigid metal duct allow the best airflow.
2. Joining the metal duct with metal duct tape instead of sheet metal screws, which can catch lint.
3. Using the fewest 90-degree elbows possible. Every elbow creates as much resistance as 10 ft. of straight duct.
4. Insulating any part of the dryer duct that passes through an unheated area. Otherwise, condensation will form inside the duct, snare the lint and greatly increase lint buildup.
5. Installing a 4 x 4-in. vent hood, instead of one with the standard 2-1/2-in. opening. Installing this larger vent hood is the equivalent of shortening the total duct run by 6 ft.

Clean the dryer's vent system once a year following these three steps:

1. Sweep the inside of the external dryer duct with a 4-in. dryer vent brush (see photo). Get this brush for $15 at an appliance parts store.
2. Vacuum the dryer's lint chute with a homemade attachment made with a piece of 3/4- or 1-in. garden hose fixed through a hole in the plastic cap from a can of spray paint (see photo above, right). In dryers with a top-mounted filter screen, lint tends to collect at the bottom of the lint chute in front of the blower.

3. Scrub the lint screen with a brush and soap and water. Even if you fastidiously remove the lint after each cycle, using fabric softeners in the washer clogs the mesh and restricts airflow.

Vacuum the area under the drum inside the dryer once a year.

This is the real key to avoiding dryer fires and making your motor last. For dryers with a front-mounted lint screen, just remove the kick plate from the bottom front. For dryers with a top-mounted screen (like the one shown), remove the two screws that hold the lint screen chute to the dryer lid. Lift the lid, then remove the two screws at the top of the sides to release the dryer front. Once you have access, use a vacuum with a brush attachment to clean the dryer floor and the motor. If you have a gas dryer, be especially careful. The igniter (glow arm) is extremely fragile. Consult your dryer's instruction manual to locate this delicate piece, then stay away from it.

Note: If the onset of your dryer's inefficiency problem is sudden, check the vent hood outside. Your dryer's vent hood should have a flap that opens only when the dryer is in use. When the flap is missing or stuck open, critters are likely to use this handy shelter to build heated nests.

3/4" OR 1" GARDEN HOSE

ANGLED TIP

SEA OF LINT ON FLOOR

3/4" OR 1" GARDEN HOSE

MOTOR

OLD, FLEXIBLE PLASTIC DUCT

BLOWER

METAL DUCT TAPE

90° ELBOW

4" X 4" VENT HOOD

RIGID METAL DUCT

Quick tip*

DRYER VENT LOGIC

If your outside dryer vent doesn't close tightly, replace it. A vent that seals well will keep energy-wasting cold air out in the winter, and unwanted warm air out in the summer.

HOMEMADE GARDEN HOSE ADAPTER

DRYER LID

LOCATION OF DRYER-FRONT SCREWS

LINT CHUTE

METAL DUCT TAPE

WHERE LINT GATHERS

Energy-Saving Q&A

Better washers and dryers

Q Both my washer and dryer are on their last legs. I'm particularly interested in the pros and cons of a front-load washing machine. What's the story?

A You'll pay more up front for a front-load washing machine, but when it comes to performance and energy savings, they can't be beat. Front-load machines, like the ENERGY STAR-qualified GE model shown below, use less water, so it requires less energy per load to heat the water. It also has a faster spin cycle, which means the clothes come out drier and need to spend less time in the dryer—saving more energy.

Front-load washers offer other bonuses. They're quieter, gentler on clothes (since there's no agitator), handle unbalanced loads better and have a larger capacity.

Quick tip*

ATTENTION ALL DRYER SHOPPERS

When shopping for a new dryer, look for one with a moisture sensor that shuts off the machine automatically when your clothes are dry. You'll save energy—and extra wear and tear on your clothes.

Feel cooler this summer with a
dehumidifier
tune-up

A dehumidifier removes humidity from a home by drawing warm, moist air over cool condenser coils inside the unit. Then, in the same way that humidity collects on a cold glass of lemonade, this humidity drips off the condenser coils into a water collec-tion pan and drains out a hose into a floor drain or fills the pan for emptying. Invest about 30 minutes to improve your dehumidifier's performance and efficiency by conducting a seasonal checkup.

For this dehumidifier model, pull off the humidistat knob, and then unscrew the hex head screws around the unit to release the front grille and cabinet cover from the chassis. Remove the rear grille and the water pan, then lift off the cabinet cover to gain access to the inner parts (Photo 1).

One reason condenser coils ice up is that accumulated dust "insulates" them and reduces their cooling efficiency, forcing the condenser to work overtime. Prevent this by vacuuming the coils, then any other interior parts (Photo 2). If your unit has a washable filter inside the rear grille or adjacent to the coils, clean it—plus all plastic parts on and inside the unit—with warm water and mild detergent.

> **tip** Avoid another cause of condenser coil icing by running the dehumidifier only in spaces where the temperature is at least 65 degrees F.

Dehumidifiers have a pressure-sensitive spring at the back of the cabinet that flattens as the water pan fills up. If the pan is spilling over, change the position of the spring to allow the shutoff switch to activate well before the pan is full (Photo 3).

Caution: Begin all appliance maintenance by unplugging the power cord.

WATER COLLECTION PAN WITH DRAIN HOSE

FRONT GRILLE

CABINET

REAR GRILLE

1 UNPLUG your appliance Before disassembling the unit, thoroughly read about the maintenance procedures in your owner's manual. Scrub mineral scale out of the water pan and check the drain hose (if used) for kinks.

DUST ON CONDENSER COILS

WATER PAN HANGING BRACKET

BACK OF UNIT

2 VACUUM the condenser coils and other parts inside the dehu-midifier. For a bet-ter job, wash the coils down with warm water and mild detergent, then thoroughly rinse and dry them.

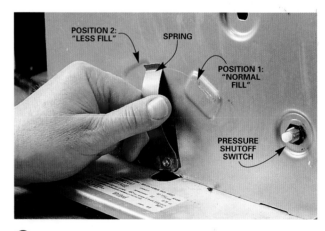

POSITION 2: "LESS FILL"

SPRING

POSITION 1: "NORMAL FILL"

PRESSURE SHUTOFF SWITCH

3 CORRECT water pan spillover (on units without drain hoses) by changing the position of the pressure spring to "Position 2." When the pan is full, the spring fully deflects—activating the shut-off switch and killing the power to the unit until the pan is emptied.

Feel warmer this winter with a
humidifier
tune-up

When heating season approaches, it's time to tune up the portable humidifiers you use to add moisture to the dry air inside your home. Periodically, you need to remove the mineral scale that builds up on the humidifier's electrical heater element and in the water reservoir pan.

The more fouled a heater element becomes with mineral scale, the less efficiently it vaporizes water. Eventually, the element builds up so much scale it stops working. Don't throw it away or buy another humidifier. Invest about 30 minutes of elbow grease and a dollar's worth of white vinegar to get your humidifier up and running. Afterward, clean off accumulated scale once a month to keep it running efficiently.

Most portable humidifiers can be tuned up by following cleaning steps similar to those in Photos 1 – 3. Your humidifier may differ from the one shown, however, so check your owner's manual.

> ✳ **tip** Work carefully around the heating element so it doesn't get damaged. Don't chip mineral scale off it with a hammer or screwdriver.

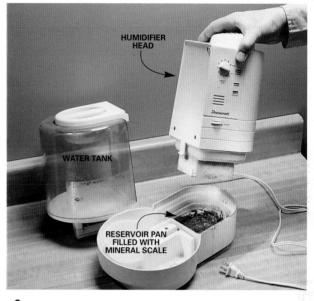

1 UNPLUG the humidifier empty the water tank, and pull off the humidifier head to reveal the reservoir pan. Empty out the water, loose mineral scale and sludge, then give the pan a quick scouring and rinse it well.

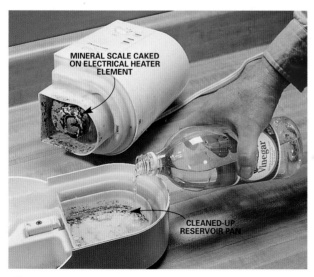

2 FILL the reservoir with white vinegar and reinstall the humidifier head. Leave the humidifier unplugged and soak the heater element in the vinegar overnight to loosen the mineral scale.

3 SCRAPE the mineral scale off the heater element with a utility knife and toothbrush. It's not necessary to scrape down to bare metal everywhere to accomplish your task.

Saving Energy:

There's no better or easier time to integrate energy-efficient building products into your home than when you add on, remodel or build new. The wall and ceiling cavities are readily accessible. And since you'll be buying new windows, doors, appliances and other components anyway, you'll find that energy-efficient models usually cost only a little more and are often no more difficult or expensive to install than non-energy-efficient components.

Of course, if you're starting from scratch, do it right. Using 2x6s instead of 2x4s for your walls will allow you to up the level of insulation. Low-E windows and windows with higher insulating qualities are widely available and are rapidly becoming the norm rather than the exception. New products that help cut down on air infiltration around outlets and switches will make your home less drafty and more energy efficient.

And in the end you'll have a home that's not only more energy efficient but more comfortable as well.

Remodeling

Building and remodeling the "green" home

It's the next big thing. But what is it?

PHOTOS COURTESY OF GE

Above: Solar made simple. GE's Brilliance solar electric power system kit has everything you need to generate your own electricity at home. Learn more at www.gepower.com.

Above, right: Natural, warm, renewable. Cork flooring is do-it-yourself friendly and available in a wide variety of styles. Learn more at www.wicanders.com, www.expanko.com, and www.wecork.com.

Ten years ago, building healthy, energy-efficient homes using environmentally friendly materials was expensive, time consuming and something only a small number of builders, remodelers and consumers were interested in. Things have changed. Today more than half the members of the National Association of Home Builders consider themselves "green builders," and the demand for their homes and remodeling services has grown dramatically.

"Green" is a loose term, which means different things to different people. It can include designing projects to be more energy and water efficient, using sustainable and natural building materials, building smaller, using solar and other alternative forms of energy, or combinations of all of these. Although there are many definitions, the common thread is to build in a way that uses and conserves natural resources wisely in both the short and long term.

Here's a look at the main elements:

PHOTO COURTESY OF ENVIROGLASS PRODUCTS, ALAN KLEHR PHOTOGRAPHER

Left: Terrazzo countertop by Enviroglass Products, made out of porcelain from old toilets and sinks. www.enviroglassproducts.com

Below: Bamboo—a truly renewable resource. Almost 20 percent of a properly managed bamboo forest can be harvested each year—forever. Materials made from bamboo are super-durable, sustainable, unique and stylish in appearance. The most popular use of bamboo in the U.S. is for tough-as-nails flooring. www.teragren.com

Use of sustainable, reclaimed and natural building materials

Most green builders keep a close eye not only on which materials they use, but also how much energy is consumed in their manufacture and transporting them to the site.

Those focused on natural building may avoid formaldehyde-based carpets, cabinets and sheathing materials and use more natural and sustainable products like bamboo and cork flooring. Using reclaimed materials such as timbers, doors and trim can be another element of building green. Wood composite decking, trim and other materials made of recycled plastic may also be used.

Generating less waste and scrap, and recycling or repurposing leftover materials is another issue to which green builders give greater consideration.

A more energy-efficient building envelope

Most green homes are built so they require significantly less energy to heat and cool than standard homes. Energy efficiency starts with a properly constructed building envelope or shell, including well-insulated (or super-insulated) walls, high-performance windows and doors, and well-sealed interior vapor barriers and exterior air infiltration barriers, often called "house wraps."

In warm climates, materials like light colored shingles and attic radiant barriers—both help reflect heat—are often included to help lower cooling costs. In cold climates, more attention may be paid to triple pane, or other types of high-efficient windows.

Some energy-efficient building components—like windows—cost more, while others simply require more meticulous care in their installation.

Today more than half the members of the National Association of Home Builders consider themselves "green builders."

Better design and site planning

Many green homes are designed and strategically positioned on the site to increase energy efficiency and decrease impact on the land. Orienting the house to maximize solar gain in the winter, along with designing roof overhangs to provide maximum cooling in the summer are two often-included elements. Positioning operable windows to provide good cross-ventilation can also help lower cooling costs.

Taking advantage of natural light through skylights and windows can help lower lighting costs. Even planting trees strategically to block sun in the summer and block cold winds in the winter can make a home more energy efficient.

Use of alternate sources of energy

In addition to taking advantage of passive solar heating and cooling, many green homes use other forms of alternative energy. Some incorporate roof-mounted photovoltaic cells to generate electricity or solar panels for heating or pre-heating water.

Other alternatives include geothermal heat pumps that extract heat from the earth via a network of pipes buried in the ground, as well as fuel cells and wind power. The combination of building an energy efficient envelope and incorporating alternative forms of energy can make some homes so efficient that heating and cooling costs approach zero.

High-efficiency heating and cooling

Energy-efficient furnaces, boilers and air conditioning equipment are found in most green homes. The best units have efficiency ratings of up to 94 percent, offering substantial energy and dollar savings over furnaces older than 20 years (which may be as little as 50 percent efficient). Since around half of the typical utility bill goes for heating and cooling, the long-range savings are substantial.

High-efficiency appliances and water heaters will also substantially lower energy bills. See "Understanding ENERGY STAR" on p. 26 for more specific details.

On-demand water heater

Heat Exchanger

Valve

Burner

Fan

Flow Sensor

Gas

Hot Water Out

Cold Water In

Increased water efficiency

Incorporating water saving faucets, toilets and showerheads is the first step toward water efficiency; purchasing water-efficient washing machines and dishwashers is the second.

Some will go the extra mile and incorporate a smaller lawn or plant drought-resistant plants in order to minimize outdoor watering needs. Gray water recycling, which involves using water from showers, baths, kitchen, laundryroom and other sources for watering lawns is yet another green tactic, but one that should be used following certain precautions. More information can be found at www.graywater.net.

Healthier indoor air quality

A tightly sealed home excels at keeping heated or cooled air inside, but it also excels at keeping mold, moisture, smoke, radon and bacteria in. Some studies show that the level of air pollution inside the home can be two to five times greater than the air outside. Since people spend an average of 90 percent of their time indoors, healthy indoor air is critical.

With a tightly built house, it's important to include some system for exhausting moisture-laden and stale indoor air and bringing in fresh outside air. An air-to-air heat exchanger which uses outgoing warm air to preheat incoming colder air is one product frequently used. These systems require a mini-duct system, so are best installed during new construction or extensive remodeling.

HEPA air filtering devices, that can remove over 99 percent of even the smallest airborne particles, are often included and may be used as freestanding units or integrated into the whole-house heating and cooling system.

Costs and payback

Since building green can be defined in so many ways, pinning exact dollar amounts on the increased initial costs versus the subsequent long-term savings is impossible. Most studies show that costs can range anywhere from 2 to 15 percent more than conventional building, but this varies greatly on degree of homeowner involvement, materials used and design. Federal, state and local governments, along with utility companies, are increasingly offering incentives by way of tax breaks and rebates for those building green.

One should look at building green as an investment: An investment that will pay dividends for as long as you own your home.

Should I buy new windows?

Consider comfort, energy efficiency & the "hassle factor"

Q **Many of the windows in my 1964 home are hard to open and don't close tightly. Is it time to chuck them and buy all new windows?**

A Tough question. New windows are tempting because they offer so much—smoother operation, lower maintenance, energy savings, fewer drafts and easier cleaning. But they're expensive. Typical residential windows cost $150 to $400 each, depending on their size, materials and features. If you add in the $100 to $300 per window that a pro charges to install them, you're facing a major investment.

Ask yourself the following three questions to evaluate your old windows and weigh the benefits of new ones.

1
Are your old windows a hassle?

Are you sick and tired of nursing your windows along, or are you OK with the minor maintenance jobs that go along with them? Consider:

- **Ease of operation.** Do they lift, swing or slide easily, or do you hesitate to open them when you want fresh air and ventilation?
- **Scraping and painting.** Painted windows require regular maintenance. Otherwise they'll rot and fall apart. New windows with aluminum or vinyl cladding or that are made from vinyl or a composite eliminate this chore.
- **Condensation.** Does condensation regularly collect on the glass, cloud the view and soak the window trim? Higher-efficiency glass in new windows will help reduce this problem.
- **Storm windows.** Do you mind cleaning, maintaining and putting up and taking down storm windows? Do your storms need replacement?
- **Cleaning.** Is this so difficult that you avoid doing it? Many new windows are designed to make cleaning a snap.

2
Are your old windows comfortable?

Single-pane windows often leave rooms feeling chilly and dry in cold weather and overheated in warm, sunny weather. Windows with double-pane glass (p. 233) can greatly improve the comfort of your home. They can block much of the heat of direct sunlight but still allow the light to come through (less need for shades). They'll reduce cold drafts and the chill of cold glass. And they'll reduce condensation, so you can keep the indoor humidity at a higher, more comfortable level in cold weather.

New energy-efficient windows will also save on your fuel bills, but they're expensive. Carefully weigh the pros and cons if your old windows are still in good shape.

VINYL TRACKS FOR SMOOTH OPERATION AND AIRTIGHT FIT

New windows offer a host of benefits— smooth operation, low maintenance, fewer drafts, easier cleaning and modest energy savings. But they're expensive, so evaluate the repair and maintenance options for your old windows before taking the plunge.

TILT-OUT FEATURE FOR EASY CLEANING

VINYL- OR ALUMINUM-CLAD EXTERIOR FOR LOW MAINTENANCE

3
Are your old windows worth repairing?

You can almost always repair and restore old windows if you're willing to set aside the time and can find replacement hardware. But it's not always worth the effort and expense. Major problems include:

- **Rot.** Once rot starts, it's tough to stop unless you commit yourself to replacing rotted wood (a difficult job) and then maintaining it regularly. Consider replacement.
- **Sagging casement (crank-out) windows.** You can usually replace worn-out crank mechanisms, but bent or worn hinges are tougher and replacements don't always solve the problem. Consider new windows.
- **Fogged double-pane glass.** The fogging that occurs between the glass panes can't be fixed. Glass replacement (sometimes the entire sash) is the only solution. This is often difficult and it's expensive if a pro does it. Compare the "fix-it" cost with the cost of a new window.
- **Hard-to-find replacement hardware.** Call the window manufacturer or local window dealer if you can identify the window brand and model number. Many hard-to-find parts are available from Blaine Window Hardware (see Buyer's Guide, p. 233). But often new windows are the only option.

Q What's the best way to replace my windows?

Option 1

A The easiest way to replace windows is to remove the old sashes and slip a window insert into the old frame (photo below). You get the benefits of high-efficiency glass, weathertightness and a maintenance-free exterior with minimal impact on the appearance of your home.

We show two ways to do this in an article on p. 146. You simply measure the frame and order a new wood or vinyl unit to fit it. This always works for double-hung (slide up and down) windows but only sometimes for casements (crank out) and sliding windows. A window dealer will advise you on your options. Or you can opt for sash replacement, which works for double-hungs only.

You can complete the changeout this way in about an hour per window (or much less after learning the ropes on the first one!). But this approach has several drawbacks. The old frame must be rot-free and reasonably square. And you still have to maintain the exterior wood frame and trim.

Option 2

A Completely tear out the old window and frame and put in a new one (photo below). You usually have to go this route with casement and slider windows. This project takes longer and is more difficult because you have to remove the exterior and interior trim, make the new window weathertight and then replace the trim. Plan on spending a whole day per window.

On the plus side, this method allows you to start fresh with a new, weathertight, low-maintenance window. And you have the option of reframing the opening and changing the window size while you're at it.

Keep in mind that complications can arise if your old window doesn't have exterior trim. Sometimes brick, stucco, vinyl siding or other siding materials butt right up against the window frame. In these situations, you may have to remove or cut siding to get the old window out and the new one in, and then patch or restore siding to finish up.

OPTION 1: Wood or vinyl window inserts cost about the same as complete new window units but are easy to install because you leave the old frame and trim intact.

OPTION 2: With new window units, you replace all the old parts with new, ensuring weathertight, long-term performance. But installation is more difficult.

Q How do I know I'm getting a quality window?

A Quality is a matter of detail. It's best to visit a showroom where you can compare windows of different brands or different models within the same brand. Check these features and answer these questions:

Appearance. Imagine the windows in your home. Does the style of the windows blend well on the interior and exterior? Are the wood or vinyl joints well made? Do the muntins (grids that divide the glass) fit tightly and cleanly? Is the hardware attractive? Unless you're trying to match existing window colors, choose a low-maintenance exterior (such as vinyl or aluminum) so you'll never have to scrape and touch up the paint.

Operation. Try out the display windows. Do they open and close smoothly? Are the cranks, runners and locking devices solid and do they look as though they'll withstand heavy use? Does the window latch firmly without too much effort? Does the weatherstripping fit snugly? Are the screens solidly built and easy to remove?

Cleaning. If cleaning is a priority, can you easily reach both interior and exterior glass? Remove or rotate the sashes to test them.

Service. Are parts available if something should break or wear out? Can you replace the weatherstripping when it wears out? Both these questions favor window companies with long track records because they'll serve their customers well into the future. If the glass breaks or fogs, how difficult and costly is replacement?

Warranties. Compare the warranties for parts and finishes. Probably the most frustrating (and expensive) problem is the failure of the seal between double-pane glass and the resulting fogging. Look for a warranty that covers glass replacement up to 20 years. **Note:** Keep the receipt for your window purchase and the warranty in your records.

Glass selection. Energy-efficient double-pane glass is fairly standard now. But it's almost always worth paying a bit extra for two additional features: a low-E coating and argon gas between the panes. Most manufacturers have two variations of this type of glass, one designed for cold climates and one designed to control sunlight in warmer climates. If you spend more for air conditioning than for heating, choose the warm-climate type, and if you spend more for heating, choose the cold-climate type.

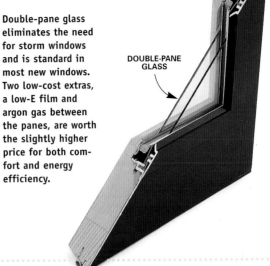

Double-pane glass eliminates the need for storm windows and is standard in most new windows. Two low-cost extras, a low-E film and argon gas between the panes, are worth the slightly higher price for both comfort and energy efficiency.

DOUBLE-PANE GLASS

Q Should I replace them all at once?

A Balance your home's appearance with your budget. Even if you try for a close match, new windows will probably look a bit different from the old. And even the glass itself (we recommend the low-E) usually looks somewhat different from clear glass. So replacing one or two in a conspicuous area may look bad. One good strategy is to replace all the windows on one side (or level if you have a two-story house) to retain a consistent appearance. Often the windows on one side of a house deteriorate much faster than the others.

Buyer's Guide

REPLACEMENT HARDWARE:
Blaine Window Hardware: (800) 678-1919. www.blainewindow.com

VINYL WINDOWS:
Many sources available for both inserts and complete units; look in your local yellow pages under "Windows, Replacement."

WOOD REPLACEMENT WINDOWS:
Many sources available for complete units. The following manufacturers will custom-size inserts to fit in old frames.

Andersen Corp.: www.andersenwindows.com

Caradco: www.caradco.com

Kolbe & Kolbe Millwork: www.kolbe-kolbe.com

Marvin Windows and Doors: www.marvin.com

Pella Corp.: www.pella.com

Weather Shield Mfg.: www.weathershield.com

2x6 vs. 2x4
wall construction

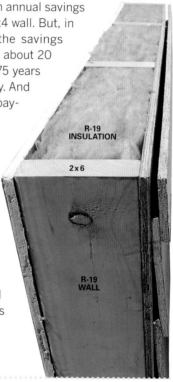
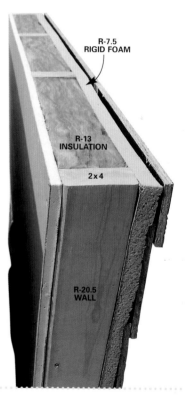

R-7.5
RIGID FOAM

R-19
INSULATION

R-13
INSULATION

2 x 6

2 x 4

R-19
WALL

R-20.5
WALL

According to an Energy Efficient Building Association study, for an average home with frame construction in a cold climate, 2x6 construction would yield an annual savings of $30 compared with a similarly constructed 2x4 wall. But, in mid-America, where the winters are milder, the savings would be much less. Because a 2x6 frame costs about 20 percent more to build than a 2x4, it would take 75 years to reach the payback point, according to the study. And that's for an entire home; for an addition, the payback would take even longer.

A much better option is to use rigid foam sheathing on a conventional 2x4 wall. A wall built this way costs 10 percent less than a typical 2x6 wall and can be even more energy efficient (see photo at right to compare R-values). The rigid foam sheathing also provides an uninterrupted envelope of insulation to prevent thermal bridging. Thermal bridging occurs when heat is lost by conduction through the studs and nails, lowering the effective R-value of the wall. Another benefit: The rigid foam acts as a wind barrier, stopping cold drafts from sneaking into your walls.

Pay extra for energy-saving features

With energy prices rising, many contractors are offering energy-efficiency upgrades (at an additional price). These might include higher-efficiency windows; guaranteed air sealing; extra-thick insulation; and higher-efficiency heating, cooling or other appliances. If they don't offer this, you can ask what additional measures they (or you) can take to improve your home's energy performance. Then compare the estimated energy savings with the cost of each upgrade. A payback period of seven to 10 years is good. (Simple payback is the time it takes for the savings to equal the original cost.) Keep in mind that upgrades done during the remodeling process always cost less than upgrades added later.

Airtight electrical boxes

Q Our building inspector told me that I need to use airtight electrical boxes. What are these?

A Some building codes now require these special boxes to reduce air and moisture movement in exterior walls. Here are three options:

First is a large plastic box (Photo 1) that you nail to the face of a stud, then install a standard electrical box inside it. It's large enough to handle multi-gang electrical boxes. Cut a slit in the side of the box and push the cable through it and wire the box as you normally would. Caulk around the cable where it penetrates the box to seal it. If you're using a plastic vapor barrier, seal it to the box apron with an acoustic (nonhardening) caulk. If you're applying drywall without the vapor barrier behind it, caulk the drywall directly to the box.

Another option is an airtight electrical box (Photo 2) that uses a soft rubber gasket that seals to the drywall. The box also is wrapped in a rubber skin that seals the cables. Make a small slit in the rubber and push the cable through. Install and wire it as you would a standard box.

You can also order these boxes at electrical supply stores.

Foam blocks stop air infiltration

Simple foam insulation blocks that fit around electrical boxes (inside the wall cavity) also stop air infiltration.

The blocks save you the time and hassle of buying airtight boxes or caulking regular boxes.

1 The Lessco Air-Vapor Barrier Box is nailed to the stud and allows use of standard electrical boxes. Slit the top to insert wire, then use caulk to seal as shown. These boxes cost $2.25 to $2.50 each. (Visit www. lessco-airtight.com to find a local dealer.)

VAPOR BARRIER

CAULK

SPECIAL PLASTIC BOX

VAPOR BARRIER

RUBBER FOAM

2 Other airtight electrical boxes use a foam gasket around the drywall flange and where the cable enters to seal out air. These boxes are available at most home centers and well-stocked hardware stores.

FOR SINGLE BOXES

FOR MULTIPLE BOXES

FOR CEILING BOXES

ENERGY BLOCK

3 Foam insulation boxes stop air infiltration and install quickly. The units shown cost $2.15 to $3.50 each. (Visit www.energyblock.com for more information.)

Insulate
rim joists
and cut heat loss

FLOOR JOIST

FOAM INSULATION

RIM JOIST

1 CUT rigid foam insulation into strips with a table saw or a circular saw. Cut the strips to fit between floor joists using a box cutter.

BOX CUTTER

In just a couple of hours, you can seal and insulate your rim joists, which are a major source of heat loss in many homes. Properly insulating and air-sealing rim joists takes patience, so most builders simply stuff in some fiberglass and walk away.

If you have an unfinished basement, you can properly insulate the rim joists in two or three hours. (This will also block tiny passages where spiders and other insects enter your basement!) The materials will cost about $1 per foot of rim joist. Call your local building inspections

EXPANDING
FOAM

CAULK

2 RUN a bead of acrylic caulk around each section of foam to form an airtight barrier. Fill gaps larger than 1/4 in. with expanding foam sealant.

RIGID
FOAM

RIM
JOIST

CAULK

EXPANDING
FOAM

SILL PLATE

FIBERGLASS
INSULATION

HOLLOW
CONCRETE BLOCK

Airtight insulation reduces heat loss through the rim joist. Fiberglass insulation and expanding foam seal the open top of hollow concrete blocks.

department before you begin this project. The inspector may require you to cover the new insulation with drywall (as a fire block) or leave some areas uncovered to allow for termite inspections. You can insulate second-floor rim joists following the same steps shown here if you happen to tear out a ceiling during remodeling.

Rigid foam is the best insulation for rim joists. Shown here is 2-in.-thick (R-10) "extruded polystyrene" ($20 per 4 x 8-ft. sheet). Don't use "expanded polystyrene," which is a less effective air and moisture barrier.

Cut the foam into 8-ft.-long strips 1/8 in. less than the height of the rim joist. A table saw is the fastest way to "rip" these strips, but you can also use a circular saw. Then cut the strips to length to fit between the joists, again cutting them 1/8 in. short (Photo 1). A heavy-duty box cutter ($6) is the best knife for making short cuts and trimming foam; the long blade slices cleanly

through the foam (a utility knife blade is too short). Use long sections of foam to cover the rim joists that are parallel to the floor joists (Photo 2). Don't worry about cutting the foam for a tight fit around pipes, cables or other obstructions; you can seal large gaps with expanding foam sealant later.

It's important to create an airtight seal around each section of foam using caulk or expanding foam (Photo 2). Otherwise, moist inside air could condense on the cold rim joist. The resulting dampness can lead to mold and rot. If you have a solid concrete foundation, also run a bead of caulk where the sill plate meets the concrete. If you have a concrete block foundation, also seal the openings on top with expanding foam. Stuff a wad of fiberglass insulation into each opening to support the foam as it hardens (see Figure A).

Replace a bath fan switch with a timer

After a shower, you should run your bath fan for 10 to 30 minutes to clear out moisture, which causes mold, mildew and condensation. Returning later to turn off the fan is a nuisance, but leaving it on is an energy waster. The solution is a timer switch. Old-fashioned rotary timers ($15) produce an annoying buzz and eventually wear out. Silent and reliable electronic timers are a better choice. Models like the one shown here are available at home centers, hardware stores and online at www.rewci.com/timinout.html ($27 plus shipping). Make sure the timer you choose is rated to control electric motors, not just lighting. You'll also need a new cover plate ($3). If you like, you can use this opportunity to upgrade any light switch that shares the same junction box.

Installing a timer isn't difficult, but you should know wiring basics such as how to make connections and detect live wires before you start. Turn off the power to the circuit at the main panel and make sure it's off using a noncontact voltage detector ($8 at home centers and hardware stores). Remove the switch and disconnect the two wires leading to it. Next, you have to determine which of the switch wires is "hot" (supplying power) and which is the "load" leading to the fan. Connect a test light ($4; Photo 1) and turn the power on at the main panel. If the light glows, it's connected to the hot wire. If not, it's connected to the load wire. Turn the power off and mark the hot wire with electrical tape (Photo 2).

To complete the job, connect the timer following the manufacturer's instructions (Photo 2). Don't straighten the hooked ends of the switch wires. Instead, cut them off and strip the insulation to expose fresh wire. You'll have to remove the electrical connectors on the existing neutral (white) and ground wires.

1 With the power off, clip a test light to the ground and to one of the switch wires. Turn on the power. If the light comes on, the wire is hot. If not, the other switch wire is hot.

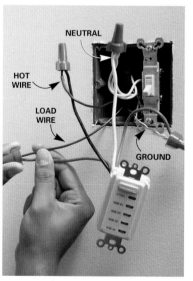

2 Turn off the power again. Connect the timer and tuck the wires neatly into the junction box. Screw on the timer and the cover plate.

Curb heat loss in cathedral ceilings

Light fixtures aren't airtight unless they have an "airtight" rating. But don't plug the holes (see photo). Manufacturers submit fixtures to Underwriter's Laboratories (UL) to receive a safety rating for their designated use. (You'll see a UL rating somewhere on the fixture.) Altering the fixture in any way may compromise its margins for safety.

Recessed lights in cathedral ceilings waste the heat from the lightbulb and the warm air that leaks through the fixture. Also, moist, warm air will flow up against the cold roof sheathing (see photo). Chances are that it'll condense there, wet the wood and eventually cause rot. Unfortunately, there isn't any easy way to know if you have moisture problems and rot until you find water dripping from the ceiling, stains or soft spots in the drywall.

Builders often try to prevent the problem by leaving a 1- to 2-in. airspace for roof ventilation (see photo, right). Roof venting can help dry the wood again in warmer weather, and it'll flush out some of the moisture in cold weather. But it often doesn't work well.

The best solution is to avoid putting any recessed lights in cathedral ceilings. However, if you want them, use type IC "airtight" fixtures (available for $20 at lighting stores and home centers). These fixtures are sealed to stop airflow. In addition, they have gasketed edges to seal them to the drywall.

Replacement can be challenging. If you're lucky, you can pull the old mounting bracket out through the existing hole. Otherwise you have to tear open the ceiling. It's usually best to hire a licensed electrician for this tricky job.

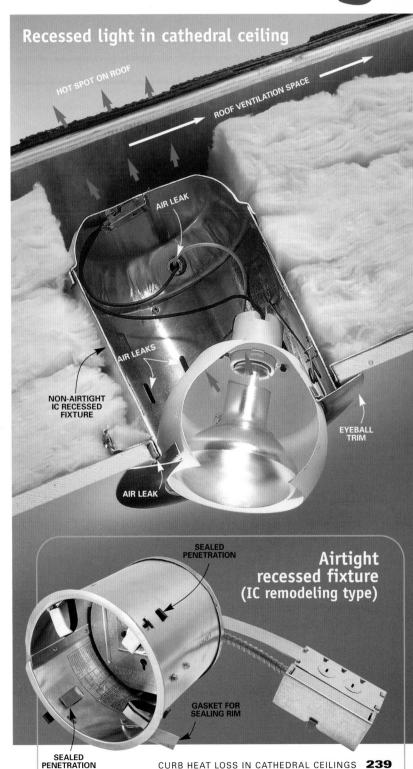

Recessed light in cathedral ceiling

HOT SPOT ON ROOF

ROOF VENTILATION SPACE

AIR LEAK

AIR LEAKS

NON-AIRTIGHT IC RECESSED FIXTURE

EYEBALL TRIM

AIR LEAK

SEALED PENETRATION

Airtight recessed fixture (IC remodeling type)

GASKET FOR SEALING RIM

SEALED PENETRATION

Energy-efficient heat for an

Does your furnace have enough oomph?

If you're looking for an energy-efficient way to heat an addition, weigh your options carefully. If a main rectangular (trunk) line is adjacent, you can tap into the top of it. If it's a round 6-in. branch duct, you should not. However, keep in mind that air distribution within a home is very complex. It's based on how your furnace performs, the local climate, structural features, and the heating and cooling loads of individual rooms.

First, you need to know if your furnace has enough heat output as measured in Btu (British thermal units) and enough blower capacity in cfm (cubic feet per minute) to handle the added square footage.

Next, you must determine the duct size that will deliver the needed cfm and how accessible your basement/crawlspace/attic will be for running new branch ducts from the supply air part of the furnace. Plus, you may need a return air duct to achieve a steady, balanced airflow.

Assuming your head isn't spinning yet, you may need to increase the size of the existing supply trunk line, then step it down to increase the air velocity so properly heated air enters the new room. Then you must decide how many supply lines the room will need, based on variables such as the number of windows and outside walls, the climate, whether your home was built on a slab or basement (heated or not?) and more.

You also have to test the system to avoid a heating system imbalance. The job is even more complex if you have air conditioning in the same ductwork.

Because the job is complex, you're likely to make a mistake and be disappointed by drafts or a

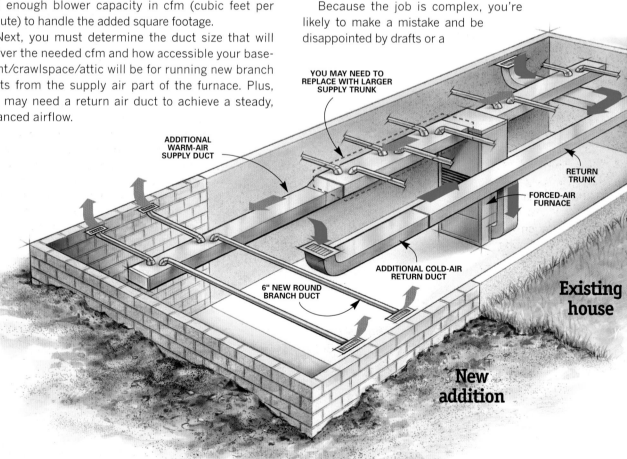

YOU MAY NEED TO REPLACE WITH LARGER SUPPLY TRUNK

ADDITIONAL WARM-AIR SUPPLY DUCT

RETURN TRUNK

FORCED-AIR FURNACE

ADDITIONAL COLD-AIR RETURN DUCT

6" NEW ROUND BRANCH DUCT

Existing house

New addition

addition

cool room. The two biggest DIYer mistakes are (1) tapping a new duct into a 6-in. round adjacent branch duct and (2) not adding return air ducts.

Best advice? Call in a heating pro. First, pros determine the heat loss/gain for the entire house and for the room addition. That tells them whether the furnace is big enough and how much heat (and cooling) the room needs.

Next, pros size up the existing furnace and duct system, then map and calculate whether a system can handle the added load.

Older furnaces can usually supply the extra heat needed, but the return air ductwork often needs improvement. Newer high-efficiency, forced-air furnaces often don't have spare capacity, so you may have to replace the furnace with a higher capacity one.

If capacity exists, pros size up the new ductwork to make sure heated air reaches the new space at the proper velocity to keep the room at a comfortable temperature and avoid drafts, while maintaining the comfort of other rooms in the house.

Rather than have you replace a furnace that's too small, a pro may recommend other, less expensive options, such as an independent system or electric baseboard heating.

Energy-Saving Products

Energy-wise kitchen appliances

New appliances are usually an integral part of a kitchen-remodeling project, so it's the perfect time to upgrade to more energy-efficient models. For starters, look for the ENERGY STAR label—it's your first indication that the appliance meets strict energy-efficiency standards.

Many new dishwashers save energy in smart new ways. The GE Profile dishwasher, for example, includes a single-rack wash cycle that allows you to wash only the upper rack, using less water. It also has a sensor that automatically adjusts the cycle time and water temperature for each load. All said and done, an energy-efficient dishwasher can save you more than $25 on hot water costs annually.

Since refrigerators can account for up to 15 percent of your annual electric bill, an energy-efficient refrigerator is a wise investment. Door-mounted ice and water dispensers mean less door opening, resulting in less cool air escaping. Some models have condensers that don't require cleaning (which translates into higher energy efficiency) and digital displays that allow you to monitor actual temperatures.

Visit the "Refrigerator Retirement Savings Calculator" at www.energystar.gov to find out the cost of running your old refrigerator versus a new model.

FORCED-AIR
HEATER

Heating a garage

There are two types of natural-gas heaters that will work to heat a garage: a forced-air garage heater (shown above) that blows warm air like a conventional furnace, and a "low-intensity" infrared tube heater (photo, opposite) that radiates heat. (Avoid "high-intensity" infrared heaters—which visibly glow red—because most aren't approved for residential use.)

Both will burn natural gas (your most economical choice) or LP gas, and both are available in several sizes, so you can choose the one that best heats your space. Both require an electrical hook-up, and both require venting to the outside as well. But the similarities of the two types end there.

Your garage walls and ceiling need to be insulated (minimum of 4 in. thick in the walls, 6 in. thick in the ceiling); otherwise you'll waste energy and money. The basic differences are how the heaters perform and how they feel in terms of comfort.

If you plan to work on woodworking projects in the garage, an infrared heater may work better because it doesn't raise dust or keep dust airborne. A forced-air heater will stir up sawdust, which is a big problem when you're painting or staining.

You won't feel warm as quickly with an infrared heater because it heats objects first, then the air. However, once your concrete floor warms, you'll feel more comfortable because infrared heat is more uniform. But you must keep all objects 3 to 4 ft. away or they'll overheat—and so will you. With forced-air heat, the air is warmer at the ceiling and cooler at your feet. And a forced-air heater will take longer to reheat the space after the garage door has been opened and shut.

Another big difference is the initial cost. Most forced-air units cost half as much as low-intensity infrared tube heaters. The 60,000-Btu Modine Hot Dawg forced-air unit shown cost around $625 (not including the vent kit and thermostat), and the 30,000-Btu Caribe infrared unit shown (including the vent kit) cost around $1,000. However, it's usually less expensive to run the infrared unit, so the cost difference will decrease with frequent use. Check with the manufacturers or a local heating pro for a more exact estimate.

Installation is markedly different too. Infrared heaters must be installed a minimum of 7 ft. above the floor, and must hang down a minimum of 4 in. from the ceiling (check the manufacturer's instructions, as these measurements vary with the size of the heater). It's critical that you make sure objects below are not too close. The 30,000 Btu unit shown requires a minimum 3-ft. distance from heater to objects below. Most infrared heaters are installed at the back of a garage pointed toward the garage door, then aimed downward at a 45-degree angle. They can also be installed between car bays if the garage door opener rail allows and you don't have a tall vehicle.

With a forced-air heater, the installation details aren't as exacting. Most are placed in a corner, near a gas line and an electrical outlet (needed to power the blower). The instructions will indicate the exact spacing required between the unit and the sidewalls or ceiling.

INFRARED TUBE HEATER

How many Btu you need depends on variables such as the garage size, your climate zone and the temperature you want to work in. A basic rule of thumb for forced-air heaters is 45,000 Btu to heat a two- to 2-1/2-car garage, and 60,000 for a three-car garage. The makers of low-intensity infrared tube heaters say that 30,000 Btu can heat a two- to 2-1/2-car garage, and suggest 50,000 for a three-car garage. Check with a local heating pro or the heater manufacturer for a specific recommendation to fit your needs.

Both heater types need to be vented if powered by natural gas or LP gas. Check the instructions for specific vent pipe sizes and lengths (some models include a vent kit, or you can purchase components separately). Most can be routed either through sidewalls or through the attic and roof.

One other option is an electric infrared heater, if venting or gas-powered heat isn't what you want. Granted, electric heat may cost you more to run, but check with your local electrical utility to see if it offers any type of rebate or off-peak rates that would make this option more cost efficient.

Hot Dawg model HD60 from Modine Mfg., (800) 828-4328 (to locate dealer). Caribe model CGTH-30, Roberts Gordon, (800) 828-7450 (to locate dealer).

Forced-air heater:
PROS
- Less expensive initial cost (50 percent less than comparable infrared heater)

CONS
- Noisy
- Loses heat quickly if garage door is opened (longer recovery time)
- Heat rises and stratifies (the air is warmer at ceiling, cooler near floor), but you won't notice it with a 7- or 8-ft. ceiling
- Air movement tends to blow airborne dust around (woodworkers will have to shut down unit before staining and finishing projects)

Low-intensity infrared tube heater:
PROS
- Little noise
- No air movement (dust settles)
- Lower cost to operate
- More uniform heat distribution (no stratification)
- Quicker heat recovery if door is opened/closed (floor and objects retain heat)

CONS
- Higher initial cost (50 percent more than forced-air)
- Correct location of heater is critical (minimum 7 ft. from floor, 3 ft. from objects). Adequate headroom is also critical, because you can overheat if you're working near the unit.

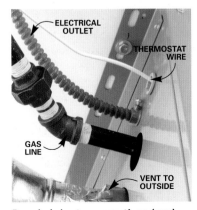

ELECTRICAL OUTLET

THERMOSTAT WIRE

GAS LINE

VENT TO OUTSIDE

Forced-air heater connections (rear)

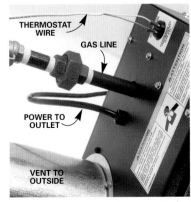

THERMOSTAT WIRE

GAS LINE

POWER TO OUTLET

VENT TO OUTSIDE

Infrared heater connections (rear)

Electric resistance
floor heat

A smart do-it-yourself heating alternative for additions & major remodels

Tile floors are popular in bathrooms for their practicality and durability, but even in mild climates, they tend to be too cold for bare feet. Imagine the comfort of stepping out of the shower onto a warm floor, and you'll understand why in-floor electric heating systems have become so popular. For small residential spaces such as bathrooms, simple electric-heating mats borrow the principle of commercial hydronic (water-filled tubing) systems to provide a reliable, affordable heat source.

Embedded in the thin-set mortar used to secure the tile, these mats feature a continuous loop of resistance heating cable amid a thin plastic mesh. There are different systems and types of heating cable available, so shop around. Like other heaters, the system can be controlled by a thermostat, a timer or even an on-off wall switch. Be extra cautious during installation to avoid nicking any wires. Insulate the joist cavity under the floor, if possible.

TILE

THIN-SET

CEMENT BOARD

ELECTRIC RESISTANCE FLOOR MAT

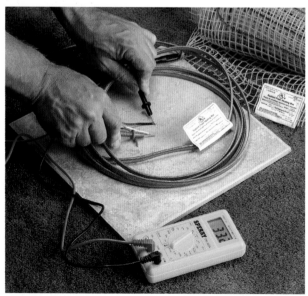

1 TEST the heating cable with a volt-ohm meter to make sure the resistance reading is within 10 percent of the rating on the product label. If it's not, check the manufacturer's instructions before you proceed.

2 AFTER LAYING a cement-board subfloor, test-fit the mat, making sure the heating cable is at least 4 in. away from any walls, fixtures or cabinets. Do not cut the heating cable or allow it to overlap itself.

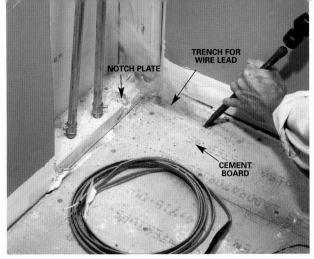

3 CHISEL a shallow trench in the cement board near the wall where the line wiring is, to make room for the mat's thicker wire lead. Also notch the bottom plate for the thermostat cable and power lead.

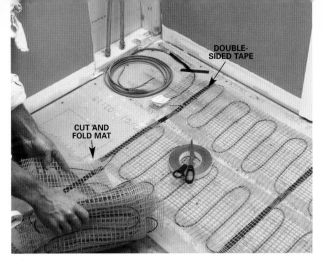

4 SECURE the mat to the cement board subfloor with double-sided tape. At the end of each run, cut the mat, not the heating cable itself, so you can fold it over and reverse direction to start the next course.

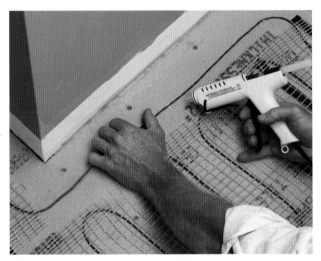

5 FOR SECTIONS where the mat won't fit, such as around a fixture, cut the plastic mesh away and secure the heating cable to the floor with hot-melt glue. Glue down any loose ends or humps in the mat, too.

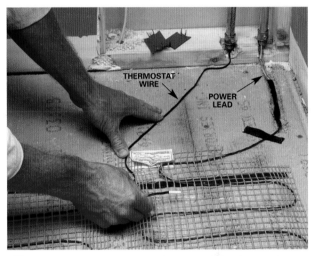

6 FEED the power lead and the thermostat wire through the conduit and to a wall-mounted electrical box. Connect the power lead to the house wiring (it may require a new circuit) and install the thermostat wire and sensor.

7 WITH THE MAT SECURED, use a notched trowel to apply thin-set mortar to cover it and provide a bed for the tile. Take care to avoid nicking or cutting the heating cable with the trowel's sharp edges.

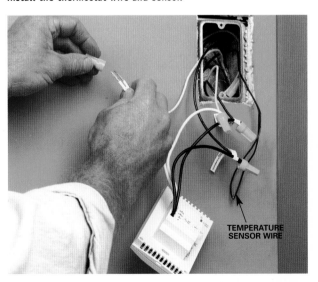

8 AFTER SETTING the tile and doing another continuity-resistance test, wire the wall thermostat. Shut off power to the thermostat while you're working on it. Let mortar cure one week before you turn on the power.

Cozy heat
for an addition

Hydronic radiant heating is a good option to consider when adding on to a house with a furnace already working at full capacity. Unlike forced-air heating, which works by blowing warm air through large ducts, hydronic radiant heating circulates hot water through tubes attached to or embedded in a flat surface, usually the floor. The heat then radiates evenly throughout a space, making this arguably the most comfortable way to heat a room.

For truly even heat, choose a system that circulates hot water through code-approved plastic tubing (like PEX) that's embedded in a layer of material and covered by ceramic tile flooring. The material can be lightweight concrete, Gyp-crete or dry-tamped mortar. This cement-like layer, combined with the tile, makes up a great mass that stores the heat for a long time and continues to radiate it even when the water's not circulating. This constant warmth can greatly increase the comfort of a room, especially in a cold climate.

The cost per square foot for a hydronic system

will depend on where you live and the size of the job. With a 300-sq.-ft. addition, expect to pay at least $1,500 to have the actual system installed (including water heater, tubing, pump and manifold). Then there's the cost of embedding the tubing. For a fairly small job, the most economical choice is to hire a tile professional to embed the tubing in dry-tamped mortar. That should cost from $3 per sq. ft. on up. Then add the cost of the finished floor. Tile is the best choice.

The cost of a hydronic system for an addition may be about the same as the cost of adding a furnace (vs. replacing). However, operating costs will be lower for the hydronic system, the water heater won't take up as much space as a furnace and ductwork, and you'll probably be more comfortable. To find a hydronics specialist, look in the yellow pages under "Heating Contractors."

During installation, the PEX tubing is laid down in long loops spaced about 9 in. apart and carefully stapled to the floor. The mortar or concrete will then be installed on top of the tubing.

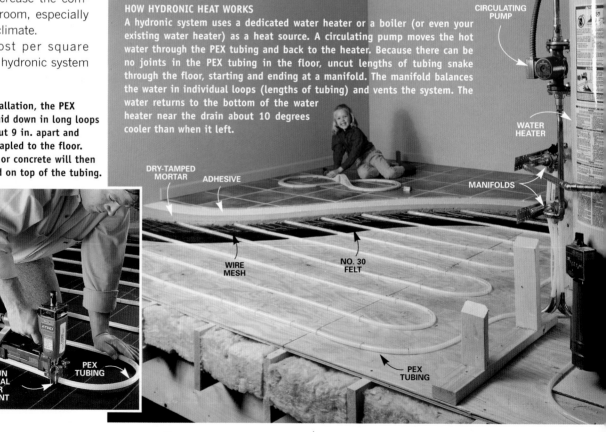

HOW HYDRONIC HEAT WORKS
A hydronic system uses a dedicated water heater or a boiler (or even your existing water heater) as a heat source. A circulating pump moves the hot water through the PEX tubing and back to the heater. Because there can be no joints in the PEX tubing in the floor, uncut lengths of tubing snake through the floor, starting and ending at a manifold. The manifold balances the water in individual loops (lengths of tubing) and vents the system. The water returns to the bottom of the water heater near the drain about 10 degrees cooler than when it left.

CIRCULATING PUMP

WATER HEATER

MANIFOLDS

DRY-TAMPED MORTAR

ADHESIVE

WIRE MESH

NO. 30 FELT

PEX TUBING

STAPLE GUN WITH SPECIAL FASTENER ATTACHMENT

PEX TUBING

Understanding
heat-recovery
ventilators

Tightly built energy-efficient homes can experience problems with lingering odors, stale air and high humidity resulting in damaging condensation. Generally, these problems can be solved with ordinary ventilation or by cracking open a window. If you live in a moderately cold climate with high utility rates and conventional methods don't solve your problem, your home may be a candidate for a heat-recovery ventilator (HRV), also called an air-to-air heat exchanger.

Compared with opening a window, an HRV provides continuously controlled ventilation. Heat from stale exhaust air is used to temper the incoming air so fresh air enters your home closer to room temperature; about 70 percent of the heat is transferred. The airstreams don't mingle or contaminate one another, but weave and bypass one another through a series of chambers. Operating costs are about the same as those for a 100-watt incandescent lightbulb.

Most HRVs are designed to ventilate the entire home. Typically, four to eight supply-and-return ducts connect to the HRV. The ideal system exhausts air from moisture-laden rooms, such as the kitchen, bathrooms and laundry room, and dumps the fresh air into a closet, hallway or other space where the cooler air and increased movement won't affect comfort. Adding this kind of whole-house ventilator can be expensive and is normally done by a professional.

It is also possible to install a small plug-in single-room HRV on an exterior wall or in a window. Some models include multiple filters that clean the air as well. For the most effective air mixing, install a wall-mounted unit high on an outside wall, but avoid mounting it up against the ceiling. Keep it away from thermostats and seating areas, in a spot where some fan noise and cool air movement won't be a bother.

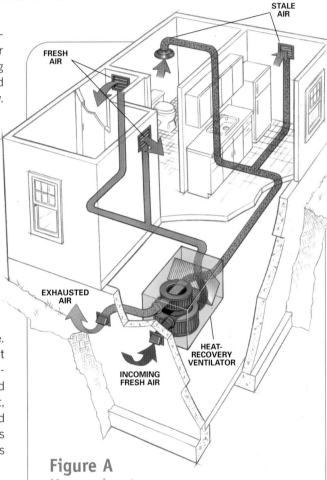

STALE AIR

FRESH AIR

EXHAUSTED AIR

INCOMING FRESH AIR

HEAT-RECOVERY VENTILATOR

Figure A
How a heat-recovery ventilator works

In an HRV, one fan exhausts stale, moisture-laden indoor air while another draws in fresh outside air. Both air streams pass each other, separately, through a core of many thin metal or plastic surfaces. As it passes through the core, exhaust air from the house transmits its heat through core walls or fins to the cooler outside air coming in. A heater can be added to a supply duct in some systems to further warm the incoming air during severely cold weather. In summer-operating mode, HRVs work in reverse. A drain carries away any condensation.

10 great resources

for learning more about energy efficiency

Lighting

To calculate your savings when replacing standard incandescent bulbs with compact fluorescent bulbs, check out the "Light Bulb Calculator" on the New York Energy Smart Website at www.getenergysmart.com. Enter the number and types of bulbs you'll be replacing and the calculator will give you your estimated yearly savings. Visit: www.getenergysmart.org and type "light bulb calculator" in the search box.

The Energy Federation is a nonprofit organization that offers energy-efficient lighting and other products to consumers at reasonable prices. You can visit their online catalog at www.energyfederation.org.

Recycling

For information on where and how to recycle batteries from cellular and cordless phones, laptops, camcorders, digital cameras, cordless power tools and other devices, visit the Rechargeable Battery Recycling Corporation Web site at www.rbrc.org. Their Call2Recycle program has established 30,000 collection sites nationwide. Most Lowe's, Sears, Best Buy, Home Depot, Radio Shack, Office Depot, Batteries Plus, Target, Wal-Mart and wireless stores serve as battery drop-off sites.

Energy-efficient appliances

ENERGY STAR is a joint program run by the U.S. Environmental Protection Agency and the U.S. Department of Energy with the goal of making homes and businesses more energy efficient. One of the ways they do this is to set energy-efficiency guidelines for appliances, heating and cooling equipment, and other products. For more information on specific appliances: Visit their Web site at: www.energystar.gov, call (888) 782-7937, or write U.S. EPA, Energy Star Hotline (6202J), 1200 Pennsylvania Ave NW, Washington, D.C. 20460

Refrigerators

To find out how much your refrigerator costs to run per year and how much you can save by replacing it with an energy-efficient model, check out the "Refrigerator Retirement Savings Calculator" at www.energystar.gov. Click on "Home Appliances," and then "Refrigerators and Freezers." Enter the year, size and configuration of your refrigerator and the program will calculate your savings over one- and five-year periods.

Insulation

To determine how many inches of insulation you need to add to your attic and/or walls to meet U.S. Department of Energy standards, visit the Owens Corning Web site at www.owenscorning.com and click on "Tools and Resources." To determine the number of square feet of material you'll need, visit www.lowes.com and under "Project Center," (on the left side of the home page) click on "Interactive Design Tools: Rolled insulation calculator."

Energy-efficient and solar products

"Real Goods" carries a wide selection of alternative energy products including solar electric, wind power and transportation. View their online catalog at www.gaiam.com/ realgoods.

Education

The Solar Living Institute offers a wide array of workshops including those on solar and renewable energy, green and natural building and alternative transportation. For more information, check out the "Workshops" area at www.solarliving.org or call (707) 744-2017.

Kids can learn more about conserving energy by playing interactive Energy Hog games at www.energyfederation.org.

Water

One drippy faucet can waste 20 gallons of water per day; if it's dripping hot water, you'll also be paying to heat all the water that's going down the drain. And a leaky or running toilet can waste 200 gallons per day. For complete information on how to fix or replace a drippy faucet, enter "Repair a Kitchen Faucet" in the search box at www.thefamilyhandyman.com. You'll also find articles on repairing running toilets and dripping showers.

Kids

Your kids can go on a home energy scavenger hunt, become an Energy Hog Buster, watch super heroes in action, and read the Green Schools Gazette at the Alliance to Save Energy Web site. Visit www.ase.org and click on "Consumers: Kids." The Web site also includes information on shopping for energy-efficient products, remodeling and tips for lowering energy bills.

Fuel Efficiency

Visit www.fueleconomy.gov for information on getting better gas mileage through better driving habits, maintenance, planning and new car purchases. Their Fuel Economy Guide lists mileage estimates for cars built between 1985 and 2008. The site also offers links to Web sites that keep track of the lowest gas prices in your area.

Index

Nails

Nail lengths are identified by numbers from 4 to 60 followed by the letter "d" which stands for "penny." The imperial and metric equivalents are listed here.

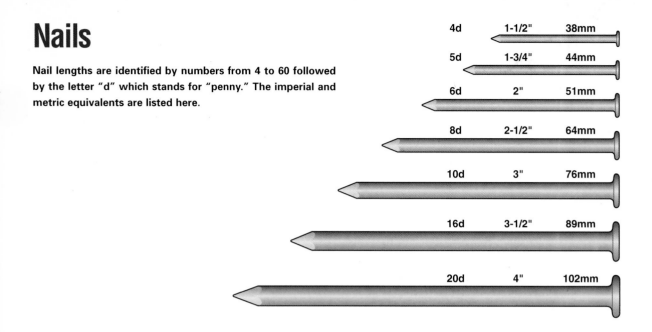

4d	1-1/2"	38mm
5d	1-3/4"	44mm
6d	2"	51mm
8d	2-1/2"	64mm
10d	3"	76mm
16d	3-1/2"	89mm
20d	4"	102mm

Fractions and metric equivalents

Fractional inches

Inches (in.)	1/64	1/32	1/25	1/16	1/8	1/4	3/8	2/5	1/2	5/8	3/4	7/8
Millimeters (mm)*	0.40	0.79	1.0	1.59	3.18	6.35	9.53	10	12.7	15.9	19.1	22.2
Centimeters (cm)*							0.95	1	1.27	1.59	1.91	2.22

Whole inches (1–12)

Inches (in.)	1	2	3	4	5	6	7	8	9	10	11	12
Feet (ft.)												1
Millimeters (mm)*	25.4	50.8	76.2	101.6	127	152	178	203	229	254	279	305
Centimeters (cm)*	2.54	5.08	7.62	10.16	12.7	15.2	17.8	20.3	22.9	25.4	27.9	30.5
Meters (m)*												.30

Selected large measurements

Inches (in.)	36	39.4
Feet (ft.)	3	3-1/4†
Yards (yd.)	1	1-1/12†
Millimeters (mm)*	914	1,000
Centimeters (cm)*	91.4	100
Meters (m)*	.91	1.00

*Metric values are rounded off.   †Approximate fractions.

Metric conversions

Use the tables on these two pages to convert the "English" or "standard" measurements in this book into metric form.

In the "English system to metric system" and "Metric system to English system" charts below, multiply the number in the first column by the number in the third column to arrive at the conversion number in the middle column.

English system to metric system

To change:	Into:	Multiply by:
Inches	Millimeters	25.4
Inches	Centimeters	2.54
Feet	Meters	0.305
Yards	Meters	0.914
Miles	Kilometers	1.609
Square inches	Square centimeters	6.45
Square feet	Square meters	0.093
Square yards	Square meters	0.836
Cubic inches	Cubic centimeters	16.4
Cubic feet	Cubic meters	0.0283
Cubic yards	Cubic meters	0.765
Pints	Liters	0.473
Quarts	Liters	0.946
Gallons	Liters	3.78
Ounces	Grams	28.4
Pounds	Kilograms	0.454
Tons	Metric tons	0.907

Metric system to English system

To change:	Into:	Multiply by:
Millimeters	Inches	0.039
Centimeters	Inches	0.394
Meters	Feet	3.28
Meters	Yards	1.09
Kilometers	Miles	0.621
Square centimeters	Square inches	0.155
Square meters	Square feet	10.8
Square meters	Square yards	1.2
Cubic centimeters	Cubic inches	0.061
Cubic meters	Cubic feet	35.3
Cubic meters	Cubic yards	1.31
Liters	Pints	2.11
Liters	Quarts	1.06
Liters	Gallons	0.264
Grams	Ounces	0.035
Kilograms	Pounds	2.2
Metric tons	Tons	1.1

(actual size)